Form, Art and the Environment

Form, Art and the Environment: Engaging in sustainability adopts a pluralistic perspective of environmental artistic processes in order to examine the contributions of the arts in promoting sustainable development and culture at a grassroots level and its potential as a catalyst for social change and awareness.

This book investigates how community arts, environmental creativity, and the changing role of artists in the Polis contribute to the goal of a sustainable future from a number of interdisciplinary perspectives. From considering the role that art works play in revealing local environmental problems such as biodiversity, public transportation and energy issues, to examining the way in which artists and art works enrich our multidimensional understanding of culture and sustainable development, *Form, Art and the Environment* advocates the inestimable value of art as an expressive force in promoting sustainable culture and conscious development. Utilising a broad range of case studies and analysis from a body of work collected through the international environmental COAL prize, this book examines the evolution of the relationship between culture and the environment.

This book will be of interest to practitioners of the environmental arts, culture and sustainable development and students of Art, Environmental Science, and International Policy and Planning Development.

Nathalie Blanc is Director of Research at Paris Diderot University, France.

Barbara L. Benish is an artist and Founding Director of ArtMill: Center for Sustainable Creativity, Czech Republic.

Routledge Studies in Culture and Sustainable Development

Culture as an aspect of sustainability is a relatively new phenomenon but is beginning to attract attention among scholars and policy makers. This series opens up a forum for debate about the role of culture in sustainable development, treating culture and sustainability as a meta-narrative that will bring together diverse disciplines. Key questions explored in this series will include: how should culture be applied in sustainability policies; what should be sustained in culture; what should culture sustain; and what is the relationship of culture to other dimensions of sustainability?

Books in the series will have a variety of geographical foci and reflect different disciplinary approaches (for example, geography, sociology, sustainability science, environmental and political sciences, anthropology, history, archaeology and planning). The series will be addressed in particular to postgraduate students and researchers from a wide cross-section of disciplines.

Series Editors:
Katriina Soini, University of Jyväskylä, Finland, and Natural Resources Institute Finland
Joost Dessein, Institute for Agricultural and Fisheries Research (ILVO) and Ghent University, Belgium

Culture and Sustainability in European Cities
Imagining Europolis
Edited by Svetlana Hristova, Milena Dragićević Šešić, and Nancy Duxbury

Theory and Practice in Heritage and Sustainability
Between past and future
Edited by Elizabeth Auclair and Graham Fairclough

Cultural Sustainability and Regional Development
Theories and practices of territorialisation
Edited by Joost Dessein, Elena Battaglini and Lummina Horlings

The Politics of Cultural Development
Trade, cultural policy and the UNESCO Convention on Cultural Diversity
Ben Garner

Form, Art and the Environment
Engaging in sustainability
Nathalie Blanc and Barbara Benish

Form, Art and the Environment

Engaging in sustainability

Nathalie Blanc and Barbara L. Benish

LONDON AND NEW YORK

First published 2017
by Routledge
2 Park Square, Milton Park, Abingdon, Oxon OX14 4RN

and by Routledge
711 Third Avenue, New York, NY 10017

First issued in paperback 2018

Routledge is an imprint of the Taylor & Francis Group, an informa business

British Library Cataloguing-in-Publication Data
A catalogue record for this book is available from the British Library.

Library of Congress Cataloging-in-Publication Data
Names: Blanc, Nathalie, author. | Benish, Barbara L., author.
Title: Form, art and the environment : engaging in sustainability / Nathalie Blanc and Barbara L. Benish.
Description: Abingdon, Oxon : New York : Routledge is an imprint of the Taylor & Francis Group, an Informa Business, [2017] | Includes bibliographical references and index.
Identifiers: LCCN 2016018659 | ISBN 978-1-138-96040-4 (hbk) | ISBN 978-1-138-96041-1 (pbk) | ISBN 978-1-315-66037-0 (ebk) Subjects:
LCSH: Human ecology in art. | Environmentalism in art. | Art and society.
Classification: LCC N8217.E28 B59 2017 | DDC 701/.03—dc23
LC record available at https://lccn.loc.gov/2016018659

ISBN 13: 978-1-138-59752-5 (pbk)
ISBN 13: 978-1-138-96040-4 (hbk)

Typeset in Goudy
by FiSH Books Ltd, Enfield

We dedicate this book to our respective daughters, and their generation, who are already carrying on the tradition of fostering change in the world, in their own creative ways: Louise, Gabriela, and Natalia.

Contents

List of illustrations   xi
Series introduction   xiv
Acknowledgements   xvi

Introduction   1

PART I
Metamorphosis: art and the environment   9

1   **Expeditions, Earth and an emerging ecology**   11
    Nature expeditions and documentation as art 11
    An image of Earth's life 12
    Double practice 13
    Landscape paintings 14
    1200 bags of coal 17
    Emergence of environmental art 20
    Ecological art/land-art 21
    Multi-cultural hybrids 25

2   **State of the art**   28
    Manifestations 28
    Discourse 29
    Sustaining histories 31
    Reading keys 33

3   **Mysteries, tensions, questions**   38
    Division by perception 38
    Issues at stake 40
    Therefore 43

PART II
Deciphering emerging forms   **47**

4   **Three green threads**   49
     Re-assessment of art: protecting life's inventiveness 51
     Arts, crafts and re-embededness 52
     Aesthetic qualities and alternative value measure in the public sphere 54

5   **Towards a new epistemology**   57
     Environmental aesthetics 58
     A dynamic reinvention of places 59
     Aesthetic public space and formal commons 64

PART III
Experiencing the living and arts transformation   **67**

6   **Depictions of the living**   73
     Deformed animals and mutated organisms 74
     Sound 76
     Histories of ecosystems 77
     The farm as laboratory 78
     An olfactory experience 79

7   **An aesthetic of repair**   81
     Shaping the flux of the city 82
     Time landscapes 84
     What about invasive species? 86
     Feeding the cities 87
     Rural cultivators 90

8   **The demiurgic gesture**   93
     The wonder of living processes 94
     Bio-art: 'Artists-in-Labs' 96

PART IV
The actors of the art-ecosystem   **101**

9   **Making new local economic cycles: Artist as player and catalyser
     of civil society**   105
     Global organisations and activism 106

Civics 101: food, waste, and the lesson of the bees 109
1989: a case study 112

10 **Creative individuals: local production, lifestyle and
    Robinson Crusoe**   117
    A Parisian frame, no longer golden 118
    Post-modern lumps of coal 121
    Jacques Cousteau meets Robinson Crusoe 122

11 **Macro to micro: artists as scientists, engineers and designers**   128
    György Kepes 130
    Environmental art and science 130
    Tropes to incite curiosity 132
    Sculpture underwater 134
    Survival 136
    Birds and beehives 137
    The plastic pollution battle 139

PART V
Re-embedding forms: a transformed public   **143**

12 **Deception: Dada to Smithson**   145
    Ubu's belly 145
    Spirals 148
    Monolithic stones of anthracit coal 150
    A lake at the Halles 151

13 **Taking it seriously and the refusal to accept permanence**   154
    Space and light 156
    It does matter 157
    Soil remediation 159

14 **Passive audience/acting public**   162
    A new public 163
    Sustainability +++ 163
    De Runde stories 164
    Dare-Dare 166
    The Experimental Building 166
    Capabilities, an aesthetic process 169

PART VI
Markets to micro-utopias: contextualising values   **171**

15 **The contextualisation of value**   173
    Copy from Cameroon 174
    O2 Canal 176

16 **The great divide: artist and art**   184
    In the belly of the beast 184
    Manifest destiny 186
    Gorillas/guerillas 188

17 **Micro-utopias: value scales**   191
    Parallel structures: art without a market 191
    Denunciations from North to South: justice at a global scale 193
    Utopias: for what to hope now? 196
    Micro-utopias 197
    Responses to the ecological crisis 201

    Conclusion: art's sustaining blossom   204
    Response to the future 205
    The ecological transformation (or metamorphosis) 207
    Art and community 210

    Bibliography   212
    Index   219

Illustrations

Figures

1.1	Marcel Duchamp, *1200 Bags of Coal*	18
1.2	Alan Kaprow, *Yard*, 1961/1998	21
1.3	Mierle Laderman Ukules, Touch Sanitation Performance "Handshake ritual" with workers of New York	24
2.1	Cai Guo-Qiang, *The Ninth Wave*, COP 21, Paris	30
3.1	Albrecht Dürer, *Self-Portrait at 13, Made with the Use of a Mirror*, Vienna	41
4.1	Leonardo da Vinci, *A Bear Walking*	49
6.1	Brandon Ballgengée, *Reclamation Series*	74
6.2	Lilian Cooper, *Coastlines Lobster Cove Head, Newfoundland, Canada*	78
7.1	Alan Sonfist, *Study, Time Landscape*	84
7.2	Hans Haacke, *Bowery Seeds*	86
7.3	Mathew Moore, *Lifecycles-Nuit Blanche*	91
8.1	Karine Bonneval Houle, *Chambres d'ecoute du vivant, cam thermique*	98
9.1	Wangari Maathai, U.N. Safe Planet Campaign Launch, U.N. Climate Conference, Bali, Indonesia	106
9.2	Chris Jordan, "What Will Be" exhibition, Universidad Technologica de Cancun, Quintana Roo, Mexico, at the U.N.F.C.C. (Climate Conference)	108
9.3	Guthrie/Pope, *What Will the Harvest Be?*	112
9.4	Margita Titlova-Ylovsky, *Movement of Tree and Body*	115
10.1	Lucy Davis, *Teak Road project* (Ranjang Jati: The Teak Bed that Got Four Humans from Singapore to Travel to Muna Island, Southeast Sulawesi and Back Again)	124
10.2	Lucy Davis, *Ranjang Jati: Bedprint & DNA*	125
11.1	Francisco de Goya, *El sueño de la razon produce monstruos (The Sleep of Reason Produces Monsters)*	129
11.2	Mel Chin, *Revival Field Maquette*	132

11.3 Wightman, studio shot of the Hudson River, Newtown Creek, and
        Gowan's Canal   133
11.4 Nicolas Floc'h, Structure productive, récif artificiel – 23m, Japon   135
11.5 Jon Wyatt, *Bamboo (Six Seconds)*   141
12.1 Alfred Jarry, *King Ubu Roi*, "*Véritable portrait de Monsieur Ubu*",
        Paris, Éditions du Mercure de France, 1896   146
12.2 Robert Smithson, *The Fountain Monument, Bird's Eye View,*
        MONUMENTS OF PASSAIC   149
13.1 Ana Mendieta, *Guanaroca (Esculturas Rupestres)*, Siloutes series   155
14.1 Dan Peterman, *Plastic Bones*, post-consumer reprocessed plastic,
        76 bags, 40lb each   168
15.1 Hans Kalliwoda, *the Polliniferous Project, the World in a Shell*   180
17.1 Valentina Karga, *The Institute of Placemaking, Summer School of
        Applied Autonomy*   201

Plates

The colour plates are found between pages 46 and 47

1   Carl Gustav Carus, *Full Moon near Pillnitz*
2   Thomas Cole, *Clouds*
3   Thomas Moran, *Minerva Terrace, Yellowstone*
4   Enrico Baj, *Bum-Manifesto Nucleare*
5   Nancy Holt, *Sun Tunnels, Avignon Locators*
6   Fabien Bouchard, *Climate March silent protest*, COP21
7   *African Mask, Tikar tribe of Cameroon*
8   Lucy and Jorge Orta, *Antartica*
9   Thierry Boutonnier, *Prenez racines!*
10   Spagna et Caretto, *Pedogenesis*
11   Maria Caolina, *Pino Ahumada*
12   Stephan Shankland, *Atelier* TRANS305
13   Theaster Gates, *Stony Island Arts Bank Vault*, original condition
14   Guthrie/Pope, *What Will the Harvest Be?*
15   Ring, Urban Orchard, *Community Build*
16   Asa Sonjasdotter, *High Diversity*
17   Tomas Ruller, *Chimera*
18   Kim Abeles, *Smog Plates*
19   Celia Gregory, *The Coral Goddess*
20   Tony Cragg, *New Stones*, Newton's Tones
21   Maartin Vanden Eynde, *Plastic Reef (2008–12)*
22   Ivan Kafka, *Lesní koberec pro náhodného houbaře (A Forest
       Carpet for a Chance Mushroom Hunter)*
23   Mark Dion, *Neukom Vivarium*, production still from the "Art in the
       Twenty-First Century" Season 4 episode, "Ecology"
24   Jeroen van Westen, *De Runde project*

25   Nso Dance, *Nso, Kumbo, Cameroon*
26   Martin Eynde, *I Want That You Want What I Want That You Want*
27   Sonny Assu, *Breakfast Series*
28   Minerva Cuevas, *Egalité*
29   Timothy Farstou, *True-Cost-Market-checkout-mockup*

Series introduction

Katriina Soini and Joost Dessein

Finding pathways to ecological, social and economic sustainability is the biggest global challenge of the twenty-first century and new approaches are urgently needed. Scholars and policy makers have recognised the contribution of culture in sustainability work. 'Cultural sustainability' is also being increasingly discussed in debates in various international, national and local arenas, and there are ample local actor-driven initiatives. Yet, despite the growing attention, there have been only a very few attempts to consider culture in a more analytical and explicit way in scientific and political discourses of sustainability, probably as a consequence of the complex, normative and multidisciplinary character of both culture and sustainability. This difficulty should not, however, be any excuse for ignoring the cultural aspects in sustainability.

The series 'Routledge Studies in Culture and Sustainable Development' aims to analyse the diverse and multiple roles that culture plays in sustainability. It takes as one of its starting points the idea that culture serves as a 'meta-narrative', which will bring together ideas and standpoints from an extensive body of sustainability research currently scattered among different disciplines and thematic fields. Moreover, the series responds to the strengthening call for inter- and trans-disciplinary approaches, which is being heard in many quarters, but in few fields more strongly than that of sustainability, with its complex and systemic problems. By combining and confronting the various approaches, in both the sciences and the humanities and in dealing with social, cultural, environmental, political and aesthetic disciplines, the series offers a comprehensive contribution to the present-day sustainability sciences as well as related policies.

1   The books in the series take a broad approach to culture, giving space to all the possible understandings and forms of culture. Furthermore, culture is not only seen as an additional aspect of sustainability – as a 'fourth pillar' – but also as a mediator, a cross-cutting transversal framework or even as a new set of guiding principles for sustainability research, policies and practices.
2   The essence of culture in, for and as sustainability is being explored through the series in various thematic contexts, representing a wide range of practices and processes (e.g. everyday life, livelihoods and lifestyles, landscape, artistic practices, aesthetic experiences, heritage, tourism). These contexts

concern urban, peri-urban or rural contexts, and regions with different socio-economic trajectories. The perspectives of the books will stretch from local to global and cover different temporal scales from past to present and future. These issues are valorised by theoretical or empirical analysis; their relationship to the ecological, social and economic dimensions of sustainability will be explored, when appropriate.

The idea for the series was derived from the European COST Action IS1007 'Investigating Cultural Sustainability', which ran between 2011 and 2015. This network was comprised of a group of around a hundred researchers from 26 European countries, representing many different disciplines. They brought together their expertise, knowledge and experience, and based on that they built up new inter- and trans-disciplinary understanding and approaches that can enhance and enrich research into culture in sustainable development, and support the work of the practitioners in education, policy and beyond.

In the field of culture and sustainability, art is often mentioned. Yet, art and the aesthetic dimension have often been treated narrowly only as means to communicate environmental problems and raise awareness of sustainability. The present book opens up a different view: it takes the readers to explore everyday life environments through their artistic forms using examples from across the world from different periods of time. It brings these works into dialogue with the history of environmental art as well as with many social and environmental theories, and in that way, it radically extends our understanding of the essence of the ecological crises and the roles of the artists in the ecological movements. In the broadest sense, the authors show how the seeds for social and ecological transformation can be found in the aesthetic and sensitive judgements of the forms.

Acknowledgements

Collaborations can be a little bit like a love affair: there are disagreements and heated debates, fuelling even more discussion and dialogue, dancing around shared concepts and entrenched intellectual commitments, resulting in a passionate output. This book was first proposed as an idea for the COST series of publications with Routledge on 'Cultural Sustainability', following the authors meeting at a presentation in Skopje, Macedonia in 2013. Our shared backgrounds in Eastern European history, art, and social change, and deep commitment to the environment sealed what has become not only a professional relationship but a friendship. Over the past three years of working between Paris, Czech Republic and California, the authors have framed what they believe is one progressive path out of the current ecological crisis. We are first and foremost indebted to all the artists in this book, (and so many others that we could not include), who are working 'on the ground' to create environments of new community, hope and health for the future of this planet.

Dr Blanc's extensive science background as a leader in France on the ecology issues facing our times, as Director of research at Le Centre National de la Recherche Scientifique (CNRS), France, is balanced by her long involvement as a trained artist. Barbara Benish, a US-born artist has a 30-year residency and history tied to Central Europe, is founding director at ArtMill Center for Sustainable Creativity and the NGO ArtDialogue born in Prague (after the political changes of 1989). Both authors have been involved with various United Nations and UNESCO policy campaigns over the past decade, and have lectured extensively. It was at the UNESCO Conference in Hungzhao, China (2012), that the leader of this COST action on Cultural Sustainability, Dr Katriina Soini, now at the Center for Environment, University of Helsinki, first invited Benish to join the COST action #1007. Both authors are deeply indebted to Dr Soini, and Dr Joost Dessein, for the conferences and dedicated input towards the series' publication. We are also grateful for the thorough work of PhD candidate Clara Breteau, who spent part of her summer and then an extended editing month in California to work on the manuscript (French/English). Her input was crucial during the formative stages of the book's organisation, and we are indebted to her for her perseverance across exquisitely challenging language and nuanced structural decisions.

We would like to thank the LADYSS (CNRS), France; the Social Practice Arts Research Center at the University of California, Santa Cruz who supported several lectures and activities surrounding this work; the COST *Investigating Cultural Sustainability*, (European Cooperation Brussels in the field of Scientific and Technical Research), COAL, Coalition pour l'art et le développement durable; the continued enthusiasm of ArtDialogue's team, especially Lexy Strong; Dee Hibbert-Jones and her students at UCSC; Lucy Lippard for her helpful feedback on the manuscript; Helen and Newton Harrison; Michael Shapiro, an enduring mentor; and finally, Karl Harrington and the FiSH Books editors as well as Rebecca Brennan and all the other great folks at Routledge.

Introduction

Over the past forty years, the relationship between 'art' and 'environment' has attracted growing attention, reminding us that the term 'environment' had already emerged in the 1960s on the Pop Art scene. Via its embrace of recycled everyday objects or waste, artists such as Warhol, Oldenburg, Raushenberg, Johns, Oppenheim and Polke, and the lesser known women artists such as Lee Bontecou, Carolee Schneemann, Nancy Rubins or even Collette (Levin, 2010), would already utilize the environment as both a resource bank and a treasure trove – as something which, much like an artwork, could be recreated, inhabited and transformed.

Echoing the not so well-known origins of the term, the two authors of this book share, articulated in their common interest in contemporary art, an intent to explore its artistic origins and evaluate the crossovers between art and environment this intimate historical link suggests. For a start, this means asserting an understanding of environmental change as a transformation happening simultaneously in and outside of us, as a change not only challenging our surroundings but the very way we personally and collectively organize our *oikos* and our lives. From this perspective, what we would rather call the 'ecological' crisis appears not only as an increasingly intensive series of disasters and catastrophes unfolding in our 'environments' at the macro scale but more generally as a form of radical exteriority that works in and outside of us to manifest some sort of power over our lifestyles, our economies, our stories and our dreams.

This translates into navigating life in a state of perpetual precariousness and uncertainty, while requiring more and more from local communities to invent – aside from institutional top-down systems and so far feeble efforts to manage the crisis – new forms of resilience and self-re-creation. What is at stake here goes far beyond striving to maintain more or less stable political and economic organizations at the local scale to ensure mere survival. It also implies being able to comprehend and deal with the new ethical and aesthetic implications of such transformed lifestyles, considering how they can impact both institutionalised and marginal artistic 'milieux', while figuring out more generally which forms of non-consumerist cultures and values can emerge and prevail with the demise of the pursuit of infinite economic growth in the optic of a whole metamorphosis.

The main question this book will ask therefore is the following: how do current or in-the-making artists not only harness their skills to build representations of environments, their histories and their destructions in a mimetic way, but also engage more profoundly to help empower societies to reinvent themselves, and how do these involvements transform and reframe what is understood as being an artist and his or her positioning within a given society? How do the aesthetic dimensions of currently reorganizing micro-societies articulate themselves with what was known thus far as 'art,' and how does this renegotiate the frontiers, not only between varied understandings of art but between a diversity of aesthetic regimes?

Indeed, we are no longer talking of artistic representation, nor even one that is subversive, because art has moved beyond the 'mimetic regime of art', or a 'representative regime of art'. This corresponds roughly with French classicism, known as the Belles Lettres and the Beaux Arts – where the question about the relationship between art and life is settled in advance by the idea that art is a representation – to establish what has been now theorised as an 'aesthetic regime'. Displacing the focus on the interface where art and life mingle, this new regime is characterised by its directly producing new worlds of value, where artistic products in particular find themselves redefined by 'a sensible mode of being' considered as specific to them (Rancière, 2013, p.18).

While we undeniably find ourselves confronted here with a double-edged movement, with on the one hand a new collective aesthetic and artistic dimensions emerging in grassroots social experiments and on the other hand transformed social and community missions and conditions of production for recognized artists, we chose for this book to try to embrace this twofold dynamic while anchoring ourselves at one end of the spectrum, using the works of current artists as a basis for reflection as well as a stepping stone to gain an understanding of the broader phenomenon.

In the following pages, we will therefore set off to investigate thoroughly a corpus of artistic works produced over the last decade and explicitly inscribed by their authors with an ecological perspective. It goes without saying that it is impossible within the limited scope of this book to cover the vast and varied number of artistic and ecological movements in the field, yet we hope to cover the general thrust of what is propelling contemporary aesthetic dialogues, and raise some questions.

Starting with the specifically European context and its association with the influential history of environmental art in the United States, this book includes dozens and dozens of case studies, gleaned from the International COAL Prize (Coalition for the Arts and Sustainable Development) corpus with its collection of hundreds of projects. As a member of the selection committee, where the artist's projects are read extensively, Dr. Blanc first became aware of the professionalisation of the artists tackling these issues. We were also startled by the place artists were giving to living beings. In order to be able to make sense of it, we tried to embrace the change, from an art history that progressively moved outside of the privacy of collections, or museums, to an art that seeks to escape the realm of luxury objects. Among the hundreds of projects, we selected those highlighting some peculiar aspects of these practices, that is linking them to contextual needs, and living beings. To complete this collection of case studies, we also included art practices in various other parts of the world (West Africa, Czech Republic, Indonesia, Brazil, Japan, etc.) whose knowledge comes from a long lasting relationship with the professional art world. Interviews were conducted in order to support and explore some of our thoughts.

As a geographer and an artist, we could have analysed the spaces created by these works of art, or the spaces that support them, or the sociological world of these very specific artists. Our view is more global, less academic. One of the authors is a geographer with an ecopoetic practice, the second is an artist with a social- and human-sciences training, favouring a reflexive approach. This book is born at the crossroads of our respective practices. The main objective is to account for these artistic developments in their diversity, multiplicity and richness. This book is formatted as a manual inviting art students and teachers to become aware of these modes of exploring environmental issues. These discussions and analyses will allow a more global and comprehensive understanding of the developments of art trends related to environmental and ecological transformations, while enlightening more essentially some of the contemporary artistic ways of bringing new 'worlds of value' to life.

While an overview will enable us in Part 1 – Metamorphosis: art and the environment – to set the scene of arts and environment crossovers and to delineate the series of problems attached to it, Part 2 – Deciphering emerging forms – will offer a space to develop and put forward a few hypotheses and concepts to be tested and tried out further along in the book, as case studies unfold and nourish the discussion with their richness and ambiguities. Whereas the first and second part are devoted to setting the stage, the third, fourth and fifth parts shift the focus to the case studies and their in-depth analysis. While we begin by addressing the historical and conceptual stakes, we will then address how artistic practices have been renewing the understanding of art in the direction of a practice of living beings, with the actors of civil society, embedded in local culture, renewing the idea of value, and art links to the market. But first we give a broad definition on how terms should be understood throughout the book. We choose to define the term of nature as *physis*, that is not as substance, but a set of relationships in which human beings are included: an entanglement process. The term 'environment' refers to the interactionist dimension, not the objectified part of our relationship with places and territories, or a set of objects as they are sometimes referred to in public policy (pollution, biodiversity, climate change, etc.). 'Ecology' is defined as a science studying the interactions that govern the distribution and the number of living organisms or as a political view defining a new relationship to the planet. The term 'sustainability' is defined as a commitment to maintaining stewardship of the planet and its limited resources. This stems from its original Latin root *sustinere*, which is literally from *sub*, 'from below,' and *tenere*, 'hold'. We will not use the term of 'sustainable development' as we are opposed to the idea of 'development' as such, as it has been historically associated with the depletion of the planet's resources toward that end.

Similarly, we use the term 'environmental art' insofar as it refers to artistic practices that integrate environmental issues as defined in the public debate, or which relate to the environment under the interactional dimension of what surrounds us. Mostly it is an umbrella term for a range of artistic practices encompassing both historical approaches to nature and more recent politically and ecologically motivated types of work. The expression of 'ecological art' relates more specifically to the art that integrates the reflections of scientific ecology or deep ecology into artistic work. Earth-Art and Land-Art bring together artistic practices where the landscape is intrinsically part of the work, but do not involve the dimensions of a scientific ecology, or environmental issues. Each artist is individually positioned within these large currents designed primarily for analytical purposes. It is therefore still difficult to produce a schematic criticism due to the complexity of the individual trajectories of artists.

Part 3 – Experiencing the living and arts transformations – will be devoted to understanding how artists develop a formal vocabulary linked to sustainability and the reproduction of a living planet, and with what means. It is clear that this goes along with the elimination of a certain kind of art object, conceived as perfect, in itself its own end; but also merchandise, toward a better understanding of life processes and an intensification of their experience by the viewer. How to consider life and living beings is an important part of the artistic debate. Numerous artistic practices tackle these preoccupations involving scientists and/or local communities. The artworks do not try to represent life, such as still-life paintings or living paintings, shunning the idea of simulacra. The role of the artist today is not only to present life but to make it happen. Bio-art, urban farming and other types of these practices are creating new art forms and, sometimes, different kinds of living beings. This opens the dialogue on sustainable alternatives to the formerly closed structures of creative endeavour. While the first chapter uncovers how formally framing the issue can be very diverse, a second chapter highlights the place of living phenomena as well as of contingency and unpredictability staging. It will also emphasise how the living is supposed to be the source of symbolic and material repair of the urban and rural area, with an emphasis on how poetic practices turn out to be at the heart of artistic repair-oriented activities. A final chapter will study the handling of living beings by artists. Whether playing with genes or simulating worlds through digital practices, bio-art and digital art are the object of much criticism and fascination alike. This section will at least show the extreme diversity of ways that artists have to frame and enact ecological micro-utopias.

In Part 4 – The actors of the art-ecosystem – a specific focus will be made on who appears to be the actor of ecological or environmental art. Interestingly enough, artists are not only engaging in their work with engineers and scientists, but also with civil society. This last become engaged sometimes as public and sometimes as co-author of art works. Whatever this specific relationship turns out to be, art practices' novelty often consists in promoting some sort of anonymity or in producing different types of actions, should they be technical, scientific or even included in the range of ordinary activities. At this point we then ask ourselves to what extent these activities refer to a history of 'art' or renew that history – deeply changing what art and aesthetic experience is about. Besides the long history that these practices inherit and beyond the contemporary promotion of art as being primarily an aesthetic experience, these practices highlight the multifaceted dimensions of our environment: they dramatize it and weave narratives around it, in a singular and *sui generis* move which, we will argue, distinguishes itself radically from technical or policy fixes offered by engineers and scientists in an attempt to manage the environmental crisis. First, artists are increasingly becoming involved in communities contributing somehow to their identification and identity in the public sector. They participate in local economies, sometimes with scientists of different disciplines, bringing forth separate scientific field studies such as water issues, food production, marine conservation, climate change, etc., so as to have a global impact based in science. Second, a way of bringing about new economies is to create local economic cycles and/or emphasise and support creative individuals within the local production and lifestyle. Through these looking glasses, the issue of singularity versus universality of the work of art in theoretical terms is also examined.

Pushing this reframing and reassessment further, Part 5 – Re-embedding forms: a transformed public – reconsiders the space of artistic commitment, as part of an already long-standing evolution started in the West by, among others, the Dada movement. Stemming from these Dada roots with ironic overtones, up until the modernist works of Land Artists (viewed at the time as 'environmental' artworks), the paradigm shift over the past three to four decades is outlined. With the postmodernist refusal to accept the permanence of artworks, valorising the experience, which uses the art object as a medium to intensify emotions and feelings, the public (and market) are put into new roles.

Today's artists' practices that eliminate the permanent material objects, besides the documentation of the process, can be valued as creating a new audience. The work of art is therefore part of a double temporality. It is an object of the physical universe and is indeed the product of a past completed and definitive process. But it also participates in a temporality that is not defined by the continued existence of something in time and space, but by the constant capacity to be updated, and even enriched as it is discovered by a receiver and being, thus to be conceived as an experience. What is at stake is not only to take artistic works out of privileged, separated spaces for contemplation such as museums or art galleries; it will also be to reject the reduction of art pieces to consumer products for luxury, decorative or investment markets subject to financial speculation, in favour of an emphasis on the process, attitude, and way of life, as well as a new form of social criticism with the fabric of micro-utopias. Thus being involved in local communities, with scientists and planners, or perhaps even playing these roles themselves, more and more environmental artists do produce artworks that are processes without traces apart from their documentation. They are imbued, influenced by, and dependent upon the local culture. The definition of the term 'community' is very different: whether, for example, in Europe, New Zealand, South Africa or the United States. There are local communities, geographically speaking, in the USA or in the UK, whereas the political community was mainly the nation state, in more centralized countries (Czech Republic, Russia, Vietnam, etc.). As this slowly evolved in recent years, the artists contribute by means of their aesthetic trade, whether to the politicisation, or to the geographicisation of local communities.

Finally, Part 6 – Markets to micro-utopias: contextualizing values – questions the value of aesthetic and artistic productions from the perspective of economic re-localisation. Indeed, more than the art itself, we will focus on aesthetic contributions to the ordinary environment. Such issues interest the artist, often involving him/her in communities protesting against developments in the name of 'betterment', but also, and more generally, the way places are used or usurped. Besides their property or financial value, these places develop in a finely braided game made of history and geographical use values that need their forms and opportunities to develop on a practical level. This last part will broaden the issue to the point of transforming the artistic challenge in aesthetic issues more widely. The aesthetic concerns any respect for the values in acts of daily life (Dewey, 1980), the style of human life that has an ethnic basis, the proper way for a community to take and score forms, values and rhythms. Human emotions are developed from thoughtful productions of rhythms and values in artistic activity (music, poetry and so forth) but display their own characteristics in all the activities of a culture (culinary tastes, dress, architecture, comfort, social attitudes and etiquette) and symbolic activity. Aesthetics is not therefore reduced to the question of representation and creation of images but to a vast range of physiological value judgments that engage all the senses, including smell, sound, touch and taste, and find figurations increasingly externalised in symbolisation.

We will also review how artistic practices play aesthetic value against financial value and consider how access is currently, and could be in the future, granted to the production of environmental aesthetic values. Local art reflects the growing conflict between local and global economies. Co-operative movements in Europe, and the former 'parallel structures' (which thrive/d in former Soviet Bloc countries and other totalitarian regimes) offer alternatives. The crossing of the two worlds of art and environment play a role in the redistribution of values, not only of local production, but engaging larger social and economic issues. New values of life, local production, environmental imagination and experience are exemplified. Artists play in each cultural section; art objects refer to different socio-economic scales. In terms of class goods, it is a way to try and install a new price (or value) on objects. Cultural objects are now produced globally and locally. Art is a way to return to local production with meaningful economics.

The conclusion – Art's sustaining blossoms – provides us with the opportunity to consider on a theoretical level the role of artistic practices in the integration of culture toward sustainability projects as being able to raise the issue of the formal commons, and of an aest/ethic way of life. Thus the implications of our work and findings on a larger scale, are not only bureaucratic and technocratic but social and political. We hope to have proven that environmental art, beyond addressing environmental issues, signals a change of culture and aesthetics, meaning an aesthetic that is inbred in social change. We understand the multiplication of these practices in the context of a broader r/evolution while artists find alternatives that allow them to break with the capitalist system. Thus our book can be useful for artists, activists and academics, but also hopefully for people working in and for civil society, dedicated to change on a larger scale, which by definition today *must* include the environment in that equation.

In the discussions that follow, we give in parentheses the year the respective artists entered the COAL prize. Some quotations are taken from the proposals the artists made at the time of submission.

References

Dewey, J., 1980. *Art as Experience*. New York: Perigee Books.
Levin, K., 2010. 'Where are all the Great Women Pop Artists?' *ArtNews*, www.artnews.com/2010/11/01/where-are-the-great-women-pop-artists/
Ranciere, J., 2013. *The Politics of Aesthetics*. London: Bloomsbury.

Part I

Metamorphosis

Art and the environment

What is the role that an environmentalist approach can give to art, and how important can that resulting art be to nature? In their sometimes competing or compared concepts, the relationship between art and nature has been little studied in its historical continuity. And yet there is a very dense field of artistic practices involving nature as well as related to environmental problems. The exclusion of nature from the discourse regarding the construction of subjectivities – such as artists display – shows that it is difficult to relate nature's elementarity and its absorption by the subject. Yet, environmental art also can, in specific locations, take many forms and corresponds to commitments as varied as the ethical and aesthetic.

While there may be meetings with wilderness that are represented as diverse landscapes and fantasised as wild nature or not, the question for the artist is how to create a form of mediation, reporting on nature, or unveiling a way of representing the human being on earth. This is not necessarily ecological restoration, but calls for environmental creativity and artistry. The artist's work is singular, totally specific and highlights a way to order the emergence of life. In the words of Goethe, life forms refer to the conditions of possibility of their singularity. It is therefore neither Earth-Art or Land-Art, nor Bio-Art, but approaches a theoretical and empirical level that artists are living in, redefining environmental forms. Indeed, environmental art borrows from political ecology its chain of subjects and objects transforming their agentivity, the animal and the food, the planet and the world. This first chapter elaborates on the historical crossovers of art and environment; the second chapter addresses the state-of-the-art; while the third chapter sums up the mysteries, tensions and questions brought by this field of study.

1 Expeditions, Earth and an emerging ecology

When modernism's largely white and western paradigm started to crumble at the end of the Cold War, a subtle opening up and broadening of the very definition of art began to unfold. Today, a conjunction of global events and thought coming out of postmodernism has brought us to an exciting moment in time when art is not only off the traditional museum pedestal, both literally and figuratively, but also is engaged in the social fabric of human activity. Questioning the hierarchies inherent to existing economic systems, art works that were not marketable or that challenged commodification – installation art, performance, sound art, and other ephemeral forms – re-established a paradigm of art embedded in the living world's puzzle, as opposed to being a supplier of aesthetic satisfaction in the market economy.

The steps developed briefly below reflect moments in the history of art related to environmental or ecological issues. It is neither a linear story, nor an exhaustive history, but historical moments to which most of the artists and curators working on environmental issues refer. This story deeply binds art and science, giving them each their respective roles, yet differing in history. We begin our story in the nineteenth century between an effort to document nature and scientific expeditions, and the idea of a renewed vision of the landscape, thanks to a few individuals, but also as part of a richer movement to change the view of nature. If representations of nature are at first mainly processed through landscape paintings, ecological representations on their side go hand in hand with the rise of a new symbolic meaning allocated to the various elements of nature: clouds for example become a symbol of pollution or radioactivity; the panda epitomizes the fragility of life; the polar bear, global warming and rising sea levels. Is this evolution towards the symbolic a true turning point? What does it mean? It is worth pointing out here that besides artistic practices strictly related to the environment, many art works that do not claim any commitment towards ecology appear to be nonetheless using natural elements as symbols associated with ecology.

Nature expeditions and documentation as art

Natural science and art are linked over centuries, especially thanks to artists' contribution to the description of the natural world. Their role as recorders of foreign lands was reflective of their royal patrons who tried to expand their power. Numerous expeditions throughout the seventeenth and eighteenth centuries propelled them all over the globe. Indeed, they were the artists documenting the colonial expansion, which exploited natural resources and wonders as well as indigenous cultures. Icons and images are at the forefront regarding the change and rise of new depictions of nature guided by the ideal of objectivity. 'Art and science converged in intertwined judgments of truth and beauty. Eighteenth-century scientific atlas makers referred explicitly and repeatedly to coeval art genres and criticism' (Daston and Galison, 2007, p. 79). The artists play with all kinds of technical constraints, such as the painting material or the geometric perspective, and describe elements of nature and the world around us through aesthetics norms. These representations value codes, visual standards that will not cease to evolve until the separation between art and science giving their autonomy to both but minoring their respective contribution to knowledge. The perspective vision will allow the viewer to be closer to a perceived optic reality, gradually objectified, and serve as a tool to represent landscape elements. The images then go from a representation of the natural anomalies to an objectification through photography, far from the temptations of artistry. In the age of science, mechanization trumped art. Conversely, historians of art call attention to the aesthetic context that shaped the making and seeing of photographs, even scientific and medical ones. This vision of a science that seeks to avoid the subjectivity of the artistic eye will sign the separation of Arts and Sciences, and the birth of aesthetics in 1750. After the eighteenth century, aesthetic becomes an independent discipline and art claims autonomy – art for art's sake – and develops a critical and creative perspective. The disembeddedness of the fields of activity such as art and science towards a specialised productive activity and public will encounter thwarting attempts by the inventors of cross paths utopians (Saint-Simon, for example with his disciples), seeking to reconcile the human dimensions of rationality and emotion. The two examples below illustrate attempts to reconcile art and science.

An image of Earth's life

Trying to link art and science, the naturalist Carl Gustav Carus attempted to substitute the term 'art of the image of the life of the earth' to the word 'landscape painting' with (Erdlebenbildkunst). This idea, which appears in his *Letters on Landscape Painting* (1815–35), shows a move away from the egotistical risk of subjectivity claimed by the landscape painters. According to Carus, if his practice of science itself must resource to the aesthetic sense, this last one may be a projection instance (landscape) that says nothing of the real (country). So he wants to be a close observer of the characteristics and dynamics of the natural world, particularly detectable in the history of rock formations and geographical specificities (see Plate 1). If his idea is still dominated by a theological and visionary geology, attention to changes in the nature converged with the work of Alexander von Humboldt, which he approaches in the 1820s and he quotes in his *Letters on Landscape Painting*.

Humboldt, naturalist and explorer of plant resources of Spanish America, is not only recognized for having laid the beginnings of modern plant ecology, before the term was invented but also he acknowledged a role for the imagination and art in his great work of synthesis, with the significant title, *Cosmos: Essay on a Physical Description of the World* (Humboldt, 2014). So, if we cannot deny the mystical and religious dimension of German Romanticism – the power of religion is transferred there to art in its capacity to link human beings or communities to the divine – its participation in debates on environmental ideas from its outset should be noted. The arts already contribute fully.

Double practice

Following the example of Carus, the poets, artists and philosophers of Romanticism were sometimes also scientists. They are, for some, engaged in a double practice and intend to reconcile art and science. They are also often walkers, in contact with nature, aiming to collect materials for their thinking during their walks. Novalis tried to find the seeds of his art working with reality rather than representing the real. Geologist, mathematician, cartographer, poet and philosopher, Novalis deploys in his last poetic literary projects more a vision of diversity and its various combinatorial modes than giving a tale of unity and totality. His approach, showing the infinite heterogeneities, is based on a logic of diversity and multiplication of assumptions, a practice of individual seriation and accidental cases.

Rather than eliminating chance (according to a Hegelian or Mallarméen plan) and reaching the heart of pure necessity, or any substance or the improbable 'thing in itself', Novalis' philosophical and poetic project was to multiply collisions, rattling the singularities and causing accidental encounters. Many contemporary artists could reclaim the open and largely non-doctrinal aspect of Novalis' writings, which mixed philosophy, science and poetry, thought and sensitivity, understanding of the environment as part of a game, more than a necessity at work in nature.

Novalis considered an enlarged human sensitivity. The reduction of the optical perception is particularly challenged by the use of the concept of *Stimmung*, frequently translated as 'atmosphere'. Referring by its etymology to the idea of a musical chord ('gestimmt', originating from 'Stimmung', also positions sound against an optical conception of the atmosphere.), the term comes precisely at the turn of the eighteenth and nineteenth centuries to designate a form of unstable resonance between the self and the world, different from the harmony of the Ancients. The *Stimmung* questions the hegemonic position of man as the master and owner of nature for the benefit of the interrelationship and instability. The work on the interaction of the senses, or synesthesia, is also tested in 'multimedia' experiments, exceeding the purely optical input of a world ruled only by easel painting. This trend continues in the following centuries where the use of sound and the idea of 'soundscape' continue to question the boundaries between art and reality. Today, many artists such as Michael Brewster (1946–2016), Miloš

Voytěchovský and Paul Panhuysen offer facilities or sound recordings to bring a global experience of the environment.

Novalis also considered Goethe as both a poet and a scientist:

> Goethe is a completely practical poet ... His observations on light, on the transformation of plants and insects are at once confirmations, and the most convincing proofs that the perfect didactic essay also belongs to the realm of the artist. One would also be justified in maintaining in a certain sense that Goethe is the first physicist of his age – indeed that his work is epoch-making in the history of physics.
>
> (Novalis, 1997, p. 111)

With Novalis, we move from a formative theory (*Bildungslehre*) to a study of force fields. This brings him closer to Schelling, who founded a new philosophy of nature from his observations of physical phenomena such as magnetism and electricity. Thus, romantic inventiveness frequently turns into an almost hypnotic capture of the senses, which replaces the real rather than opens the individual to the real and its hazards. The perceptive individual is expected to become an amazed spectator of his or her own internal and autonomous psychophysiology. But is it different from some contemporary artists? Overstating the phenomenon of human perception, James Turrell and Olafur Eliasson, for example, seem to leave intact the gap between the individual and the environment.

Landscape paintings

On the other hand, far from a scientific perspective, in Europe and in the United States depictions of nature have been mainly related to the history of landscape painting, and not necessarily as a way of seeing nature *per se*. Suffice it to say that landscape painting was not always linked to a representation of nature. If we put aside the important beginnings of the artistic invention of landscape during the Renaissance or even before, the eighteenth and nineteenth centuries saw the birth of an artistic interest in nature other than as a *decorum* for human actions. The new concept of landscape implied an aesthetic ordering of nature. While mankind is seen as the crowning glory of creation, romanticism seemed to question this anthropocentric view, valuing the significance of natural elements. Romanticism's legacy to modern landscape painting consists precisely in this convergence of interest in nature and the desire for a specific kind of representation. In the nineteenth century, the main symptom of this trend was the gradual demise of the principle of historia, and subsequently of the human figure itself, a process that cleared the way for formal experimentation.

Julie Ramos writes:

> In Germany, Philipp Otto Runge (1777–1810) and Caspar David Friedrich (1774–1840) were tending to subvert, rather than break with, the old rules. The former proposed a subtle role reversal in which human attributes were

transferred to landscape. While his work was not pure landscape, he saw his conception of Landschafterey as paving the way for a style of painting that did not include the human figure, and his Times of Day cycle, combining symbolic compositions and painted settings marks a departure from the classicist approach to landscape. The latter, by making landscape the subject of an altar piece, gave the genre historical status. The focus was no longer on the direct representation of the human figure, whose role was to dignify the surrounding landscape, but on a perception of landscape that now gave it a symbolic dimension.

(Ramos, 2000)

On the American side, the more penetrating of these examinations into the changing landscape emerged during the 1850s and 1860s in the writings of Ralph Waldo Emerson and Henry David Thoreau during the early era of the American Renaissance, which was influenced in part by British Romanticism. Nature was once again a subject for American art and letters, but the perceptions of it had shifted to reflect the new American concern with the changes in the landscape. Rather than presenting nature as an obstacle to the establishment of a civilization, American authors and painters alike upheld nature as the source of the animating spirit behind the American character. At this time, the English painter Thomas Cole (1801–1848), founder of the Hudson River School, depicted the industrial and agricultural threats to the scenic Hudson River Valley landscape of New York (see Plate 2). Cole symbolically painted the Hudson's demise and brought his vision to the public, urging patrons to save native landscapes; an early form of artistic environmental protest (Matilsky, 1992), which raised public awareness of critical eco issues. The paintings of Thomas Moran (1837–1926) in the Yellowstone region, executed during an 1871 expedition made at the invitation of Ferdinand Hayden (director of the United States Geological Survey) strongly contributed to the creation of the eponymous national park when presented to the United States Congress in 1872, and which acquired the work *The Grand Canyon of the Yellowstone* (see Plate 3):

> The first congressional acquisitions of landscape painting for the Capitol were the powerful images of the American West done by painter Thomas Moran. Moran had accompanied two geological surveys to the West and provided visual images of the unbelievable descriptions that surveyors and travelers alike were reporting in letters to the East. The allocation of $10,000 for Moran's first painting, *The Grand Canyon of the Yellowstone*, suggested the importance of both the idea and the land of the West and also served as a federal endorsement of wilderness as the wellspring of American nationalism (which included an expansive colonialism). Other paintings would follow Moran's, but the pioneering work of this artist carries with it the complex history of America's relationship to its environment during the late nineteenth century – suggesting that more than sublime Nature alone is enshrined in the Capitol building.

(Johns, 1996)

The Romantics believed that nature was the inherent possessor of abstract qualities such as truth, beauty, independence and democracy. In the natural world, people could reclaim or at least approximate the lost innocence of their origins, both individual and national. The image of America as a garden could apply to the Romantic perspective of nature, but the grid-work of civilization had to be stripped from the landscape. Albert Bierstadt, Frederic Church and Thomas Moran jointly founded a school of American art that freed itself of European conventions by painting the rough beauty and uniqueness of wilderness for its own sake. These landscapes experiment with new subject matter and brush techniques, but the focus of the scene still speaks to the white heritage. It ignores the indigenous people whose lands were being portrayed in the pictures. These scenes illustrate the notion of uninhabited, virgin wilderness, seen for the first time by European explorers and American pioneers alike. Though as the European painters were pushing westward, the United States military was simultaneously erasing native culture from these very territories romanticised in the paintings. This could be one reason why there is a link between the importance of landscape in Modernity and the divorce of the modern white man with the old Cosmos; indeed, the further the gap expanded, the more the landscape was fantasised. It is also the result of abandonment by conventional science of the question of the sensible and the supernatural.

These two ideas have not entirely disappeared from contemporary concerns. This would make it a link between the spread of Newtonian physics and the emergence of aesthetics. The conclusion seems pretty close to what current artists see as the grip of a scientific or technical approach to environmental issues. Science is limited in some way to 'spell' natural phenomena, the understanding of belonging to nature would be transferred to the art. By assigning a value to the aesthetic landscape considered as the part of a country that nature presents to an observer, the romantic man perceives nature as through the categories of art. In other words, he does not see nature, but sees the landscape, that is to say a reorganized nature according to aesthetic laws. The questioning of an anthropocentric worldview stumbles from its beginnings on dualistic thought. The critique of the chasm between nature and culture, which seems to deny the existence of reality in favour of art, is often implicit in the words of the artist since the 1960s, especially those who abandon traditional artistic mediums and opt for natural materials, or involve science in their works. The contemporary critique of landscape, which could also be that of land art and Earth art, tended to agree on a morphological and static vision of visual elements of the natural and built environment. The living elements, the fluid nature of life and landscapes both constructed and natural, were not taken into account. Formally, art was limited to painting and sculpture and tied to two or three dimensions. Dependent upon retinal input, the experience of art in the West was a dialogue of audience and artist in the context of the gallery, museum, palace, church or living-room decor. Even public art was generally limited to sculptural monuments of Empire, until the events of the World Wars began to unravel and question boundaries and ownership. According to our hypothesis, environmental artists take into account the uncertainty, complexity and unpredictability of living phenomena, breaking with the supremacy of a retinal art as well as with a patriarchal view of the world, including the 'male gaze' (Berger, 1972) with the female as an object in that dynamic. This paradigm can be extended to the romantic view of nature as an object independently of its wholeness.

1200 bags of coal

In the light of these events, and the prism of environmental art, at an exhibition in Europe in 1938, Marcel Duchamp turned a gallery and thought upside down with one of the first documented 'installations', *1200 Bags of Coal* (see Figure 1.1), hanging from the ceiling of a room at the Exposition Internationale du Surrealisme in Paris. Just as his *Nude Descending the Staircase* had broken up the visual field of painting following the cubist work of Picasso and Braque, the installation with the Surrealists challenged the visual dimension of art by opening up the context of the field. No longer 'sculpture' of three dimensions, the installation expanded to the entire four dimensions of the room and the relationship to the human body in it.

Immediately, the instrument of experiencing art was altered from the retina to the entire body. The connection to the work included an aural sense, with the smell of coal and the burning fire stove beneath it in the room. (Given the facts we now have on coal-burning, this could be also considered a pioneering eco art work.) The space itself created a sense of claustrophobia and danger, with the bags hanging at human-height level, and the viewer forced to walk under them. The context of the artwork shifted from 'viewing' to 'experience'. It was still placed in a gallery situation, but the effects were revolutionary.[1] Of course, no incident is isolated in the world, and many other such 'installations' were happening simultaneously in Europe and the Americas, stemming from the Dada movement in France, cultural exchanges with Africa and the renewed interest in Native American forms of expression. But in Europe at least, when the context of art shifted to the new relationship to our bodies, it was setting the stage for a complete opening up to the world fabric at large. The Western-centric 'art world' rushed to embrace works of 'the other' as indigenous and Western cultures were increasingly confronting one another with migrations and overlaps exceeding previous ages of 'exploration'.

The Second World War radically changed the art scene as much as it changed the configuration of world power relations between countries. Europe lost its predominance in terms of the art market, shifting the focus to where many artists had fled during the war in fear of the German advances. The atrocities committed during this war permanently changed the notion of representation. The Shoah not only upset the political, social, economic, cognitive and philosophical frames of Europe, but also its artistic frames, its modes of representation and the reception of artistic productions.

If it made difficult the representation of the body, Hiroshima and Nagasaki in 1945 also marked a breaking point in contemplative artistic perception of nature.

Figure 1.1 Marcel Duchamp, *1200 Bags of Coal*

Nuclear war begins the holistic perception of the destruction of human and environment. Moreover, the atomic cloud brings out the inseparable relationship of humans with their environment. Then, in 1951, an awareness emerged in the visual arts in Europe. Indeed, between fascination and terror, the movimento d'arte nucleare (1951–1958) was created under the impetus of Milanese artist Enrico Baj and Sergio Dangelo, and participants included Yves Klein and Lucio Fontana (Durozoi, 2002–6, p. 58). Thus, nuclear art reflects morphisms related to atomic destruction (see Plate 4). Indeed, Baj widened globally the field of art and wrote *Interplanetaere Kunst / Interplanetary Art* in 1959. On the occasion of the 2nd exhibition of Nuclear Art (Gallery Apollo, Brussels, February 1952), Baj and Dangelo issued the group's first manifesto in which they state that:

> The Nuclearists desire to demolish all the 'isms' of a painting that inevitably lapses into academicism, whatever its origins may be. They desire and have the power to recreate painting.
>
> Forms disintegrate: man's new forms are those of the atomic universe; the forces are electrical charges. Ideal beauty is no longer the property of a stupid hero-caste, nor of the 'robot'. But it coincides with the representation of nuclear man and his space.
>
> Our consciences charged with unforeseen explosions preclude a FACT. The Nuclearist lives in this situation, of which only men with eyesight spent can fail to be aware.
>
> Truth is not yours, it lies in the ATOM.
>
> Nuclear painting documents the search for this truth.
>
> (Home, 1991)

From there, the Milanese artists depicted decomposed and tortured humanoids in painting and clay. Then, the cloud is superimposed on the living forms of fetus, embryo, viruses, microbes or cells. The disintegrated and dislocated forms are representations of a subatomic and subhuman universe.

As art was objectified, vilified and marketed over a 2000-year period that coincided with the rise of capital and, not coincidentally, the colonial model of global expansion and empire, much of Western art became a cog in the wheel that raised the individual (or his/her religion) above all else. From the time of Albrecht Dürer's self-portrait in 1484 (the first self-portrayal by an artist in Western art) until Andy Warhol's silk-screened self-portraits of the 1970s, visual representation remained rooted to the artist's self, (which was more often than not, white male). Although, as deconstruction shifted the dialectic of thought from object to process towards the latter half of the twentieth century, visual art dialogues also went through a radical upheaval. The natural world and the world outside the museum space and galleries became the centre of intervention of artists sensitive to relationships and interdependencies between the natural and built environment and their art. At first, environmental art was connected to sculpture (for example, Site-Specific Art, land art and Arte Povera), while critics considered traditional sculpture obsolete and as having no relationship with the environment. Already in 1912, Boccioni theorised in his *Technical Manifesto of Futurist Sculpture* that the new art would be carried by the environmental sculpture, which would change the surrounding atmosphere. For Allan Kaprow, the first artist who theoretically defined the characteristics of the environment in the article 'Introduction to a Theory' in *Bull Shit* magazine (1991), audience participation and intervention in the environment are only the direct result of the fusion between art and life. As the context of being in the world was re-interpreted with a new view influenced by, among other things, the feminist and civil rights movements in the United States, globalisation and mass immigrations changed the cultural as well as political climate in Europe and beyond. At the end of the Cold War and the subtle shift in the world axis from East–West to North–South, the context of how we experience art changed dramatically. With expanding technology opening up the world, we could argue that there is no longer any 'foreign', only 'difference'. Just as Duchamp's coal bags turned the room upside down in the 1930s in order to change the way we see, art is now, nearly 100 years later, creating a similar paradigm shift. But instead of the room, the context is now the planet.

Emergence of environmental art

The Green movement, spurred by the increasing realisation of the devastation of the natural environment, was, not surprisingly, inspired by an artist who played a major role.[2] When Joseph Beuys planted his 7000 oak trees in the German city of Kassel for the inauguration of the seventh Documenta in 1982, it was another turning point not only in art history, but also in how art functioned as a catalyst for social change in the West. His theories on 'Social Sculpture' contributed to 'environmental art', firmly based in a critical engagement with community, social and political change. In the main city square, directly in front of the Museum Fridericianum, he planted a young oak tree with a basalt marker, the first of what became a mass planting throughout the city of seven thousand trees; the last tree was planted by the artist's son in 1987, the year after his father's death. Through his multi-faceted practice, Beuys brokered new relations between art, performance, teaching, ecology, economics, politics and philosophy. He saw *7,000 Oaks* as a catalyst for change, a symbolic start of the transformation of consciousness, of life, of society, of the whole ecological system, in which the biosphere as a healthy atmosphere would be consistent with human needs. While the formal challenges presented in major outdoor installation works such as Smithson's *Spiral Jetty* or James Turrell's *Roden Crater* in the USA have expanded the viewer's personal relationship to the environment, they have not created the change of experience in the society at large, such as Beuys sought to inspire.

Other Earth art by artists such as Ana Mendieta (1948–1985), who used her own body in situ to echo the forces of nature around her, brought back a more ancient, primal, and spiritual connection to the earth. The celebration of the environment around her, and her connection as a female to that nature, was documented in film and photography, thus changing the context twice: from artist to land to gallery again. Mendieta, of Cuban origin, not only shifted the context of performance art from inside to outside (like Eleanor Antin or Alan Kaprow in California, see Figure 1.2), but brought an important non-male, non-white, dialogue to the table of art history and human endeavour. Her earthworks

Figure 1.2 Alan Kaprow, *Yard*, 1961/1998

of the 1970s were non-invasive, and did not destroy the very land they were cele-brating, as so much of the monumental male-dominated works of the period ended up doing. She was one of the few artists of that period in the West to begin a dialogue of 'other' that included an ancient memory of our relationship to the earth that was filled with respect, awe, worship and connection.

Alice Adams, Alice Aycock, Agnes Denes, Harriet Feigenbaum, Suzanne Harris, Nancy Holt (see Plate 5) and Mary Miss to name but a few of the pioneer female land artists of that era, changed the dialogue from 'conquest' to 'cohabi-tation'. Hungarian-born Agnes Denes' famous installation of growing, waving grains, *Wheatfield: a Confrontation* on lower Manhattan in 1982 perhaps best sums up the era's conflux of feminism, eco art, installation, land art and social change. The context of art was now so wide, that the lines between it and the fabric of living a life became more and more blurred.

Ecological art/land art

From its origins in the mid 1960s in the United-States with artists such as Alan Sonfist, Patricia Johanson and Mierle Laderman Ukeles, ecological art was lumped together with land art in a rather misleading way. Also appearing in the 1960s, this trend referred to American artists working with natural materials, often in deserted places outside art galleries, modelling monumental landscape sculptures. There were synchronistic actions occurring even behind the Iron

Curtain during this time period, as we will explore later in this book. Meanwhile, in the USA ecological artists decided to make nature their medium and the object of their works and thoughts. Although the intentions were very different from the beginning, nature being a common denominator, ecological artists were assimilated to land art, which in fact was very problematic: it propagated the usual confusion between a retinal spectacular landscape inherited from painting with a nature which is to be thought of as a process – and not as a substance – studied by natural scientists and claimed by poets. Furthermore, if we look at the range of artworks associated with these two movements, the similarities are difficult to find. What is there indeed in common between the *Spiral Jetty* (1970) by Robert Smithson, the *Sun Tunnels* (1976) by Nancy Holt, minimal sculptures urging the surrounding landscape and connecting to natural circadian temporality of the Utah desert and *Time Landscape* (1965–78) by Alan Sonfist? Or, what connects a small urban garden to a New York native forest, reconstituting it in an archaeological approach, in order to install a green lung in the northern SOHO district?

The differences are even more obvious when art works involve a universal time and imperious orders of nature in a remote area, while Sonfist is orchestrating an ordinary version of a communion with nature. This difference may well explain our difficulties with the term of Anthropocene, which we relate to land art. The hypothesis of Anthropocene is the following: through history, human beings became over time a comprehensive geological force related to the most powerful natural forces. Deep reverie about a dramatic and romantic vision of man, the hypothesis of the Anthropocene now accompanies many artistic representations. The confusion goes back to the origins of the two movements, when the gallery owner John Gibson created the exhibition entitled *Ecological Art* including works by Carl Andre, Christo, Jan Dibbets, Peter Hutchinson, Will Insley, Richard Long, Robert Morris Claes Oldenburg, Robert Smithson and Dennis Oppenheim. In France, this original confusion seems deeply imprinted: the updating of the reference book *Land Art*, edited by Gilles Tiberghien (Pareyson, 2007), maintains the prevalence of this movement, offering a chapter entitled 'Out of scope' covering a broad spectrum ranging from landscaping arrangements of Nils Udo up to rehabilitative works by Patricia Johanson, a choice that maintains the final amalgams and subordination of ecological art to land art.

Several difficulties explain the obstacles associated with the recognition of ecological art, which are linked to its feminization, the importance given to the ordinary as well as its efficiency in creating ecological change. These are the same three criteria that hold our attention: the three American artists briefly presented below are women, with a concern for ordinary life, who share the idea of taking care of the environment, which is translated into support for living species or the characteristics of living species.

Mierle Laderman Ukeles, who in 1969 wrote the feminist manifesto *Manifesto for the Maintenance Art!* deeply conceptualized the idea of maintenance between life and death: it combines the life of the unit, the eternal return to the perpetuation and maintenance of the species. Her work has led to relating her personal situation – the person responsible for her life – to the general condition of living beings and to the earth that needs to be taken care of. It was one of the first to link environmental care to transforming technocentric environmental design (see Figure 1.3). In 1976 her piece *I Make Maintenance Art One Hour Every Day* was a collaboration with the 300 or so workers who cleaned and maintained the 3.5-million-square-foot building where the show was held. She asked them each to conceptualize their work as an act of art for one hour each day, and she took photos with a Polaroid camera. She has been the artist-in-residence of the Sanitation department of the city of New York since 1977 and helped to convert the Fresh Kills area of Staten Island into a park. To her, maintenance isn't about beautification or cleanliness. It's not superficial, but basic – it's survival. Mierle Laderman Ukeles explains about the *Maintenance Manifesto*:

> The first part/floor is personal: that I would live in the museum, and the artwork would be my taking care of the museum, like washing, feeding people, sweeping, dusting. And that was art. I saw this in the Whitney Museum. So one floor would be focusing on his personal dusting, feeding, washing the dishes. Then the second part/floor would be general: I would have to interview many people: what do you do to stay alive? Those will be posted up all over the museum. Also visitors who came to the museum, they would be interviewed. And then, the third floor, I saw, was taking care of the earth. That everyday, different kind of pollution would come into the museum. A container of one garbage truck, container of polluted air, container of polluted water. And they would be transformed by what I said were scientists and pseudo scientists by who I meant 'artists'. What I was really saying that the museum is a place for transformation itself, that active transformation can occur in the museum itself. That's where the culture reinvents itself. And actually, in my case, with what I was talking about, it is the culture that is going to invent how we're going to stay alive on the earth. People have misunderstood. They thought that maintenance art is about cleaning. But it was never just about that, it was about the personal, the social and taking care of the all planet.
>
> (Ramade, 2011)

For Patricia Johanson art is very much about survival too. She, like many other artists, uses the line of drawing as a compositional basis creating interwoven structures of nature and culture. She designed hundreds of sketches for environmental projects. In 1969 she originated plans for water gardens (made from flood basins, dams, reservoirs and drainage systems), ecology gardens, ocean-water gardens, dew ponds, municipal water-garden lakes and highway gardens, even though she had no particular clients in mind. Some of these ideas influenced her organization of *Cyrus Field* (1970), which linked a geometric marble path to a redwood maze configuration to a concrete pattern. Created in the woods near her Buskirk, New York home, the forest's irregularity disrupted this work. Like

Figure 1.3 Mierle Laderman Ukules, Touch Sanitation Performance "Handshake ritual" with workers of New York

Haacke's *Grass Grows* (1969) or Sonfist's *Time Landscape* (1965/1978–present), *Cyrus Field* inspired visitors to focus on ecological processes. Whereas the traditional art object is based on the idea of perfection, this art piece is alive, growing and changing, thus engaged in a metamorphosis (Spaid, 2002). In 1978, Harry Parker, then director of the Dallas Museum of Fine Arts, got the idea to invite her to restore Leonhardt Lagoon, after seeing her 'Plant Drawings for Projects' exhibition at the Rosa Esman Gallery. There, Johanson rehabilitated a large body of polluted, murky water in the middle of the city, bringing it back to life with sculptural forms as well as pathways. They were drawn to simultaneously control bank erosion, serve as paths and bridges over water and create micro-habitats for a wide variety of plant and animal species. Today, this popular lagoon is a meeting ground between species, human and non-human. Feedback on the work over time, confirms the 'sustainability' and permanence of this environmental work.

Lynne Hull also specialises in sculpture that doubles as wildlife habitat. She has made safe roosts for raptors in Wyoming, butterfly hibernation sculptures in Montana, salmon-spawning pools in Ireland and nesting sites for wild ducks and geese in the Grizedale Forest Sculpture Park in England. Carved hydroglyphs capture water for desert wildlife, and floating art islands offer an inviting habitat for all sorts of aquatic species, from turtles and frogs to ducks and herons, to songbirds, swallows and insects. For over 35 years, Hull's mixed-media work has focused on ecological realities in the American West and at sites around the world. Her prime spectators include hawks, eagles, bats, beavers, spider monkeys

and migratory birds traveling from Canada to Latin America, but she pays attention to even the smallest creatures. For instance, in 1993, she made perches for
frogs, toads and newts, which were having trouble climbing out of an abandoned
swimming pool. She placed rocks for shelter and basking, planted aquatic vegetation, created a driftwood island and wittily entitled this new world *The Uglies
Lovely*. For the roosts, she consulted with raptor biologists who understand the
specifications that the birds seem to need or accept. She worked out the
aesthetics within those parameters. Her background as a potter contributed to
this approach. Similarly, birds have certain needs, like the size and height of the
nesting platform necessary for the specific nest to fit. If the elements are too big
or too small, certain birds won't use the sculpture. She often builds a model and
experiments with the shapes until they look right. *Lightning Raptor Roost* was
inspired by lightning strikes, which are a dominant element in that landscape.
Raptor Roost L-2 was inspired by found objects from a deserted homestead, and
the colours came from the landscape.

Moreover Hull's work is symptomatic of the great differences between environmental art and land art. As Suzi Gablik emphasised:

> Where early site-specific sculpture was in a sense a parasite of nature, absorb-
> ing surrounding beauty but contributing little to its continuity, Hull's work
> functions within that environment, exchanging beauty with that of the
> surroundings.
>
> (Spaid, 2002, p. 76)

The work *Entre La Dame Blanche et L'Homme*, which was a nest box for owls
inside a castle turret indicated by a ladder on the outside, created in 2003 as she
helped French scientists to restore a wetland near the residence of Atelier des
Arques, highlights the gap between environmental art and land art. Lynne Hull
presents her work as having to 'provide shelter, food, water and space for wildlife,
such as remedial action for the loss of habitat to human beings' (Spaid, 2002, p.
75). Scientists are closely following these projects. Note however that the success
of Lynne Hull's work is also due to the way it is able to produce works of art from
a fairly simple concept and materials found in nature, such as her ability to
attract attention of non-specialists on specificities of small landscapes. In these
cases, the audience is made up of all those interested in ecological phenomena
and art, but also by the 'inhabitants' of the area, prospective employees of the
nature park and the animals themselves. Its reception is constantly re-invented.

Multi-cultural hybrids

Contemporary artists like Rikrit Tiravanija (born in 1961), whose feasts cooked
in the gallery, blurred the lines of community-building, cultural exchange and
art, and continued the opening up of artistic context into the world at large. As
a Thai, born in Buenos Aires and raised in Ethiopia, Canada and Thailand, with
an art education from New York, Tiravanija also represents a multi-cultural

hybrid thinking of the postmodern world that has literally changed the face of the former 'art-world'. Committed to 'bringing people together', Tiravanija's work has spurred the 'relational art' movement, which builds its strength on human interactions. 'It is not what you see that is important but what takes place between people' (Buck, 2009).

This thought stems from Wittgenstein, also echoed by the California light and space artist Robert Irwin in Lawrence Weschler's seminal book of 1982, *Seeing is Forgetting the Name of the Thing One Sees*. As the object became less important than the experience created, the context became the work itself. When in 1970 Irwin filled a storefront gallery space in Venice, California with 'nothing' (the effect produced by a scrim across the front of the store and natural light), the artist questioned the 'thingness' of art and reality. This again pushed the context of public (and private) experience, and re-framed an ephemeral natural element – light – into a non-traditional place. The element of surprise and simplicity in much of the installation work of the 1980s and 1990s helped the audience, on one hand, to broaden the experience of art viewing to include the natural world. Our definition of art in the West has been deconstructed to include everything of Derrida's 'eccentricity' that opens up the context to the all, everything. There is no sub-text, says the first quote of this chapter; every deconstruction operation comes from inside. Would it mean that metamorphic possibilities and the potential for social transformation should also come from the inner folds of the art world?

> The very condition of a deconstruction may be at work in the work within the system to be deconstructed. It may already be located there, already at work, not at the center, but at an eccentric center at a corner whose eccentricity assures the solid concentration of the system. Participating in the solid construction of what it, at the same time, threatens to deconstruct. One might then be inclined to reach this conclusion: Deconstruction is not an operation that supervenes from the outside, one fine day. It is always already at work in the work.
>
> (Dick and Kofman, 2002)

On the other hand, the audience strongly reacted against conceptual art, wondering, as happened previously when confronted with avant-garde movements: is that art, and why? The accusation of elitism incurred by contemporary artistic work is paradoxical: it draws art towards its traditional forms such as paintings realized for the church or the royal court, in its more decorative functions, but at the same time accuses art of being useless and a product of a capitalist market. In response to these discourses, many of the political and socially conscious works of the late twentieth century began to reflect the human impact upon that natural world. As the effects of climate change, pollution, water shortages, loss of bio-diversity and the rise of sea-levels became more visible and evident, artists have begun to reflect the change of that context. As our planet changes, so has the relationship of the artist to it.

Notes

1 *Air of ... (1919)*, Duchamp aims to offer a rare and precious gift to his American friend, the collector Walter Arensberg. With the help of a Parisian pharmacist he empties a glass ampoule of 50 cm3 containing serum. This gesture takes on meaning in the 21st century. Indeed, what would be the value of this Parisian exotic air gift today? (Macel and Guillaume, 2007, p. 32).

"Appeal for an alternative", first published in the newspaper *Frankfurter Rundschau* in December 1978, was a lengthy manifesto that embodied the ideas, realisations and demands that Beuys had debated over the years at the FIU and during the congresses at Achberg. He also used the text in several multiples. In turn, this manifesto became a fundamental document for the Green Party, Germany's grassroots alternative to a political party, in consolidating certain vital social and ecological aspects of their platform.' www.walkerart.org/collections/artworks/aufruf-zur-alternative-appeal-for-an-alternative-1

References

Berger, J., 1972. *Ways of Seeing*. London: Penguin.

Buck, L., 2009. 'The group show that takes to the stage'. *The Art Newspaper*, 10 June, 4.

Daston, L. J. and Galison, P., 2007. *Objectivity*. Cambridge, MA: MIT Press.

Deléage, J.-P., 1991. *Une histoire de l'écologie*. Paris: Editions du Seuil.

Derrida, J., 1967. *Of Grammatology*. Paris: Les Éditions de Minuit.

Dick, K. and Kofman, A. Z., 2002. *Derrida*. (Film)

Durozoi, G., ed., 2002–2006. *Dictionnaire de l'art moderne et contemporain*. Tours: Hazan.

Home, S., 1991. *Assault on Culture: Utopian Currents from Lettrisme to Class War*. Edinburgh: A. K. Press.

von Humboldt, A., 2014. *Cosmos: A Sketch of the Physical Description of the Universe*. s.l.: Create Space Independent Publishing Platform.

Johns, J., 1996. 'Nature and the American Identity'. Available at: http://xroads.virginia.edu/~cap/NATURE/cap2.html

Kaprow, A., 1991. *7 Environments: Introduction to a Theory*. Milan/Naples: Fondazione Mudima and Studio Morra.

Macel, C. and Guillaume, V. eds., 2007. *Airs de Paris*. Paris: Centre Pompidou.

Margantin, L., 1999. *Système minéralogique et cosmologie chez Novalis, ou les plis de la terre*. Paris: L'Harmattan, Ouverture Philosophique.

Matilsky, B. C., 1992. *Fragile Ecologies: Contemporary Arists' Interpretations and Solutions*. New York: Rizzoli.

Novalis, 1997. *Philosophical Writings*. Albany: State University of New York Press.

Pareyson, L., 2007. *Esthétique: Théorie de la formativité*. Paris: Éditions Rue d'Ulm.

Ramade, B., 2011. 'Mierle Laderman Ukeles: après la révolution, qui ramassera les poubelles?' *02*, Autumn, 36–49.

Ramos, J., 2000. 'Romantic Landscape in Europe'. *Naturopa*, 93, 10–11.

Spaid, S., 2002. *Ecovention: Current Art to Transform Ecologies*. Cincinnati: Contemporary Arts Center.

2   State of the art

Although environmental art is still to be recognised by a wide audience, exhibitions,[1] events and books on this topic have been numerous in recent years, since the pioneering exhibition 'Fragile Ecologies' organized by Barbara Matilsky in the New York-based Queens Museum of Art opened the way in 1992. From the late 1990s onwards, curators and writers started mobilising: Hildegard Kurt discussed the aesthetics of sustainability in Germany (Kurt, 2004), Shelly Sacks pursued Beuys' work on social sculpture in the UK; Maja and Reuben Fowkes focused on the environmental art history and aesthetics of East European art from the art production of the socialist era to contemporary art in Hungary (Fowkes and Fowkes, 2006); and Stephanie Smith from the United States developed her work around art and sustainability (Kagan, 2011, p. 345). In 2005, the 'Groundworks' exhibition[2] presented works that had been generated through collaborative or participatory approaches, which saw inhabitants of specific sites actively involved in processes of physical and creative transformations. This aspect was reflected by one of the pioneer books in the field, *Ecovention: Current Art to Transform Ecologies* by Sue Spaid (2002). As opposed to other conventional categories (land-art, earthworks, environmental art, ecological art defined below), the author comes up with the notion of ecovention (ecology + invention), which she uses to refer to any project initiated by artists who would employ inventive strategies to physically transform specific local ecologies. Going in the same direction, the book *Land, Art: A Cultural Ecology Handbook*, distributed at the first of this lecture series in 2006 at the London School of Economics, reflected a renewed environmentalism, primarily focused on creativity and not only on the risks, constraints and limitations very often brought forward together with environmental concerns. A UNESCO report published the same year also confirmed this trend (Brown, 2006).

Manifestations

In 2007 a conjunction of several landmark exhibitions took place on the international Western scene at the same time: 'Timeout: Art and Sustainability' on show in Liechtenstein, (curated by Friedemann Malsch at the KunstMuseum of Liechtenstein), 'Everything Will Be Fine' offered at the University of Lüneburg

The book *Art and Ecology Now* (Brown, 2014), profusely illustrated, goes beyond the limited use of beautiful books with an apparatus of text while not engaging in environmentalists' usual and obsolete 'visual sermons'. Although his expertise in the field of environmental art seems recent, Andrew Brown engages in drawing a panoramic synthesis, presenting the history of environmental art's pioneers while emphasising the wealth of thematic and methodological practices, and with a concern for the non-Western, which makes his book stand out compared to many other works in the field. Brown reframes the debate rather clearly, organizing the book into six thematic entries – Re/View, Re/Form, Re/Search, Re/Use, Re/Create, Re/Act – which allow him to renew angles and ways to consider his case analyses ranging from photography or urban performance to gardening and documentary survey in a very interesting way.

Sacha Kagan has published the results of his research on art and sustainability as part of a PhD in cultural theory at the Leuphana University of Lüneburg. *Art and Sustainability: Connecting Patterns for a Culture of Complexity* (2011) unfolds all mechanisms and philosophical issues of this complex concept that combines social justice, ecological integrity and economic welfare. Kagan displays a deep knowledge of his subject in theory and articulates its reflection with the fundamental antagonism of unsustainability versus sustainability. Yet his analysis seems to be more of an overview of the field from a theoretical point of view while showing only a secondary interest for practices. By searching for the logic of sustainability in the exhibitions of the first decade of this millennium, he nonetheless engages in a relevant update of the contextualisation of practices, without further reflecting on their critical reception.

In *The Ethics of Earth Art* (2010), Amanda Boetzkes takes a deductive and inductive approach from theory to artistic work and vice versa. The author adopts the term of earth art, referring to the 1967 Robert Smithson essay 'A Tour of the Monuments of Passaic, New Jersey' to describe the extremely diverse works. While it is true that all Earth art involves outdoors and dematerialised displays, the intentions of the two authors are very different. The assimilation of works such as those of Michael Heizer and Betty Beaumont brings a certain discomfort that dominates while reading the book. Malcolm Miles, in *Eco-aesthetics, Art, Literature and Architecture in a Period of Climate Change* (2014), proposes to read cultural events, exhibitions, books, films in the light of a personal commitment for a political ecology. The argument put forward, while focusing on the aesthetic value of art in a time of environmental despair (Bloch, 1995), on an individual and collective level, also shows however, the many difficulties of such a thesis.

Sustaining histories

These works are presented in a few lines to evoke the multiplicity of approaches to writing and thinking about environmental art. Their reading reports on a field of practices evolving under the constraint of multiple and contradictory injunctions. Before being able to discuss the main keys to reading the many environmental art practices, it is important to give some clarification of the terms used. Indeed, simultaneously, understandings of key notions such as ecology, environment, nature and landscape evolved along with their scopes and articulations. This, of course, on the one hand created much confusion, but on the other it proved beneficial to the field in so far as it increased the level of freedom, invention and experimentation allowed to artists willing to embark on crossing environmental issues and artistic practices. We choose to define the term of nature as physics, that is not as substance but a set of relationships in which human beings are included, an entanglement process.

The term environment refers to the interactionist dimension, not the objectified part of our relationship with places and territories, or a set of objects as they are sometimes referred to in public policy (pollution, biodiversity, climate change, etc.). As for ecology, as problematic as the use of the term is today, it is defined as a science studying the interactions that govern the distribution and the number of living organisms. The term was coined in 1866 by the German biologist Ernst Haeckel and introduced to France in 1874 by geographers. Since the year 1968, scientifically ecology has grown considerably, while becoming a political thought regarding how to adjust the activity of mankind to environmental dynamics. The original term 'sustainability', which we refer to in this book, was coined by former Norwegian Prime Minister Gro Harlem Brundtland in 1987 at the World Commission on Environment and Development, where it set the standard for the twenty-first-century paradigm shift in environmentalism. Sustainable development, the label the United Nations uses very specifically, is now closely linked with environmental education, poverty relief, social equality and political freedom. As Brundtland said, we now strive to meet the needs of the present, without compromising the 'possibilities of our future generations to meet their own needs' (World Commission on Environment and Development, 1987).

Similarly, the expressions 'environmental art', 'ecological art', of 'Earth art' or 'land art' have been used in a confusing manner, and sometimes interchangeably, to deal with artistic practices yet they differ greatly. We use the term environmental art insofar as it refers to artistic practices that integrate environmental issues as defined in the public debate, or which relate to the environment under the interactional dimension of what surrounds us. Mostly it is an umbrella term for a range of artistic practices encompassing both historical approaches to nature and more recent politically and ecologically motivated types of work. The expression of ecological art relates more specifically to the art that integrates the reflections of scientific ecology or deep ecology into artistic work. Earth art and land art brings together artistic practices where the landscape is intrinsically part of the work, but do not involve the dimensions of a scientific ecology, or environmental issues. Moreover, while land artists have expanded the viewer's personal relationship to the environment, they have not created the change of experience in the society at large, such as that which environmental art strives to inspire.

Reading keys

We shall now discuss the main keys to reading the many environmental art practices. While this field of artistic practice has been expanding, its limits as well as its richness are also evident. At one end of the field is manifested the hope of a profound renewal of environmental issues through art, as well as a challenge to the great divide between culture and nature. At the other end, artists and curators express rather a real fear of exploitation of their field of expertise through political or moral activism.

The first point is the issue of guilt or environmental responsibility, also addressed by the media, accompanied by a flood of authoritarian messages, some of which are so contradictory that sensible action is impossible. The second point supports artists committed to an active environmental practice, but fun, working on mobile nomadic structures on the edge of art and design.

The curators of the 'Greenwashing' exhibition opened the catalogue with a statement:

> The most superficial, but environmentally friendly way to make a show would be not to invite any artist, not carrying anything in the gallery and to switch the lights and the heating off. Like any company, we are so used to believe [sic] that ecological practice means sacrifice and self-denial that such literal suggestions now appear full of meaning.
>
> (Bonacossa and Latitudes, 2008)

Although out of context, this reflection highlights the contradiction in which artists, curators and visitors are placed. The precaution would be to refer ecological questions to scientific research or public policy, and avoid them as much as possible in order to escape the effects of manipulation. The title of the exhibition also evokes the companies' concern about their image, labeling their activities as 'green' to mask their reality, which in fact is far removed from ecological issues. The choice of curators is to exhibit artists who do not offer solutions, but sometimes raise questions on a squeaky mode.

Sculptures, paintings and multimedia installations here deal with the waste and accumulations of a society, revealing the cycles of power and, sometimes, invisible material exchanges. At the other extreme, the introductory text of Victor Margolin to the essay collection *Beyond Green* (Margolin and Smith, 2006) invites a more general review of the role of culture in the issue of sustainability. According to him, it is the same conception of art that would prevent its participation to consider such a question:

> The hierarchy between art, architecture, design and planning remains a paradox within a culture of sustainability, where the main criterion of value is to bring into existence 'sustainable' projects and environments. The social demonstration space of these projects is still coded unsustainably following discursive hierarchies which tend to favor certain practices over others.
>
> (Margolin and Smith, 2006)

However, the author continues:

> the old categories need to fall before we are able to think aesthetic question again. The latter is not the art objects that respond to an environmental or sustainability challenge, but concerns the entire art world including many current relationships between values and forms and use values which are believed to be part of the objects of everyday life.

While attempting to map out the way this artistic field is temporarily structured, we will readily appreciate how much this evolution operates under stress because of what we will call here the three keys.

The first key, noted by Victor Margolin, concerns the definition of the modernist art of the 1950s: that of the injunction of self-determination and to abstract from social consideration. Or ecological art is in multiple ways led to, and from, the 'outside' since it obeys the solicitations of the site and nature that prevails and of politic and society offering a framework for action. It is site-specific as proposed by Miwon Kwon (2004).

The second key, noted by the curators of 'Greenwashing', lies in the mix of ecology and environmental catastrophe seen as unavoidable and as a lot of questions involving environmental and social justice, in the context of a future compromise. To avoid catastrophe, or rather pretend that we try to avoid it by inviting the practices to become 'green' is an easy and cheap way to feel good; injunction linked with the revival of a 'greenwashed' capitalism.

This can even be seen as a sign of obedience to a scientific technocracy, which already holds the main keys to a risk of becoming authoritarian (or dictatorial?). What is striking is that art and artists are confined to a double bind: of being obedient and playing the game, or of being disobedient and finding oneself in the classic position of art and the artist celebrating the rebellion as being the prime virtue leading to social renewal.

The third key, more complex, is due to a series of reflections whose main authors believe that nature is the source of meaning for human beings and helps structure a deeper inner-self core. The issues are not only to protect air, water, flora and fauna but to support a profound change of cultures of nature. Therefore one cannot be satisfied to see the kind of ethical behavioral creed to which it is reduced since one speaks of 'sustainable consumption' to give the latter new virtues. By ethics, one would then refer to the moral attitudes towards nature that would manifest more readily if human beings reconnect with it. In what way is art concerned? Art practices such as shamanic healing or by calling back a spirituality or a fundamental human being has often seemed behind this formulation of the ecological link. However, this kind of practice could be suspected of fundamentalism and even qualified as archaic in westernised cultures.

These issues accompany the practices and whereabouts of contemporary artists. They relate to a vision of the environment and ecology with this possible outcome: the idea that we live in a world we cannot fully control, bringing forth an attention to relationships and overall dynamics rather than to isolated objects or organisms, unexpected processes that emerge in the course of the action that are characteristic of the dynamics involved. To give full freedom to imagination in the wake of environmental aesthetics would be to get art out of the register of aesthetic exception and combine aesthetic experiences with ordinary life. Thus, art need not be thought of as a refuge from the impossibility to act in the real world. Neither must it be thought of as the vanguard facing the impossible alternatives to implement in a conservative context and options pre-empted by the universe's own commodification capitalism. Awakening consciousness also seems to be the main focus of many contemporary works, even though the media space is increasingly overloaded with information concerning the environment. Art is clearly seen as having translation, mediation and negotiation functions. Surprisingly, the desire of the viewer towards these artistic practices is never questioned. The question of public reception is absent from most books. The works are totally decontextualized and seem to convey only a message or a content. Yet, this does not mean to think of these practices in terms of success and failure. Basically, to assume that for environmental art to be truly concerned with ecology it must concretely transform the territories, is precisely to remain blind to the multiple meanings of ecology, to its current redefinition in terms of sensitivity and imagination, maintaining the idea that ecology is a matter of technical solutions. Therefore, distancing from different representations of environmental art is also to clearly designate the deep variety of situations and artistic modes of intervention. It is also to see aesthetics as a theoretical and empirical framework contributing to the wealth of the world, its major design.

Summing up, the history of art and environment can be traced to various kinds of artistic practices that are now rapidly changing. Nowadays, the contemporary arts suffer from specialisation, ongoing from the last decades, and have been experiencing the 'parcelisation/specialisation' as in other fields (own public, own artist, own field of knowledge, etc.). Our aim is not to discuss the different 'branches' of environmental art, nor the characterisation of the specialised fields, but to debate over the crossings that have potential impact for a sustainable future. Each of the five main sections of the book contain specific projects from the COAL Prize and others artists to illuminate and expand on examples of these crossovers in various regions of the globe.

Notes

1   On the exhibition front, 'Natural Reality' in 1999 curated by Heike Strelow presented artistic works under three headings: human-nature relations, critical-analytical investigations in art and science and social perspectives on nature and landscape (Aachen, Ludwig Forum, Germany). Other major exhibitions followed suit such as 'The Greenhouse Effect' in 2000 in London (Ralph Rugoff and Lisa Corrin, the Serpentine Gallery and the Natural History Museum), 'Ecologies' in 2000 in Chicago (Stephanie Smith, Smart Museum of Art), 'Groundworks' in Pittsburgh in 2005 (curated by Grant Kester and co-curated Patrick Deegan) and 'Beyond Green: Towards a Sustainable Art' in 2005 in Chicago again (Stephanie Smith, Smart Museum of Art), or the 'Art and Ecology' programme launched in the same year at the British Royal Society of Arts, including exhibitions, seminars and lectures.

2   The Monongahela conference on post-industrial community development held in Pittsburgh in 2004 gathered several eco-artist and associated curators and critics. Among the participants were the Harrisons and Suzi Gablik, but also Tim Collins and Reiko Goto, Grant Kester, the London Collective based Platform, Ann Rosenthal and many others.

3   In 2008, the Fondazione Sandretto Re Rebaugendo (in Turin) organised the exhibition 'Greenwashing. Environment: Perils, Promises and Perplexities', curated by Ilaria Bonacossa and Latitudes (Andrews and Canepaluna) and published in an accompanying catalogue. Two years earlier, Max Andrews had been already the guest editor of the RSA publication *Land, art: A Cultural Ecology Handbook*.

References

Andrews, M., ed., 2006. *Land, Art: A Cultural Ecology Handbook*. London: The Royal Society for the Encouragement of Arts, Manufactures & Commerce in partnership with Arts Council England.

Blanc, N. and Ramos, J., 2010. *Ecoplasties. Art et environnement*. Paris: Manuella.

Bloch, E., 1995. *The Principle of Hope*. Cambridge, MA: MIT Press.

Boetzkes, A., 2010. *The Ethics of Earth Art*. Minneapolis: University of Minnesota Press.

Bonacossa, I. and Latitudes, eds., 2008. *Greenwashing Environment: Perils, Promises and Perplexities*. Turin: The Bookmakers.

Brown, A., 2014. *Art & Ecology Now*. London: Thames & Hudson.

Brown, L., 2006. *Art en écologie - Un laboratoire d'idées sur l'art et le développement durable, rapport sommaire (report summary)*, Vancouver: UNESCO.

Fowkes, M. and Fowkes, R., 2006. The Principles of Sustainability in Contemporary Art. *Praesens: Contemporary Central European Art Review*, 1, 5–11.

Gablik, S., 1991. *The Reenchantment of Art*. London: Thames & Hudson.

Kagan, S., 2011. *Art and Sustainability: Connecting Patterns for a Culture of Complexity*. Bielefeld: Transcript-Verlag.

Kurt, H., 2004. 'Aesthetics of Sustainability'. In Herman Prigann, ed., *Ecological Aesthetics: Art and Environmental Design. Theory and Practice*. Basel: Birkhäuser Publishers for Architecture, 238–41.

Kurt, H. and Wagner, B., 2002. *Kultur - Kunst - Nachhaltigkeit*. Essen: Klartext Verlag.

Kwon, M., 2004. *One Place after Another: Site-Specific Art and Locational Identity*. Cambridge, MA: MIT Press.

Lippard, L., 1998. *The Lure of the Local: Senses and Place in a Multicentered Society*. New York:The New Press.

Lippard, L., 2007. *Weather Report: Art and Climate Change*. Boulder: Boulder Museum of Contemporary Art.

Lippard, L., 2014. *Undermining: A Wild Ride through Land Use, Politics, and Art in the Changing West*. New York: The New Press.

Margolin, V. and Smith, S., 2006. *Beyond Green: Toward a Sustainable Art*. Chicago/New York: Smart Museum of Art at University of Chicago and Independent Curators International.

Matilsky, B. C., 1992. *Fragile Ecologies: Contemporary Arists' Interpretations and Solutions*. New York: Rizzoli.

Miles, M., 2014. *Eco-aesthetics: Art, Literature and Architecture in a Period of Climate Change*. London: Bloomsbury.

Spaid, S., 2002. *Ecovention: Current Art to Transform Ecologies*. Cincinnati: Contemporary Arts Center.

Weintraub, L., 2006a. *Cycle-Logical Art: Recylcing Matters for Eco-Art*. Rhinebeck, NY: Artnow Publications.

Weintraub, L., 2006b. *ECOcentric Topics: Pioneering Themes for Eco-Art*. Rhinebeck, NY: Artnow Publications.

Weintraub, L., 2007. *EnvironMentalities: Twenty-Two Approaches to Eco-Art*. Rhinebeck, NY: Artnow Publications.

Weintraub, L., 2012. *To Life!: Eco Art in Pursuit of a Sustainable Planet*. Berkeley: University of California Press.

World Commission on Environment and Development. 1987. *Our Common Future*. Oxford: Oxford University Press.

3   Mysteries, tensions, questions

The preceding chapters allow us to understand that a project such as this book encounters obstacles. These obstacles are manifold.

Division by perception

A first obstacle is the division between art and science, and art and technology, as well as breaks between art and nature. Indeed, at least since the seventeenth century and the development of a science of aesthetics (Baumgarten, 1750), art is experienced as autonomous, and the philosophy of aesthetics has mainly developed as a science of perception. It is also true that art, specific to museums and exhibitions, was ordinarily considered as separate from nature, to the point that Kant was the first in his *Critique of Judgment* (1790) to fully formulate an aesthetic of nature. However, it is clear that these divisions, dramatic as they are, are not absolute. Artists have worked with scientists since at least the seventeenth century, if only to illustrate or to honour the wonders of nature or the natural treasures brought back from many naturalist expeditions. It took the art of photography and its ability to consider natural phenomena mechanically, and supposedly objectively, to upstage the art of drawing, betraying the subjectivity of the artist. However, this art is not completely abandoned, as shown by the work of Haeckel, the biologist who was also the founder of ecology, who published two volumes in 1904, (originally in sets of ten between 1899 and 1904), and an illustrative book of lithographs entitled *Kunstformen der Natur* (*Art Forms in Nature*). His artistic talent was marked by natural symmetry, including those of unicellular microorganisms such as radiolarians. His lithographs had a decisive influence on the course of Art Nouveau in the early twentieth century, whose principals were the reintroduction of forms from the living world in human œuvres, whether of curves and scrolls or otherwise complex geometry. Artist/scientists historically accompanied expeditions of exploration during the sixteenth and seventeenth centuries, as Europeans went in search of foreign lands and riches. The paintings of English artist John Webber (1751–93), for example, who accompanied Captain Cook to Polynesia, influenced an entire generation of interest in the 'exotic' peoples and plants of the Pacific. These illustrations, fraught with ethnocentric bias, nonetheless provide valuable historical documentation of events (Cook's death, for example) as well as botanical wonders, which in many cases are today extinct. Artists such as John White, Juan Vincente de la Cerda, B. L. Turner, and even George Catlin, to name a few, provide us today with a vision of the meeting of vastly different worlds, both cultural and physical.

If the gap between art and science is based on a story that we can circumscribe, the break between art and nature, very old, still resonates today. There are roughly two opposing traditions. The first tradition opposes nature and culture; human culture, as a set of practices and representations, enabled the development of the technical exploitation of nature. Nature is therefore considered to be a substance, or a collection of elements, not a process. The hypothesis of the Anthropocene – wherein human beings became over time a comprehensive geological force – staging a deep reverie about a dramatic and romantic vision of man, goes in this direction and inspired many artistic practices. Another tradition staged an inspired nature as a living thought process, unpredictable, akin to the genius of the artist. Our scientific and critical positioning is guided by this other tradition, aesthetic and philosophical. More than digging in to the secrets of nature, breaking its unity, it accompanies its movement, the way it processes creatively. Thus, human art is a means of knowledge of nature, since nature is itself an artistic creation.

This insight is at the heart of much philosophical reasoning, embraced by many artists in the twentieth century. Nietzsche speaks of the aesthetic instincts of nature and of a world that is entirely a work of art engendering itself. In the eyes of Nietzsche, art is the creation of any forms. If art is nature, and nature is art, the artist and the philosopher could, by the means of aesthetic experience, 'know' nature, that is to be aware of all aspects of a world perception but in two different ways. First, a careful observation of natural forms enables them to get a glimpse at the method by which nature seems to work, in other words the great laws of the emergence of forms. But this familiarity with nature can also lead to a completely different experience than the existential presence of nature as a creative source. Immersed in the creative impulse of nature, artists and philosophers will feel they identify with it. They then go beyond the search for nature's secrets, able to access the mystery and wonder of the world. This is also the creative process that holds the attention of artists like the twentieth-century painter Paul Klee: the natural processes are more important than the objective nature.

When Goethe said that art is the best exegete of nature, he is suggesting that the aesthetic experience provides a glimpse of some laws that could explain all the variety of life forms. Similarly, Roger Caillois in his general aesthetic notes that what he calls natural orders – forms of generating schemas – are few. Goethe refuses to distinguish between inside and outside, to speak of experimental knowledge, which would leave the external phenomenon to discover a mechanism in some interior that would explain the phenomenon. It would, rather, speak of the movement of the intuitive knowledge that follows the movement of the genesis, of growth, *physis* in the Greek sense, the trainer momentum. The shape is not *Gestalt* – motionless configuration – but *Bildung* – formation, growth. The scientific method consists of Goethe's careful perception of the training movement. Goethe sought to discover the standard forms of nature, and explained the natural movements by fundamental laws presiding in general, including the two forces of polarity and intensification or ascension one sees at work, for example, in the growth of the plant. This approach, often described as contemplative, could be also qualified as supportive. The question indeed is not to reject any transformation of nature, but rather to extend the natural process. Beyond these cuts of a philosophical and historical order, the previous chapters have highlighted a series of problems that play a major role in the confusing relationship between art and environment. Before promoting what artistic works could have to say facing the environmental challenges in a context of ecological crisis, we state the problems collected throughout the historical overview and the state of the art, asking for a reassessment of the 'traditional' viewpoints and discourses exposed previously.

Issues at stake

The first of these problems, as we have previously discussed in Chapter 2, is the confusion between the terms. What are we talking about? Nature, biodiversity, environment, ecology, Anthropocene? The deeply rooted confusion between land art and ecological art and the subordination of the latter to the former requires a clear, new categorization. As was discussed previously, environmental art is an umbrella expression embracing different kind of practices related to an environment, understood as a set of objects and/or politics, or as what surrounds you. Environment should be understood in its interactionist dimension; environment is what you make of it and what it makes of you. Land art, a movement that occurred first in the US during the late 1960s and through the 1970s, is mostly related to monumental art practices and landscape's transformation and doesn't so much address the phenomenological dimension of the art experience, but its more retinal, spectacular part. Much of the monumental (and male-dominated) works of the period ended up in fact destroying the very land they were celebrating.

A second issue is that, even though avant-garde art practices have referred to social change since the eighteenth century, it remains unclear to what extent art has contributed to political change. Many sociologists and economists have analysed culture (Pierre Bourdieu, 1979, 1992, 1993; Howard Becker, 1982; Paul Di Maggio and Francie Ostrower 1992; Hans Abbing, 2002; Lawrence Levine, 1988), institutionalisation and system building of fine arts (Kagan, 2011, p. 67). For Jacques Ellul (1977, p. 77), the contemporary arts, even when promoting a refusal of the consumer society, the space of the gallery and museum, or the object (Lippard, 1973), have missed their emancipatory mission. Contemporary art borrows its premises from Romanticism when promoting human genius, the exceptional nature of art, the spiritual link that describes art as a particular and specialised activity (alongside other activities of the social system: police, justice, etc.). In fact, we might conclude contemporary arts are deluded and have instead contributed to the reigning capitalism (Boltanski and Chiapello, 2006). Suzi Gablik (1984, 1991) frontally attacked artistic modernity, which, she argues, in its autonomy wills itself away from society and any ethical interaction.

Third, the word 'value' when associated with art has, at least since the Renaissance, been tied to economic systems. In indigenous cultures, value stems from embedded practices: performative, ritualistic and spiritual. The West African artisan who produced a realistic representation could even be shunned, if not punished, as realistic portrayal is not within the artistic tradition (Wingo, 2010) (see Plate 7). This is diametrically opposed to the rise of idealisation of beauty in Western art over the last 2000 years, and the eventual glorification of the individual artist and his portrait (reflecting the rise of the individual in general in the West) since the Renaissance. Albrecht Dürer's self-portrait in early 1500 opened the door, symbolically and literally, to the new-found era of European exploration, exploitation, individualism, mechanical reproduction

Figure 3.1 Albrecht Dürer, *Self-Portrait at 13, Made with the Use of a Mirror*, Vienna

with printing, and the rise of industrialisation. Dürer's bold, frontal realistic representation of himself placed the artist on a pedestal of capital and commerce, where he remained until the modern era. Western art objects have personal value, monetary value, and perhaps cultural 'collateral' over time, but steward-ship of the land, or valuing the environment has come late in the westernized cultures that have (obviously) profited from its exploitation. Environmental art offers a critique of the capitalist structure of desire and demand.

On the other hand, the 'unknown' that contributes to the aesthetic of these traditional works, and therefore maintains social control within its native context, becomes devoid of power when removed to a museum or private collec-tion. Or does it? What is the hidden element that allows works of art to create social change? And what are the repercussions for contemporary artists working in the field of environmental aesthetics? The displacement of objects from their tribal lands has been an ongoing battle over the past decades, as more legal battles are enacted over ownership and cultural heritage issues. Native Americans battle the French even as this sentence is written, over an auction in Paris of sacred Indian ceremonial objects (Reuters, 2015). Private collectors in the US sent the Hopi ceremonial masks and statues to auction in France, possi-bly hoping to avoid press and legal repercussions from the tribal leaders back home. A spokesman for the cultural heritage organization Survival International explained that 'Hopi Indians are totally opposed to the trade of these objects and for these objects to be shown, published and scattered … According to them, they are not marketable items, they are what they call "friends", "spiritual friends", which have to return to their homeland' (Reuters, 2015).

A fourth problem could be the inefficiency of art regarding ecology. A ques-tion, often more implicit than explicit, dominates the analyses: do artistic practices contribute to a local and global ecology? Are they efficient? Many of the works that could fit into this field are of little help in the rescue of animals and plants. More generally, they avoid environmental issues and many new issues in the field of action, including the public. Basically, to assume that environ-mental art truly concerned with ecology is actually transforming the territories, is precisely to remain blind to the multiple meanings of ecology, to its current redefinition in terms of sensitivity and imagination, and to maintaining the idea that ecology is a matter of technical solutions (Guattari, 2005). Environmental art issues resurrect the need to hark back to the roots of the different terms; indeed, beyond the great divide between nature and culture, other terms might evoke possible alternative pathways. Reflecting this, artistic practices differ according to their position in relation to art, the environment and their juxta-positions. Their commitment is not always linked to an ecological cause. It can also be critical of political ecology, a discourse of many injunctions.

A fifth problem is environmental art's history. Several difficulties explain the obstacles associated with the recognition of this art, which are linked to its femi-nisation, the importance given to the ordinary as well as its calling back a fundamental human being, which has often seemed behind the formulation of the ecological link.

Therefore

The current idea of 'environmental art' can therefore only collect this series of definitions and redefinitions. Beyond the idea of ecological restoration, which is central to the definition, lies the question of the languages of art as a possible interpretation or invention of shared worlds. It is impossible to completely rule out environmental art painting (for example, Alexis Rockman, the painter of Brooklyn, and Chester Arnold), photography (among others, David Maisel, Chris Jordan, Edward Burtynski and Peter Goin) or videographers providing new representations of nature or human in nature. They are also essential to the imagination of the environment, but are part of a more classical tradition of artistic intervention.

Ecology, meaning "how to live" cannot and should not avoid the fact that we live in all kinds of places, and that one of them is the Earth, made of biochemical-physical material. But we also live in a world of languages that offer us the opportunity to represent ourselves at work in this environment. Ecology is dealing with bubbles, atmospheres and moods, all of which cannot qualify after the subject/object relationship, but should lead much more widely to undertake the reform of our inter-relational categories, and also of our political understanding, which takes into account objects to administer. Environmental art thus falls into a deep review of our dynamic world views as it should be understood as the art of the environment. At least that's the assumption in these pages that is being tested with the artistic works.

Modernist interpretation then leads us to consider the history of environmental art as an impossibility, or even a perversion of the artistic avant-garde. The more contextual interpretation meanwhile stresses the slow and healthy return of art away from museums in the lap of reality. Is this fundamental dichotomy – 'pure' art versus 'committed' art – always relevant? Jacques Rancière shows the artificiality of pitting one against the other with the rupture brought about by the French Revolution and the invention of an aesthetic regime of art. What is there to say? The birth of aesthetics is the time of the invention of a continuity between art and non-art, no longer based on different ways of 'doing' or on a distinction of tastes but on the invention of a 'distribution of the sensible'. In other words, art provides unique body settings, in space and time, 'that define ways of being together or separated, in front of or in the middle of, in or out, close or distant' (Rancière 2010). These devices should allow to oppose the established order.

How are these difficulties overcome today? Have they been subsumed by something else? The dozens of case studies, gleaned from the International COAL Prize corpus, which collected hundreds of projects, as well as the art practices in various parts of the world will help us find an answer. Our challenge is the re-embeddedness of art into aesthetics and the reassessment of importance of aesthetics. To give full freedom of the imagination in the wake of environmental aesthetics would be to get art out of the register of aesthetical exception and combine aesthetic experiences to ordinary life. This does not necessarily mean to think of these practices in terms of success and failure, or in terms of effectiveness or efficiency, but to see aesthetics as a theoretical and empirical framework contributing to the wealth of the world, its major design. Therefore mankind should not be seen as an ontological exception of whose art, that appears proper to man, would be proof. The presentation of case studies should help us to understand the singularity and plurality of answers to these questions and problems. The artists confront not only to specific places, but show very different mediators of traditions of the past. In many parts of the world, artistic practices feed on ancient traditions, repositories of a wealth of techniques and theoretical bodies but also of many different and subtle ways of feeling, doing and seeing the world. Tapping into these cultural riches, artists can then shape up and propose new ways of beings in society.

In this sense, art and artistic promises are numerous. First of all, art builds a critique, that is it facilitates a detailed valuative distance regarding contemporary life; then it taps into this 'cultural collateral', which means that it can shape new ways of being in society and in respect to the environment. This power to act can link art with political ecology in its resistance to global capitalism, and its efforts to resist to the unique way of financial valuation (Demos, 2013). Second, the artist who calls for another sustainability cares that art be about preserving the creativity at the heart of the living world. Third, artistic practice allows the establishment of an environmental ethic that is giving value to aesthetic commitments. Fourth, art practices allow a formal link of an aesthetic value to the reproduction of a cultural-natural heritage.

The involvement of artistic practices within the field of environmental fabric is pushed emphatically, at different levels and for different reasons; the local authorities seek to better public participation; UNESCO wants to be able to recognize culture as a fourth pillar. The theory being that without human creativity, imagination and innovation, existence on this planet never would be and cannot be possible into the future. Indigenous peoples, educators, scientists and artists are leading this recognition of culture and creativity as basic factors in the equation of how the next generation will face rising sea levels, natural disasters, rising chemical body burden and water shortages.

At one end of the spectrum are manifested the hopes of a profound renewal of environmental issues through art, hence the institutional support of artists committed to an active environmental practice. At the other end, a profound scepticism doubts the contribution of art to social change.

References

Abbing, H., 2002. *Why are Artists Poor? The Exceptional Economy of the Arts*. Amsterdam: Amsterdam University Press.

Baumgarten, A. G., 1750. *Aesthetica*. Frankfurt: I.C. Kleyb.

Becker, H., 1982. *Art Worlds: 25th Anniversary Edition*. Berkeley: University of California Press.

Boltanski, L. and Chiapello, E., 2006. *The New Spirit of Capitalism*. London: Verso.

Bourdieu, P., 1984. *Distinction: A Social Critique of the Judgement of Taste.* London: Routledge & Kegan Paul.

Bourdieu, P., 1992. *Les Regles de l'art. Genese et structure du champ litteraire.* Paris: Seuil.

Bourdieu, P., 1993. *The Field of Cultural Production.* New York: Columbia University Press.

Breidbach, O., 2006. *Visons of Nature: The Art and Science of Ernst Haeckel.* Munich: Prestel Verlag.

Demos, T. J., 2013. 'Contemporary Art and the Politics of Ecology'. *Third Text,* 27(1), 1–9.

Di Maggio, P. and Ostrower, F., 1992. *Race, Ethnicity, and Participation in the Arts: Patterns of Participation by Hispanics, Whites, and African-Americans in selected activities from the 1982 and 1985 surveys of Public Participation in the Arts, Research Division Report 25, National Endowment of the Arts.* Washington DC: Seven Locks Press.

Ellul, J., 1977. *Le système technicien.* Paris: Calman-Levy.

Gablik, S., 1984. *Has Modernism Failed?* London: Thames & Hudson.

Gablik, S., 1991. *The Reenchantment of Art.* London: Thames & Hudson.

Guattari, F., 2005. *The Three Ecologies.* London: Continuum International Publishing Group Ltd.

Kagan, S., 2011. *Art and Sustainability: Connecting Patterns for a Culture of Complexity.* Rev. edn. Bielefeld: Transcript Verlag.

Levine, L., 1988. *Highbrow/Lowbrow: The Emergence of Cultural Hierarchy in America.* Cambridge, MA: Harvard University Press.

Lippard, L., 1973. *Six Years: The Dematerialization of the Art Object from 1966–1972.* New York: Praeger.

Ranciere, J., 2010. *Dissensus: On Politics and Aesthetics.* New York: Bloomsbury.

Reuters, 2015. 'Hopi sacred masks auctioned in Paris despite protests', 11 June. Available at: www.reuters.com/article/us-france-auction-masks-idUSKBN0OR1DG20150611

Wingo, A., 2010. 'The Odyssey of Human Rights: Reply to Diagne'. *Transition,* 202, 120–138.

Plate 1 Carl Gustav Carus, *Full Moon near Pillnitz*

Plate 2 Thomas Cole, *Clouds*

Plate 3 Thomas Moran,
Minerva Terrace,
Yellowstone

Plate 4 Enrico Baj, *Bum-*
Manifesto Nucleare

Plate 5 Nancy Holt, *Sun Tunnels, Avignon Locators*

Plate 6 Fabien Bouchard, *Climate March silent protest,* COP21

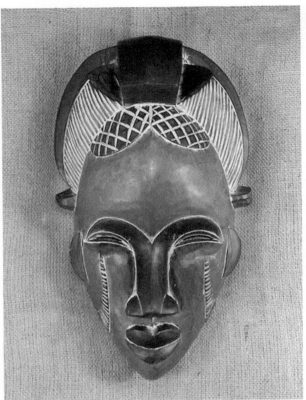

Plate 8 Lucy and Jorge Orta, *Antartica*

Plate 9 Thierry Boutonnier, *Prenez racines!*

Plate 10 Spagna et Caretto, *Pedogenesis*

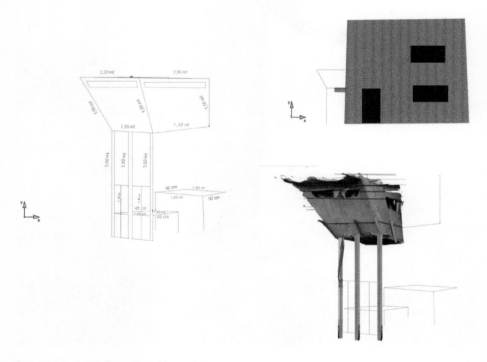

Plate 11 Maria Caolina, *Pino Ahumada*

Plate 12 Stephan Shankland, *Atelier* TRANS305

Plate 13 Theaster Gates, *Stony Island Arts Bank Vault*, original condition

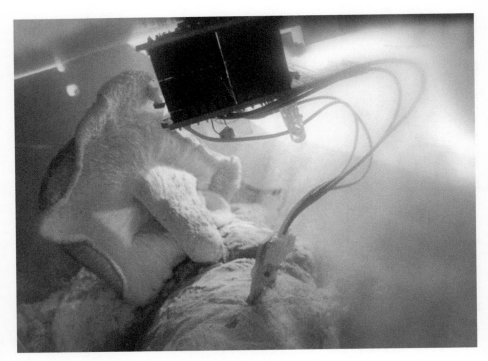

Plate 14 Guthrie/Pope, *What Will the Harvest Be?*

Plate 15 Ring, Urban Orchard, *Community Build*

Plate 16 Asa Sonjasdotter, *High Diversity*

Plate 17 Tomas Ruller, *Chimera*

Plate 18 Kim Abeles, *Smog Plates*

Plate 19 Celia Gregory, *The Coral Goddess*

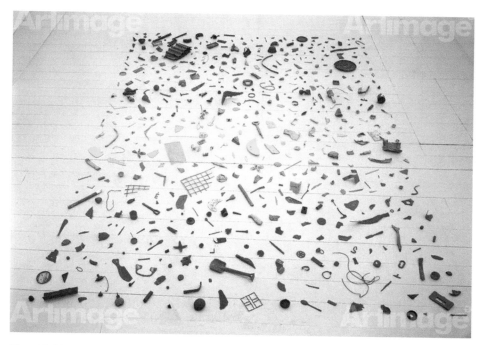

Plate 20 Tony Cragg, *New Stones, Newton's Tones*

Plate 21 Maartin Vanden Eynde, *Plastic Reef (2008–12)*

Plate 22 Ivan Kafka, *Lesní koberec pro náhodného houbaře* (*A Forest Carpet for a Chance Mushroom Hunter*)

Plate 23 Mark Dion, *Neukom Vivarium*, production still from the "Art in the Twenty-First Century" Season 4 episode, "Ecology"

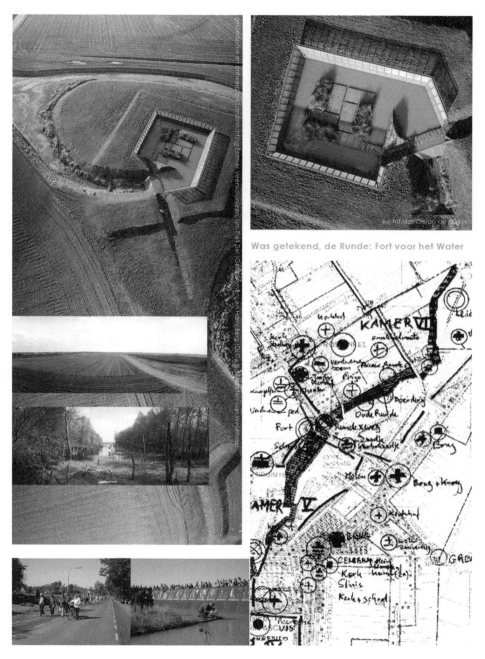

Was getekend, de Runde: Fort voor het Water

Plate 24 Jeroen van Westen, *De Runde project*

Plate 25 Nso Dance, *Nso, Kumbo, Cameroon*

Plate 26 Martin Eynde, *I Want That You Want What I Want That You Want*

Plate 27 Sonny Assu, *Breakfast Series*

Plate 28 Minerva Cuevas, *Egalité*

Plate 29 Timothy Farstou, *True-Cost-Market-checkout-mockup*

Part II

Deciphering emerging forms

Many books on art and environment present case studies, but without framing the issues at a theoretical level. The project of this book is to propose a theoretical framework, which embraces the many facets of aesthetic renewal brought by the variety of practices and artistic relationships between art and the environment. This part is therefore devoted to the formulation of some hypotheses that would be potential responses to questions and issues raised earlier, and that we will put to the test through the case studies presented in the following parts.

Theoretical threads presented below attempt to answer the break between nature/culture, and find ways to re-associate science and art. Thus, we won't seek to precisely define environmental art, or to measure the effectiveness of artistic proposals in response to environmental challenges. Indeed, the inefficiency of emancipatory artistic practices is real only to the extent of its claims. While art often has not been living up to its ambitions, many artists have, however, historically contributed to the evolutions of our time. We hope in this section, rather, to offer a broader spectrum of answers.

Our theoretical proposition is composed of three threads (Chapter 4). First of all, we would like to reassess the understanding of art as the ability to create form. Art could be considered as a specialized 'formating' activity protecting life's inventiveness. Second, we will assess how art contributes to the environment, which could bring art nearer to craft, with artists inventing new techniques in order to protect or invent lives. Then, we will discuss how an aesthetic composes a public space and renews our understanding of value, so as to be able to grasp what is at stake in public art. A second chapter (Chapter 5) is devoted to a broader level in order to theoretically reframe the evolution of artistic practices towards the environment.

4　Three green threads

Art is defined by a set of resources and conscious processes by which humans tend to a certain end and will to achieve a certain result. Art is the expression or application of human creative skill and imagination, producing works to be appreciated for their beauty or emotional power. The study of the arts is primarily concerned with human creativity and social life, such as languages, literature and history (as contrasted with scientific or technical subjects). Beyond art understood as a specialized activity,[1] and beyond any aesthetic experience that even concerns the objects of everyday life, there is a 'formative' ability, which applies to the whole experience, including objects and environmental phenomena, especially in the cities and places of human habitat. Wherever there is a creation of forms there is a demonstration of art (Pareyson, 2007; Blanc, 2016).[2]

Figure 4.1 Leonardo da Vinci, *A Bear Walking*

By 'form' we mean any momentary (event) or lasting (entity) crystallisation of a proposal of meaning and/or organised life. The forms thus conceived take shape via several processes: creation, reception (perception and appreciation) and interpretation. Environmental forms stand therefore as forms relating to environmental issues and to the production of an ordinary environment. The notion of 'form of life', in particular, is central to understanding the ecology and morphogenesis of the ways in which biological life is organised, just as much as for human communities. Between external conformation and internal essence, between principle of stability and dynamic model, between structure and genesis, and between exogenic print and autopoiesis, examining environmental forms will involve exploring the multidimensional characters of the notion of form, understood as a basic concept for any reflection on life. This reflection will be pushed further in Part III as integrating life processes, which is a major concern for many artists dealing with environmental issues.

Although the term 'form' is commonly used and scientifically discussed, when seen in a contemporary perspective taking into account the environmental problems, it could widen the interdisciplinary debate and make it possible to go beyond the *aporia* created by underestimating the potentialities of the Humanities and Social Sciences when confronted with environmental issues. In the same way, the Earth and Life Sciences could benefit from the manifold considerations of biological and physicochemical forms. Using environmental forms (such as the Earth, nature writing, the landscape, the urban garden, etc.), the artists propose knowledge modes and modes of assessment and action that are different from those usually mobilised by public environmental action. It involves bringing together cultural and environmental approaches, while at the same time respecting the diversities contained within each of them.

In environmental aesthetics, but also more widely in socio-environmental approaches (environmental humanities), both the questions of creation of art objects and their reception have been discussed at length. However, there has been a tendency to place them in opposition, as creation is seen as activity and reception as passivity. In fact, the 'public' is often viewed in this way, as the passive receiver of a production (artistic, architectural, urban, technical). It is also this view that is important in a world assessment and, more widely, in the world of action for the environment. Faced with this way of thinking about the processes by which 'forms' emerge, it is important to insist on the fact that the receptive process is an active process too, and therefore a creator or re-creator. Indeed, any reception is also interpretation, and any interpretation is a production, by the meaning attributed to it. In a more fundamental way, form is neither only one object/event, nor is it only one creation or one interpretation of this object/event by a subject. Form is the system shaped by the interaction of three clusters: (1) the producers, (2) the objects/events, and (3) the receivers/interpreters. It is a system that integrates a multiplicity of actors/producers and knowledge(s). Forms are therefore not just the source or the result; they are the crystallisation of a process of possible mediations and dialogues between different systems for interpreting the inhabited environment, its agents and its actors. They are collective, joint and 'negotiated' productions.

Re-assessment of art: protecting life's inventiveness

The notion of form, therefore, beyond the Manichean alternatives between obedience and disobedience, between object and subject and nature and culture facilitates the review of our representations by renewing our inter-relational categories along the lines of unprecedented understanding of the political. Nature is no longer this beautiful totality imagined by science in modern times, but consists of a series of problems that arise in the flow of human activity. We could respond by protecting modes of emergence of forms, valuing nature or rather a common formal tank, a system of potentialities. Ecology cannot protect nature as the inert material basis of the world, but it could well intend to preserve or protect the inventiveness that is at the heart of life in its relationship with the arts.

While reviewing our corpus, trying to investigate and emphasise the trends that characterise it, we will also see what answers they suggest to the following questions: what does protecting the inventiveness of life at the heart of environmental issues mean, on both ethical and aesthetic levels? What kind of protection could we imagine? What role do aesthetic tensions play in the formulation of an obligation regarding a living sustainability? Which questions are important to answer on this particular point thanks to the case studies? What is to find out, validate and test?

We would like to show that environmental art incorporates natural activity, and discloses not simply operations of power, but also of the entwinement of human social relations with a terrestrial realm. Thus, environmental art runs against the supposition that contemporary art is undertaking the dematerialisation of the object (Lippard, 1973). Nevertheless, environmental art has been at the forefront of the movement to challenge the definition of the art according to either its objecthood or the fixity of the medium. Environmental art is resolutely concrete as its vitalism implies the emergence of contingent forms linked with the living phenomena. Yet, environmental art differing from land art or earthworks does not only invest in specific locations. It can take many forms and corresponds to commitments that are ethically and aesthetically varied. There may be encounters with the natures represented by diverse landscapes and wilderness, but the question for the artist is to create forms of mediation, offering new tales of nature, or alternatives regarding the role of the human beings on earth. This is not necessarily meant to be thought of as ecological restoration, or even environmental rehabilitation.

Instead of merely representing the artist's relationship to nature, our aim may be also to present the irreducible character of contingency in artistic work. This contingency is philosophical (Meillassoux, 2006), meaning that it is to highlight a way of ordering the emergence of life. In the words of Goethe, life forms refer to the conditions of possibility of their uniqueness. It is therefore neither Earth-art or land-art, nor bioart, nor even ecological art nor environmental art, but to approach theoretically and empirically what artists do to life in redefining its forms. It is important therefore to distinguish two types of interventions, one that is possible to call representation and the other presentation. In the first case, the artist works with the interpretation of a given thing or scene through various media. In the second case, the artist is directly involved in the ecological factory of given places. Artists modify physical objects in real time. This is more than copying what already exists, but to be part of what produces the existence of things, which explains the abandonment of Re(presentation), as a sign of artistic distancing. Also, environmental art testifies to the artist's ability to intervene in real life. Can we then revise the historically built distance between art and craft, knowing that art might be departing from a mimetic regime? Saying that, we want to promote the biotic dimension of aesthetic and ethical relationships. Their pragmatic formalism emphasises the immersive dimension of the subject struck by the force of the situation, but also an engaged dimension of the artistic intervention, i.e. favouring the process. Whatever the considered views, these artists reflect a forgotten nature, reinvented, imagining a vanishing point obscured as needed by stories. It is a question of demonstration, even of manifestation. Therefore, a representation of nature shows what is given to forget, a 'phusis' impossible to frame symbolically. The beauty of nature holds the diversity of its manifestations. It shows a need to represent the unknown that is to be revealed, continuing the ideas of the Enlightenment.

Arts, crafts and re-embededness

Environmental forms resurrect the issue of an art that can be qualified by craft(s). The explanations are manifold: their aesthetic involvement includes the aesthetic dimension of our ordinary lives; they force art to widen its traditional field of intervention to environmental issues. The idea is not that a perfection of the model is in play, and the artist/craftsman can imitate nature with ideal productions or divine creations. Environmental art is renovating a craft merging with the context; the environmental artists need to get engaged into the matter and make forms that have values: it is not to forget a world of ideas but rather to incorporate values into a material world. This evolution explains the link between these artistic works and various trades (social and natural sciences, engineering) as well as its openness to local development in its ecological, social, economic dimensions. The goal of this art would be the reinstatement of the dimensions of social life, not in community fittings to fixed identities, opposed to each other, but in solidifying space-time constraints.

Interestingly, that said, it also allows us to go beyond the several problems identified in the previous chapter regarding (for instance) art's irrelevancy in terms of social change and ecological transformations. It also strengthens the contribution of the otherwise feeble link between art and the ordinary, helping to highlight the relevancy of those artists. This then gives it prominent importance in their work. In Part I we insisted on the break of artists with other actors of society, and their lack of capacity to intervene in the real world without degrading their art. The merging of a tradition of 'fine art' with crafts may be a turning point in broadening the arts, and transforming crafts and design in the contemporary world. The emergence in the 1980s of art 'factories' (Warhol) and fabricators, designers, builders, working closely with artists, began to blur these definitions of 'high' and 'low' art once again.

More generally, this interpretation of the concept of environmental forms opens into a broad understanding of art, technology and poetry, understanding that is rooted in a tradition: indeed, the meaning of these terms has not always designated differentiated operations. This role of form refers to the symbolic activity and practice of art, which can be defined as a type of knowledge or a predisposition to make something special (Dissenayake, 1992). Reference may be made, in addition to the work of Dewey disconnecting the aesthetic experience of art to apply it to different objects of ordinary life, or to the analysis of an anthropologist such as André Leroi-Gourhan, to an older conception of art. 'Ars' meant the conscious and intentional human ability to produce objects in the same way that nature produces phenomena (Panofsky, 1938). The activity of an architect, a painter or sculptor could still, in the Renaissance, be designated as art as well as that of a weaver or a beekeeper. Therefore, the activity that we used to call 'art' in the West is only one example among others of this founding relationship between technical forms and techniques of thought (Jauss and Shaw, 1982). Techné could also refer not only to the 'doing' but also to art in the greater sense.

The Greek word *poiesis* itself meaning the capacity to make things concretely happen, was historically not understood as a creative process. The medieval understanding of artistic *poiesis* was to imitate God's perfect creations, whereas the modern understanding means a creation which itself produces the perfect thing (or, expressed differently, the beautiful appearance of perfection). Leonardo Da Vinci, the quintessence of creative capacity and of the universality of the human spirit, symbolises the change from the classical to the modern concept of creativity. We must therefore emphasize that *poiesis* was not originally limited to verbal art but was an act of doing, producing that which was not opposed to the *physis* (Greek terminology for nature). *Physis*, synonymous with 'by which the thing happens by itself', is *poiesis*. In many cultures, arts and crafts are not separated and in many non-Western cultures the representation of perfection, meaning godliness, is prohibited. The use of ornamentation and non-representational imagery in Islamic art is a case in point.

In contrast, the young Marx elevates productive or concrete doing to the level of aesthetic activity; in other words, he interprets technical production according to the 'inherent standard' of artistic production. The fashioning of beauty in labour is to fulfil that general human need 'to be at home in the world,' which in Hegel's *Aesthetics* could be satisfied only by art. For the young Marx, labour was the true 'resurrection of nature' whenever it humanises nature as it produces beauty and through its products makes the poetically appropriated nature appear to man as his work and his reality.

Aesthetic qualities and alternative value measure in the public sphere

Engaging in an overview of the historical relationships between arts and envi-ronments allowed us, in the previous part, to touch upon some of the complexities arising around the issue of arts' value. We briefly addressed the value problem as being the problem of what's marketable, or that modern art is a specialised activity reinforcing capitalism. At a more general level, the rational economic logic of sustainability is based on attributing financial value to nature (ecosystem services) even in its cultural understandings, while artistic commit-ment in public space could well be read like an attempt to reformulate the public space following Arendt's thinking.

The artwork is the model of the object that is resistant to time erosion. This observation enriches the understanding that we may have of the term 'sustain-ability'. In elucidating the work of art, Hannah Arendt (1998) explains that nowhere does pure sustainability of the world of objects appear so clearly. Nowhere, therefore, is the world of objects revealed as dramatically as the home-land of non-deadly things. Art creates an area of activity where the things produced resist the material and ideational wear; can aesthetic value promise a good future? The hypothesis is the following: to recognise the aesthetic value of places, objects or things is to assign to them a sustainability factor. A second hypothesis is that to valorise attitudes rather than forms, the process rather than the object, in the field of art, expands the scope of objects which may be affected by the aesthetic value; yet it must first be admitted that the aesthetic experience is a testimony of the common capacity to confer aesthetic value, to experience the real world. The aesthetic experience is what allows us to be fully human highlighting our common capacity to value the environment.

Thus, aesthetic value can offset the economic value. Like money, it has an exchange function, but it opens an aestheticised public space. Because the aesthetic can't be totally objectified, it needs a public space for discussion. The idea of the museum and gallery space provided this, and still does to some extent, when not corrupted by wealthy board members who manipulate art only as an investment. Throughout these pages the authors offer a critique of this moneyed system that has rendered so many of our great public culture institutions into a circus of promotion and merchandising. But it is not to say that all museums nor galleries fit into this corruption by any means. Throughout the United States, for example, university galleries and museums are offering exciting and challenging exhibitions, devoid of collections and/or buyers. There are artist-run spaces and co-operative exhibition halls around the world today that are also outside of a mainstream art market, and maintaining this vital connection between the public and artistic creativity.

For our reflection on the relationship between art and money, Jean-Pierre Cometti explains that there is no comparison between the values of the objects of use. So they can be shared, we must lend them a common value that can be their exchange value. This is pretty much the same thing for art. The value of an artwork considered only from the point of view of one who loves or owns, is immeasurable, and that is why it is meaningless to talk about its value. A work has value as long as it can be publicly appreciated. Art is therefore an exchange value as well as money, two general equivalents. However, it seems that the terms of these two operators are opposed. Money tends to derealise the object, as we can see with the unreality of the landscape made by its monetisation. These mechanisms are strengthened when they are coupled with a classic frontal development programme that tends to obliterate the local values. Conversely, we believe that art is a translator whose terms of exchange and sharing tends to re-materialize things. The artistic exchange does not take place in the market with the price as the only indicator of value; it takes place in the public space where the sharing of assessments on forms occurs. If this discussion can escape abstraction, it is because it is not made up only of disinterested judgments as Kant thinks, but because the circulation of forms can enhance the aesthetic experience of each of the participants in the debate. The aesthetic experience is what allows us to be fully human in witnessing to our common responsibility to give value to the life we live.

What kind of value does the aesthetic experience and judgment give to things? First, permanent values; beautiful things are immortal (because they evoke the life that goes on beyond generational lives) and are part of the transmitted heritage. The legacy consists of the transmission of what is beautiful, which has value. Second, work values; the work is the result of judgment of a singularity, of the artist or of a community, governed by political action, which is to itself its own purpose. The environment as a producer of a society's reflexivity itself is now at the heart of this issue of heritage. Similarly, since the question of intention is any question underlying the separation between culture and nature, the singularity of the work being the supposed intention, is, originally, the fragile or omnipotent hand. From there, what we admire is the ability to produce. Therefore, we raise the question of cultural perspective since we addressed the question of the value that we attribute to products of different cultures. Third, creative transformation of values means possible renewal and fragility of the aesthetic work. The fragility and beauty of the work solicits creative action.

We will follow artistic processes, which have tried to embody these issues, and otherwise represent the value of an artwork, either as embedded in local territories, or as another way to create a public debate in the world that surrounds us.

Notes

1   Hal Foster, American art critic, defined the works of environmental art as:

> sculpture projects that use site-specific materials taken into the environment to create new forms or to redirect our perception of the environment; programs that include new objects, unnatural in a natural scenario; Individual activities on the landscape where time is critical; concerted action and social consciousness. Even if there were, at first, the will of environmental art to fight against the 'art system', eliminating the artistic object and its commodification, it appeared necessary to

present the achievements to obtain recognition and the status of works of art and the necessary funds. For this reason, artists have begun to consider the need to film and photograph their achievements.

(Foster, 1983)

2   For Lefebvre, 'aesthetic activity does not operate on concepts. It deals both with the making (œuvre), the living and the telling. Aesthetics is not only a discourse. It operates on a material (which can be verbal, but then the words become work material, such as colors and sounds).' (My transl.) The poetic of the city is based on a theory of art as a lifestyle (Lefebvre, 2001).

References

Arendt, H., 1998. *The Human Condition*. 2nd edn. Chicago: The University of Chicago Press.

Blanc, N., 2016. *Les formes de l'environnement: Manifeste pour une esthétique politique*. Lausanne: Métis Presses.

Cometti, J.-P., 2002. La monnaie de la pièce: remarques sur l'art, l'échange et la valeur. *Parachute*, April, May, June, Issue 106, 70–85.

Dissenayake, E., 1992. *Homo Aestheticus: Where Art Comes from and Why*. Seattle: University of Washington Press.

Foster, H., ed., 1983. *The Anti-Aesthetics: Essays on Post-Modern Culture*. Port Townsend: Bay Press.

Jauss, H. R. and Shaw, M., 1982. 'Poiesis'. *Critical Inquiry*, 8(3), 591–608.

Lefebvre, H., 1962. *Introduction a la modernite: Preludes*. Paris: editions de Minuit.

Lippard, L., 1973. *Six Years: The Dematerialization of the Art Object from 1966–1972*. New York: Praeger.

Meillassoux, Q., 2006. *Après la finitude: Essai sur la nécessité de la contingence*. Paris: Seuil.

Panofsky, E., 1938. *Meaning in the Visual Arts*. Chicago: University of Chicago Press.

Pareyson, L., 2007. *Esthétique: Théorie de la formativité*. Paris: Éditions Rue d'Ulm.

5   Towards a new epistemology

This brief presentation has led us to see the complexity and intricacy of what is called upon as environmental. It has a major link to site-specific situations and reminds one of the importance of places, being aware though of the lure of the local (Lippard, 1973). Modern science has objectified knowledge, relegating arts and humanities on the side of subjective productions. In this context, the question of nature, which is to be defined in terms of its material and conceptual production requires reconfiguring aesthetic relationships in active terms, not as liabilities associated to a contemplative state. The aesthetics of Baumgarten, subversive in his time, contest logic, this higher faculty of knowledge, to promote sensitivity, but also the capacity to live beautifully.[1]

What kind of knowledge does art or art practice allow? How to live beautifully is a kind of knowledge addressed by any aesthetic practice. It promotes a certain quality in our relationships to others, parents, family and working relationships. This position joined a scepticism that leads to a vision of one's own life with all its uncertainties and vacillations, or rather the certainty of perpetual change. The perspective of action demands to feel the moment, but also to forge an idea of an aesthetic relationship to this sensory open environment, capable of shaping the latter, which itself becomes the instrument of the knowledge and recognition. A sceptical method to live well can be summed up as a test of one's own judgments requiring an aesthetic opening to the possibility to feel otherwise. *What do I know?* is a central question for the sceptic. For us this question translates as: What kind of knowledge produces this interdisciplinary alliance between art and environment? Besides formalising landscapes, places, situations or intermediate objects, our goal could be indeed to deploy the conditions of possibility of a new knowledge on better living conditions. What I know, therefore, is only temporary, but the beauty of some of these temporary formalizations gives the measure of their accuracy. The judgment is not a final instrument but a public discussion tool, which permits to share environmental configuring. It is also the best way to dramatise this existence, to actively and passively enjoy the spectacular changes both inside ourselves and out.[2]

Aesthetics stands out as a way to imagine a renewed environmental artificiality in the light of ecological issues, that is the ability to live together in this world. The human adventure gives to environmental forms the status of guides in the formation of a new ecological commons. Human sensitivities being given, the contemporary modes of the subject's construction should be based upon the elaboration of new environmental forms.

If many of the relational thinkers, whether of relational aesthetics (Bourriaud, 1998),[3] or interpretationism (Gadamer, 2013) assumes an intersubjective public space, how could we – if we get rid of philosophical correlationism, which stands upon the nature-culture divide – think of an absolute emergence of forms? The factuality of existence and the unseizable community oblige to recreate the sense of the place with sensibility for only reason. What makes us, pushes us, sustains us, moves us, inevitably, becomes the reason of our existences. Therefore, there is no more a world that emerges in the absolute, a world outside ourselves, with which human beings would be in a relationship, but a way of being absolute, whose produced referents are forms. The fragility of contemporary knowledge is born of the multiplication and the infinite diversity of these forms. Thus brings the role of vitality, as a singular impetus.

In other words, whenever the question of life, as nonsense, is subsumed by the force of life, and we become aware that despite the absolute absurdity of life, we live, momentum becomes beautiful. Ignorance accompanies the certainty of being alive. Therein lies the issue of self-determination. Its finality is the human accomplishment in a world filled with significantly different defined forms. Because living at best is also knowing how to fully experience your life, from which emerges the need to take distance, for a rich self-awareness. Unlike Guattari (2005) dividing analytically *three ecologies*, between the consciousness, the environment and the society, it is thought necessary to conceptualise our ecologies into ecological momenta (formalised objects). Such desubjectivation and desobjectivation, where neither the subject, nor the object is called upon on a permanent basis, is to avoid the trap of natural, cosmologic or earthly essentialism, for the benefit of socio-ecological manufactures, opening them to debate and reformulations. Environmental or ecological art (and environmental aesthetic) both draw attention to the need for new environmental immersions considered as a means to reveal the environmental condition as well as to pay attention to engaged aesthetic dimensions of any environmental problem. The reformulation of a 'sharing sensitive experience' operates from claims arising from a worldly immersion.

Environmental aesthetics

Environmental aesthetics battles the threat of a double reduction: the geometricisation of the environment seen as a measurable space free of bio-physical materiality, and the confusion between eco art and land art, with the intention to promote ethical and political development of aesthetics issues, aesthetic ecological claims. What are the connections of artistic practices rooted in the environment with sustainability? What are the links between taking into account environmental, social and economic justice and art with sustainability? In addition to a responsible moral posture, concerned about the wellbeing of future generations, many of these artistic practices involve a deep aesthetic concern guiding them towards the preservation of the unique and irreplaceable quality of natural entities. These practices endorse the similarities between the loss of a work of art and the loss of an animal or plant species.

They include the local value of the premises and therefore the aesthetic and ethical singularity of their experience: they make and enrich sustainability, definitions of sustainability being as diverse as the places and stories where they originate from. The term sustainability is as strong (and therefore subject to a relative consensus) as it is coloured differently in different cultures. Sustainability represents a value system that creates strong relationships between the general and the particular. Obviously, in the absence of a fixed dogma (sustainability is rather to be understood as a flexible framework), sustainability calls for local crafts, to specific style effects, and a strong aesthetic dimension. It thus provides an other means for political wholesomeness.

Our proposition, anchored in new materialist theories (Barad, 2007; Dolphijn and Tuin, 2012) as well as new speculative theories (Blanc, 2016; Meillassoux, 2006), could be the following: the dialogue between the artist, the scientist and the public is trying to reinvent the environmental agency program, and more specifically the agentivity of living species. Aesthetics therefore address the mode of appearance that 'parcels out places and forms of participation in a common world', and reaches a moment of politicisation when conventional categories of, and separations between, the seen and heard versus the forgotten and overlooked are challenged and redistributed. The reinvention of the composition of the sensitive experience continues the revelation of knowledge in light of new artistic practices and/or hybrid art/science practices. Beyond practice, what we aim for is the question of aesthetic regimes of environmental knowledge. The use of the aesthetic term here refers to the exercise of the right to experience fundamental experience and its contents (proprioceptive, sensory, emotional experience of a committed body in an action) and not simply the judgment of taste attached to a particular type of experience – that of a work of art – that historically constitutes the factual scope of the art disciplines.

A dynamic reinvention of places

Environmental aesthetics is a science that attempts to determine how aesthetic satisfaction intervenes in the assessment and creation of natural and built environments. It also strives to gain a better understanding of contemporary aesthetic imperatives concerning the production of the environment. So, environmental aesthetics aims to understand how a collective sentiment emerges in the deployment of a shared environmental aesthetic that includes social interplay comprising know-how, power relationships and information sharing. As such, the issue concerns the type of aesthetic (and ethical) challenge that arises from the contemplation and contemporary production of environments.

Let us begin by exploring why we should be searching in this direction. Sustainable development is a phase. Rio+20 has shown how sustainable development negotiations have now reached a dead end that points up the limits of negotiated growth based on reforming development strategies and lifestyles in countries with very different historical trajectories. In 2015, France hosted the 21st United Nations Conference on Climate Change (COP21), as mentioned earlier in this book. The Conference of the Parties are, since 2005 the annual formal meetings for the United Nations Framework Conventions on Climate Change. The Paris COP was a key international meeting to negotiate an international agreement to fight climate change. Its goal was to engage all countries through a universal binding climate agreement to contain global warming to 2 degrees Celsius by 2100. While the expectations were largely met with an international consensus to keep fossil fuels in the ground, the timeline to do so is generally agreed to be too long and too late, leaving the planet to warm up by well over 3 degrees in the near future (see Plate 6). Bill McKibben of 350.org famously summed up the Paris talks to the press shortly afterwards saying that [they] 'didn't save the planet but it may have saved the chance of saving the planet'.[4]

The issue concerns a more radical change in our model of civilisation; going against the ideology of consumption that tends to impose equality on objects and things bound up with their incompressible and irreducible values in use. It also disagrees with the idea whereby the pooling of goods and property can resolve the crisis in contemporary capitalism without any negotiation or debate, thus avoiding power grabs and petty ambitions. This is opposed to the provocative elitism of a rejection of mass consumption and its voracious hedonism. It is also opposed to the impossible role attributed to participation. This, for some people, merely seeks to articulate the appetites of a market-based society (Agamben, et al., 2012). Last, it goes against everything that is opposed to the recognition (Honneth and Rancière, 2016) in its very existence (Merleau-Ponty, 2000) of the material bases of life. There is therefore a need to reflect upon a socio-political system that recognises its finite nature, limits and contingencies. Opposed to all heroism in speech as well as to any attitude seeking to impose the idea of a calculated (and calculating) possibility of surpassing the limits of human endeavour, it is bound up with incorporating material realities such as the sensorial realities likely to shed light on each person's existence. And yet the aesthetic – the aesthesis – supposes and is underpinned by the recognition of everyone as a living being in a world of diverse forms, colours, sounds, smells and precepts as well as the formal representations associated with all of these things.

In our view, aesthetics should take into account the conditions of a shared habitation, in other words, one that does not forget its rapport with milieu. This first phase in our reflection on environmental aesthetics gives us a threefold scope: one, it seeks to revisit 'sharing sensitive experience', a system of sensitive proof that simultaneously depicts the existence of something in common and the boundaries that circumscribe the respective places and parts (Rancière, 2000). Indeed, the definition of what is included within the domain of the environment, the sharing that splits it into different categories and the related choices made are what really determine the production of the environment. It focuses in particular on reviewing the categories and current state of the knowledge that underpins 'sharing sensitive experience'. Consequently, we will also have to review the conditions for using and contributing to, controlling and participating in environmental resources and their production (and assessment) that are no longer based merely on rational knowledge.

Two, it therefore seeks to broaden the environmental planning and management debate to encompass previously ignored dimensions (aesthetic and ethical values); it makes it possible to leverage the environmental resource in terms other than those associated with rational and scientific action.

And three, in the event that it fails to achieve its goal, it aims to empower people by promoting the abilities associated with the possibilities offered by their particular lives. Therefore, the scope is political insofar as it is not merely concerned with reviewing the production models of democracy in action, but with reflecting upon other possible conditions for a political regime that embraces equal participation by human beings (as citizens) in the exercise of politics, which includes the production of the environment.

Thus, the aesthetics associated with a category of problems within the sphere of public action, environmental problems (pollution, finite resources, etc.) and a new conception of the rapport with the world in general, proposes an action model that includes the idea of sharing. We believe that this idea of deferred sharing differs from that developed by Jacques Rancière (2000). It is not concerned with ascertaining how the sharing takes place or the extent to which it has always neglected a group of people who are devalued in the public debate. This sharing is associated with a desire to share with a view to testing it out. It involves the idea of objectivation of speech in the public domain for the purpose of comparing its value. This idea of sharing harks back to Hannah Arendt's interpretation of Kant's third critique. In her lectures on Kant's *Political Philosophy* dealing with the critique of the faculty of judgment published in 1790, Hannah Arendt refers to the Kantian conception of aesthetic judgment: the faculty of judging the particular when we do not have a universal – rule, principle, law or standard – within which to subsume it and define political judgment.[5] The close proximity of the two judgments only works because politics is defined by Arendt as the 'space of appearance where people share words and deeds' (Arendt, 1991). How can taste, that supposedly entirely subjective phenomenon, lead us to judgment and reveal the shared world? Kant has already answered this question. He believed taste to be a common sense; the condition for the existence of beautiful objects is the 'communicability' that begets taste. Spectators' judgments constitute the public space in which beautiful objects appear. The aesthetic associated with an experience of 'aesthetic seizure' and the desire to share the resulting feeling is part of collective art. Aside from the desire for approval, which sanctions recognition of one's judgment and possibly of the object to which it refers, communication is essential for aesthetic happiness (Doguet, 2007). The reasons for sharing need to be experienced together. These motivations vary but they all lead back to the question of sense because we share meanings, values and usage value, pleasure and disgust. We have this in common. Sharing is fundamental (etymologically the notion reflects a division into parts, and not what performing such an operation actually means, and once again today it reflects the idea of life 'in common' in the fullest sense); it cannot be solely rational, or rationally constructed; it must also be emotional and experienced. It is therefore bound up with the possibility of a broader based empathy and conditions for sharing a collective feeling (Rifkin, 2009).

This sharing is political, particularly within a democracy, which requires shared voting, political representation, common sense and collective living. Conversely, democracy underpins the idea of sharing as we understand it: the desire to share, and not simply the numerical operation of division into parts. This political regime is invoked to undertake the possibilities of a plural existence decided upon communally: what are these possibilities? Under which conditions do they play their role? As Jean-Luc Nancy has written (Agamben, et al., 2012), democracy also questions these considerations in the absence of an over-arching rule providing a definitive measure.

Why sharing? Revisiting this question involves considering that environmental aesthetics allow us to renew the idea of pleasure, to associate with others, to experience certain environments, and to feel alive under collectively challenging conditions. Starting with Kant and Arendt's interpretation of his work, but also drawing upon John Dewey's philosophy of pragmatism and his obstinate refusal to allow art and aesthetic experience to be confined to the realms of museums, environmental aesthetics seeks to open up the domain and the idea of 'political'[6] sharing to the common experience of the natural and built environments. It is also concerned with sharing its experiences, pleasure and suffering inter alia, inasmuch as particularly today, in the midst of the network era, the possibility of sharing is one of the conditions for obtaining recognition and forging a reputation. Being known and recognised is contingent on forging numerous connections. Recognition is now enhanced by sharing personal production through the networks. Still within this meaning, sharing also entails creating in common: there are different types of environmental creativity however; this expression warrants analysis and we will come back to it later. The idea is to pool the (private or public) environment created by and for the pleasure of a public yet to be created. The individual creates an environment, experiences pleasure therein, perfecting its forms and the vision of the world it represents or summarises, that are then shared as such; sharing enhances its validity. The pertinence of the environment is tested by sharing. As such, managing or controlling the sharing process (of experience in particular), necessarily involves setting oneself up as a despot, monarch or all-powerful figure. If, as Jean-Luc Nancy notes (Agamben, et al., 2012), the term democracy, as distinct from monarchy (just one) and oligarchy (a small number), is not bound up with the idea of number, this is also because it also implies defining the conditions for sharing by and with everyone, particularly from a project perspective. So, is it a coincidence that Arendt's interpretation of Kant makes aesthetic judgment one of the bases of politics and that Dewey criticizes the lack of importance accorded to aesthetics in any debate about education and democracy?

Reflecting on sharing also means reflecting upon the conditions for a more effective distribution of environmental resources both from an ideas and a material standpoint, thus the need for the expression of environmental creativity. We would contend that there is a strong link between sharing, that is a distribution of goods in more or less equal proportions in accordance with rules understood by all, and creating an environment or one's own environment. To begin with, a number of arguments support the link between sharing and creativity. The first of these – and in our view the most persuasive – is that creativity is underpinned by the deployment of new conditions for sharing sensitive experience. Continuing on, what emerges from creativity is everything that qualifies as new, that is an object, situation, joke, etc. Obviously, this newness is judged in accordance with the scenes in which it operates and the criteria specific to the actors present within it. However, one key thing is that creating involves setting up new 'sensitive experience sharing', in other words a novel way of seeing the world. Succeeding as a creative person or unit involves the allowance of sharing.

The fact that the environment is a result of collective art makes it even more necessary to publicly debate standard arrangements for designing natural and built environments. This is the 'experience of sensitive sharing', that is the manner in which sensitive elements are shared and presented with a view to being shared, that lies at the heart of designing a common strategy. It is about building a fairer society, that is one in which there is a defined order of present phenomena distributed in approximately equal portions. How does environmental creativity partake of this approach? It is the adjunct of being that must be distributed; the extreme demonstration of a modus operandi at work.

So, once again, what is environmental creativity? Let us take things a step further. We should clarify from the outset that sharing actually involves what may be displayed in the public domain and in this respect, the public domain is of fundamental importance. Displaying an object, work, product or scientific innovation means according it relevance in the public domain. Such relevance sometimes boils down to questions of effectiveness or efficiency. Occasionally, it may be associated with the criterion of its beauty – in which case it is taste that decides – or its technologically innovative character may make it a significant creation. In any case, the environment is the result of dependent interactions concerning the degrees of agency lent to contributing elements; it is important therefore not to consider it as a piece of data (Barad, 2007). We may also contend that there is an ordinary environmental creativity that operates via adjustments made in the course of actions where it is generally very difficult to break out the moment of relevance. Ordinary environmental creativity proceeds from a series of innovations without any specific authors.

We therefore need to conceive of a politics of forms that does not ignore these aesthetic environments.[7] A politics of these forms could factor in the way in which these aesthetic investments take place, break, interrupt and scar our singular and collective existences in their singularities and historical and geographical complexities. These aesthetic investments embroider the related materiality with specific contingencies and play on finite natures and limits by exploring the contingencies. This is also how these investments teach us lessons.

These conditions must be discussed and debated. There is no way that our visions of the material bases of existence and related powers can be reviewed without debate. We need to develop the tools for a collective mediation that gives life to forms.

Aesthetic public space and formal commons

Hannah Arendt (1991) proposes a design of public space inspired by the Kantian aesthetic judgment, but totally reformulated and transformed. Her reflections on public space imply taking into account aesthetics, especially her emphasis on action, common world, appearance, durability and unpredictability, as well as her passion for distinction, process, plurality and confidence.

More recently, Sue Spaid (2003) insisted on the proximity between contemporary art and the Arendtian public space. Indeed, the works of many contemporary artists incorporate the process, sustainability and plurality of spectators as well as unpredictability. In addition, because they do not resemble what is usually considered as art, an aesthetic judgment is required to hold the attention and determine whether it is art. However, we share the critique of the Kantian judgment as it was stated by Dewey (1980). Kant's anaemic conception of art is, on the one hand, too involved in a representational structure of experience (as of its conditions of possibility) and, on the other hand, limits the aesthetic pleasure to a faculty judgment, considered as entirely disinterested and disconnected from the other parts of life. This analysis, though, allowed us to formulate the hypothesis of an aestheticisation of public space (Blanc and Lolive, 2007). The idea of an 'aesthetic of public space' introduces aesthetic judgment as a democratic, non-expert, criterion in public debates. It permits a political transition between the individual and the collective, between singular and general, between aesthetics experience and aesthetic judgment.

Notes

1   Sensitivity is a mode of knowledge, which highlights the co-construction of the individual and the environment, of the self and others. In sum, knowledge and recognition are so closely associated. This approach stands out from the objectifying science that tends to separate the issue of the knowledge of nature, that of the recognition, realisation of human beings (Honneth and Rancière, 2016). Ecology becomes a technical science, the planet a laboratory, and the city a regulated, and controlled system. The eighteenth century saw us become aware of the fact that it was necessary to oppose to the increasing mechanization an aesthetic approach to nature. In 1750, Alexander Baumgarten in *Aesthetica* says that besides a logical truth, there is also room for an aesthetic truth, opposing, for example, the eclipse observed by astronomers and mathematicians, to the eclipse perceived emotionally by the shepherd who speaks with his beloved (Baumgarten, 1750).

2   To rethink sexual difference from a very pragmatic or empirical point of view. In fact, de Beauvoir introduces us to a naïve ethics that, as its point of departure, is not

willing to accept received sociobiological or socio-cultural differences between the sexes. As with Artaud, it is an ethics that starts from the soil within which a force of life that gives form to flesh and spirit is at work. In contrast to the way de Beauvoir is usually read in feminist theory, she takes here an affirmative stance, trying to think of feminism not as a critical but as a vitalist project.

3 Exhibition curator, writer, art critic and theorist especially for relational aesthetic concept, Nicolas Bourriaud (born in 1965), is the co-founder and co-director with Jérôme Sans, of the Palais de Tokyo in Paris from 2000 to 2006, co-founder of the magazine *Documents on Art* (1992–2000) and *Perpendicular* (1995–1998); he was curator for contemporary art at Tate Britain, professor at the University of Venice and from 2011 to 2015, director of the National School of Fine Arts in Paris.

4 See: https://350.org/press-release/cop21-reaction/

5 Conferences given in the New School for Social Research in New York in autumn, 1970. We have based our analysis of these conferences on both Arendt's paper and Myriam Revault d'Allonnes' excellent interpretation (Arendt, 1991).

6 It is not that everything should be political, even in a democracy, but rather that democracy forces us to continually rethink the question of sharing and in a democracy this is necessarily a political issue.

7 To our knowledge, Nicolas Bourriaud was the first to conceptualise this idea albeit from a different angle.

> Our period is lacking not a political project but rather forms that embody one. The dominant form when the French Revolution took place was the assembly, during the Russian Revolution it was the soviet. Then came protests, the sit-in, etc. Our period is lacking in forms conducive to expressing and even encouraging political projects. The dominant form at the present time – but it is not a 'political' form – is the free party or 'rave', a spontaneous and temporary assembly of individuals around the same objective who occupy a place not intended for this purpose.
>
> (Bourriaud, 2002)

References

Agamben, G., Badiou, A., Bensaïd, D., Brown, W., Nancy, J.-L., Rancière, J., Ross, K. and Zizek, S., 2012. *Democracy in What State?*. New York: Columbia University Press.

Arendt, H., 1991. *Juger: Sur la philosophie politique de Kant, suivi de Deux essais interprétatifs par Ronald Beiner et Myriam Renault d'Allonnes*. Paris: Seuil, coll. Libre examen.

Barad, K. M., 2007. *Meeting the Universe Halfway: Quantum Physics and the Entanglement of Matter and Meaning*. Durham, NC: Duke University Press.

Baumgarten, A. G., 1750. *Aesthetica*. Frankfurt (Oder): I. C. Kleyb.

Blanc, N., 2016. *Les formes de l'environnement: Manifeste pour une esthétique politique*. Lausanne: Métis Presses.

Blanc, N. and Lolive, J., 2007. *Cosmopolitiques 15: Esthétique et espace public*, Rennes: éditions Apogée/Cosmopolitiques.

Bourriaud, N., 1998. *L'esthétique relationnelle*. Dijon: Les Presses du Réel.

Bourriaud, N., 1999. *Formes de vie: L art moderne et l invention de soi*. Paris: Denoël.

Bourriaud, N., 2002. 'Les îlots et l'utopie'. *L'Humanité*, 22 February. Available at: www.humanite.fr/node/260705.

Bourriaud, N., 2003. *Postproduction*. Dijon: Les presses du réel.

Dewey, J., 1980. *Art as Experience*. New York: Perigee Books.

Doguet, J.-P., 2007. *L art comme communication: Pour une redéfinition de l art*. Paris: Armand Colin.

Dolphijn, R. and van der Tuin, I. eds., 2012. *New Materialism: Interviews & Cartographies*. Ann Arbor: Open Humanities Press, Michigan Publishing.

Gadamer, H.-G., 2013. *Truth and Method*. London: Bloomsbury Academic.

Guattari, F., 2005. *The Three Ecologies*. London: Continuum International Publishing Group Ltd.

Honneth, A. and Rancière, J., 2016. *Recognition or Disagreement: A Critical Encounter on the Politics of Freedom, Equality, and Identity*. New York: Columbia University Press.

Lippard, L., 1973. *Six Years: The Dematerialization of the Art Object from 1966–1972*. New York: Praeger.

Meillassoux, Q., 2006. *Après la finitude: Essai sur la nécessité de la contingence*. Paris: Seuil.

Merleau-Ponty, M., 2000. *Nature: Course Notes from the Collège de France*. Evanston, IL: Northwestern University Press.

Rancière, J., 2000. *The Politics of Aesthetics, the Distribution of the Sensible*. London: Bloomsbury Press.

Rifkin, J., 2009. *The Empathic Civilization: The Race to Global Consciousness in a World in Crisis*. London: Tarcher.

Spaid, S., 2003. 'A Political Life: Arendtian Aesthetics and Open Systems'. *Ethics & the Environment*, 8(1), 93–101.

Part III

Experiencing the living and arts transformation

In the 1967 poem 'All Watched Over By Machines Of Loving Grace' by Richard Brautigan, living beings are compared to machines. He writes of a 'cybernetic forest' or of 'a cybernetic meadow / where mammals and computers / live together in mutually / programming harmony' (Brautigan, 1967); the whole poem shows a movement of all things, living and non-living, towards the formation of a harmonious whole, as a cybernetic ecology. But for critics of technology, life is a movement whose organicity is contrary to technology. The rise to power of contemporary robotics and of digital technologies complete the virtualisation of the world and go against the appropriation of a power of action. Home automation has sometimes increased human powerlessness in the domestic space; the ever more perfect robot refers to the difficulty of defining what it is to be human. So why open this part focusing on the consideration of living species by artists with a poem that praises the mixture of life and the digital? Such a move is based on the idea of the artificial; the artist participates through his/her art to reproduce or invent images and processes by which beauty can be said to be at times superior to that of nature. Kant, in his *Critique of Judgment* (Kant, 1951), notes, however, that nothing beats the beauty of nature, making him one of the first philosophers to develop an aesthetic of nature. In general, we could say that no artist is free of the demiurgic gesture that involves inventing a world. Part III, regarding living phenomena, is the heart of this book. Indeed, we are not looking to create some new artistic taxonomy, but rather to redefine how living processes have deeply changed the craft of the artist at all levels, producing new ways of making art.

To extend this idea, and to identify more precisely the originality of the artists' work involved in the environmental field, a definition of life and living seems necessary. However, there is no simple definition. The process of life – which can be described both as material and non-material – is more defined by a series of characteristics and 'specific patterns of relationships', such as auto-organisation, homeostasis, growth, reproduction, adaptation, response to stimuli, etc., this list being still problematic.

The essential characteristics that distinguish living from non-living systems – the cellular metabolism – are not a property of matter, nor a special vital force. They compose a specific pattern of relationships among chemical processes. Although it involves relationships between processes that produce material components, the network pattern itself is nonmaterial … Thus, life is never divorced from matter, even though its essential characteristics – organization, complexity, processes, and so on – are nonmaterial.

(Capra, 2002, p. 72)

Moreover, according to theories of evolutionary ecology, strict genetic determinism is challenged and the environment plays a role in the reproduction of the species. The unavoidable phenotypic plasticity reveals that the same genome can result in different phenotypes in evolutionary ecology (Lodé, 2011). Why bother to talk about this? First, ecological theories of living species evolve and give environments a role. Second, the question of life and of its reproduction involves many complex factors, some environmental. Artists can play with these factors. Finally, these theories include contingency, meaning there are no other forces guiding evolution than those specific to these unique living beings and their changing decisions. Speciation is ultimately a long and loving diversification event, giving birth to a loving biodiversity. On the other hand, the theoretical approaches of 'New Materialism' concern the process of formal co-located emergency. Thus the uniqueness of living environments is highlighted beyond the extreme abstraction and generalization specific to scientific approaches: this is the case, for example, with spatial geography at the expense of local geographies or biology with genetics. Biology, by removing all reference to its object of study, has become a biotechnology. In laboratories, the important thing is how to manipulate and transform the living rather than trying to understand the specificity of life. This purely mechanistic and technical life is not without consequence since it allows for the manipulation of all life as it becomes an object like others. The philosophical dimension of the meaning of life is sometimes dismissed for fear of reintroducing religious or vitalistic notions into science. So every technical advance in biology (GMOs, artificial procreation, genetic drugs) produces philosophical questions that biologists all too often diminish to obscurantist delusions.

Obviously, there is no totally convincing definition of the phenomenon of life. However, it is possible to take an interest in artists whose art attempts to dominate or to denounce the fate that awaits the plant and animal species. It is also important to look at artists who are trying to intervene directly on living processes, either at the genetic level, or by simulating a living world. It is therefore important to see that, in this part, our aim is not to celebrate life regardless of artifices that summon its presence. On the contrary, and this is what the Richard Brautigan poem shows, which is very contemporary, art must consist of a celebration of life, its meaning, and its glorification and beauty. This section includes case studies of projects and varied artistic realisations. In addition to artists who are trying to present or intervene directly on the fauna and flora, many artists depict phenomena that have an impact on these species. The means vary, for instance it could be via the use of maps to track the progression of a species or a forest, but also with stories that narrate the quality of rivers, or that visualize phenomena that have a direct impact on biodiversity such as climate change.

This third part of the book is concerned with the contributions of art or aesthetic sensibility that cross environmental issues, and more specifically the issues regarding living species. Living species happen to live in certain geographical configurations and artists aim to make visible environmental problems and ecological relationships in varied ways, knowing that each one carries within itself a dramatic resolution regarding the life of these living species. Art is a performance rather than an object (Davies, 2008). Then, considering that societies are taking control over the subjective bodies (Foucault, 1988), the somatic practices – as self and world invention practices with a strong link to the effects of our actions – they could now be tools of empowerment in the face of current bio-politics. So many ecological artistic practices reinvent gestures of places in order to change cultures. For example, to highlight the deformities of frogs associated with chemical pollution in an exhibition, is different from creating an artistic expedition that demonstrates the mass of plastic pollution in the ocean (see Chapter 6). This way of working submits knowledge modes specific for this type of sensitivity to the public's attention, using the tools of the artist or aesthetic professional. The artist works alongside the environmentalist, the climatologist, the ecologist, the biologist, or the geographer to propose ways of knowing the problem. These are as varied as the media involved. It may be contradictory to associate pollution with living organisms, whether toxic or malformed. Such examples include both the frog and the forest, the hidden pollution and the transformed gene. These exhibitions take place indoors, and use traditional medias such as photographs, drawings, films. Knowledge is also feeling: more and more works require that public participation incarnates in a gesture. The body is invited to contribute to the artistic action. It is also called upon to be interested in space or productive activities that have become a valuable part in exposing the evils of our society; namely, food with industrial agriculture, or for example the abuse of livestock, which has serious repercussions on food production. The countryside, with its farms, is spotlighted and becomes the object of aesthetic and artistic attention that often involves the highlighting of an alternative agriculture. It is the same with climate, and issues whose abstraction is problematic yet leads to all kinds of artistic endeavors.

While acting from the territory of the visual arts, contemporary artists broaden the field, forming an ambition to be both designers, architects, sculptors, video artists and graphic designers, sowing confusion between the concepts of object and artwork and disturbing contemporary exhibition practices. The art of appropriation begins with the first 'ready-made' of Marcel Duchamp. At this time the dialectic of the creative process that focuses on the object and its craftsmanship emerges (Bourriaud, 2003, p. 11). Contemporary artists are characterised by a simultaneously critical and experimental attitude. In the period of the late twentieth century, the attitude was anti-art and against-culture, one that began to question the features of artistic creation themselves.

Second, restoration, repair or support for environmental issues led many artists situated in various places towards commitments to various stakeholders (residents, technicians, cities, planners and scientists) and transformed the conditions of artistic production in complex projects with similar issues to the ones in local development projects (see Chapter 7). This restoration or repair work is anchored in urban areas, and polluted areas, such as brownfields. These practices are creating new art forms and, sometimes, different kinds of living beings. This opens the dialogue to sustainable alternatives to the structures of creative endeavor, formerly closed. Concerned for animals and living species, artists want to restore their living conditions and habitat. These works' unique public is sometimes even these non-human species, and the ecologists' support of population dynamics, which make new entanglements with nature visible. While the representations of living beings have long been pointing towards their ability to deceive. What matters today is not to deceive, but to be truly alive. So artists explore 'environmental creativity' as being part of a human path towards inventing new conditions of life for all living beings. They craft original devices sometimes anchored in local communities, and imagine micro-utopias in the heart of the megalopolis, repairing animal and plant habitats. It is true that art has of late, been specialized into different activities such as bio-art, environmental art, etc. But that is not our concern. Rather, our concern can be described as: how do artists keep finding new narratives to invent alternative pathways towards a pseudo-envisioned catastrophic future? Their goal may be to produce a living body, in relation to what is offered by local nature, but also to bring it into existence as art. Vitalism has long been rejected by science, (such as mechanistic and atomistic biology from the end of the nineteenth century), but could be thought of as reappearing through the ecosystemic paradigm. In the following chapter, we will try to demonstrate how artists have been incorporating natural elements in their works going from the representation of nature to the unfolding of its uncanny possibilities and resources in the era of ecological change.

Third, the artists, conscious of ecosystemic flows, adopt contrasting positions. On the one hand, their work should be part of these restored flows. On the other hand, the opposite numerical modeling of ecological flow tools, or ecosystems, admit wonderful demonstrations that could resume the life flows (Chapter 8). The idea that it is possible to technologically recreate ecosystem dynamics is the subject of much criticism. Highlighting technological solutions to climate change and the irreparable loss of biodiversity is clearly singled out: the new technological cognitive capitalism is built on the development of such ideas. However, these ideas are struggling to appear realistic in the light of environmental challenges, as their development is accompanied by a capitalism without consideration for people and ways of life. The authors report briefly in these pages on the current art trends as one of the avatars of the development of technologies that encounter dramatic challenges of the era. The fact is also that many artists are fascinated by the autonomous nature of living things and transform this into an objective teleology of artistic creation. *L'Eve Future* (*Tomorrow's Eve*), a short French novel from 1886 by Auguste Villiers de l'Isle-Adam (Villiers de l'Isle, 2000), shows the difficulties of recreating a being 'almost-alive' to overcome the limitations of some living things. This seminal opus in the field of science fiction describes specific tensions of an art seizing the tools of nature. But what artists are modeling and playing with are the very same life mechanisms (rewriting the genetic code, simulating the functioning of living systems) as an ability to create something larger than life.

References

Bourriaud, N., 2003. *Postproduction*. Dijon: Les presses du réel.

Brautigan, R., 1967. *All Watched Over by Machines of Loving Grace*. San Francisco: The Communication Company.

Capra, F., 2002. *The Hidden Connections: Integrating the Biological, Cognitive, and Social Dimensions of Life Into a Science of Sustainability*. New York: Doubleday.

Davies, D., 2008. *Art as Performance*. New York: Wiley-Blackwell.

Foucault, M., 1988. *History of Sexuality*. New York: Vintage.

Kant, I., 1951. *Critique of Judgement*. New York: Hafner Publishing.

Lodé, T., 2011. *La Biodiversité amoureuse: Sexe et évolution*. Paris: Odile Jacob.

Villiers de l'Isle, A., 2000. *Tomorrow's Eve*. Champaign: University of Illinois Press.

6 Depictions of the living

As artists move out of the studio and back to the world at large to create, process, discover and join the human community, boundaries expand and old definitions die. What emerges from the encounter between art and environmental issues is the importance of the protection of life. The staging of natural elements, such as cloud, air, sun, sea, ice, the polar bear, is accompanied by the identification of environmental damage: the natural symbolism is renewed in the light of environmental problems. In addition, exposing these natural elements to public view in galleries, museums or meeting them on the oceans and in the air is associated with the re-evaluation of the contexts of artistic production. It is not so much to say, this is art or to mix art with life, but to see how the 'nature/culture' chimeric product of human activities implies an aesthetic reflection on the manufacturing of environmental forms across the globe.

Staging for example, the monstrous deformities of frogs, by the means of haptic installations of these chimeric productions, besides contemplating nature, it is a way to raise consciousness of the frog's own harmful transformation from pollution, degradation of the environment, etc. It is also a way to fight against plastic marine pollution, against deforestation and acid rain, against climate change experienced as an external problem. Showing all the gestures that make us human beings of nature, wrapped in successive environments, is also inviting the public to contemplate life on the farm as the heart of a contemporary lifestyle that depends on agricultural production. We smell old memories and listen to the sounds of nature in order to be aware of a natural expressiveness. Indeed, contemporary art achieves the transfiguration of the commonplace object by directly installing the excluded objects of art's historical imagination, into the exhibition (gallery or museum space) without changing their physical consistency. In doing so, it performs a modalisation of the action – the exhibition of contemporary art is the staging of a situation of exposure – which reinforces its spectacular efficiency, clearly differentiating it from traditional artistic actions. When art dialogues with the environment, it furthers this movement and can enrich the terms of an art exhibition.

Deformed animals and mutated organisms

An 'inventory', the depiction or description of living beings, and their exhibition is a traditional art form. Of particular historical note is the work of Aby Warburg (1866–1929), who created the *Mnemosyne Atlas*, which highlights all forms of suffering. Its value is not only as a scientific work of taxonomy, but also in its creation of a new path of aesthetic attention directed towards natural elements. Prominent in the history of 'the art of nature', naturalist painter John James Audubon (1781–1851) explored the wilderness for decades, bringing the connection between environments and animals, in particular birds, to the public via various scientific experiments. These detailed works, along with Audubon's attentive naturalist writings, influenced the evolutionary theories of Charles Darwin and popularized natural history. His philosophical views on the intrinsic value of nature laid the groundwork for the later transcendental poets. Today, the artist highlights natural deformities as being a subject of wonder, which also forces the artist to highlight their role as creator. Teratologic studies in the nineteenth century gave deformities a central role in the representation of nature. In the twentieth century, monstrosities were increasingly used to show ecological factors in body deformities.

The work of Brandon Ballengée, born in 1974 in Canada, combines his fascination with amphibians and fish, research and photographic work on the decline of frog populations and their possible morphological deformities caused by

Figure 6.1 Brandon Ballgengée, *Reclamation Series*

human activity (COAL Prize, 2013). Dissemination to a wide audience through the art network is seen as a militant commitment. *Praeter Naturam: The Environmentally Sculpted Amphibians of Agricultural Landscapes* is representative of this militancy. The project provided a laboratory and resulted in a year-long BioArt installation. The artist collaborated with school groups and the public to form participatory 'Frog Teams' and led 'eco-actions' to analyse the health of frogs and toads, in order to compare deformed frogs with healthy amphibian populations found in regional nature parks. A functioning BioArt laboratory was established to generate primary biological research experiments as well as to become an important 'open' platform for public discussion. A central praxis to this project as well as to others, is engaging local communities through a 'citizen' science; this raises awareness of the complex issues involved in environmental change while gaining a better ecological understanding of the threats that amphibians and other species face in local and global agricultural habitats.

The use of laboratory techniques, such as clearing, staining and scanner photography, highlights the 'monstrous' beauty of abnormal frog specimens. The psychological complexity of finding them in human-compromised environments is thus emphasised. The visual art response to the proposed amphibian investigations involves the creation of several high-resolution scanner photographs. These prints are part of the ongoing series *Malamp Reliquaries* (2001–current) and are created by chemically 'clearing and staining' terminally deformed frogs. After the actual laboratory work, cleared and stained deformed frog specimens are exhibited as part of a sculpture titled *Styx*. Films are directly made from recordings of laboratory procedures. Field trips and animals encountered form part of the different projects. For example *The Cry of Silent Forms: Breath* (2008) consisted of a 24-hour loop of the face of a metamorphic toad taking his last living gasp of air before dying as a result of a prior predatory injury. A more recent work *Un Requiem pour Flocons de neige Blessés* (2009–11) consisted of 21 individual portraits of short-lived beings, tiny terminally deformed metamorphic American toads found in Southern Quebec.

More generally, since 1996, Brandon Ballengée has undertaken work at the intersection of arts and sciences, building on a scientific culture, as well as a commitment to the environment and ecological art. For him, art is a way to test science and vice versa. His method is based on a participatory ecosystem activism, which requires biological surveys, and focuses on public engagement. The art itself is:

> made from diverse mediums including biological materials (chemically cleared and stained deformed specimens displayed as glowing gems, preserved specimens to represent collapsing global food webs, living plants and animals displaced in temporary mesocosms, paintings from my own blood mixed with industrial pollutants found in my own body and the living bodies of all organisms), large-scale scanner photographs representing the individuality of non-human individuals, outdoor light sculptures to encourage insect fornication and participatory trans-species happenings – all of

these try to re-examine the context of the art object from a static form (implying rationality and control) into a more organic structure reflecting the inherent chaos found within evolutionary processes, biological systems and nature herself.[1]

If these works exemplify the effects of pollution on nature, for example, the fact remains that they are solely intended to sensitise and educate a rather traditional public. The method could be compared to any state environmental policy, where most of the message seems to be to educate the masses through scientific popularised messages. Brandon Ballengée's work involves a fascination based on an ancient tradition of the 'Cabinet of Curiosities', displaying the wonders of nature. During the sixteenth and seventeenth centuries, princes, noblemen and academics founded collections all over Europe containing antiquities, art objects, ethnographic artefacts and naturalia – all kinds of zoological, botanical, geological, the strange and the wonderful specimens and samples. Sometimes these were deformed animals that made up a thematic and geographical microcosm, a teatrum mundi, which in reduced form reflected an endlessly complex macrocosm. In addition to art objects, most of these collections contained naturalia and were regularly visited by the learned scientists of the time. The curiosity cabinets of the Renaissance reflected a particular interest in rare natural and artistic phenomena, a curiosity and a deep admiration of them, of their exotic or ancient origins, their bizarre character and possibly monstrous appearance (Liebgott, 2000).

Sound

Exhibiting living beings is not the only way to make people feel the richness of biodiversity. The work of field recording exemplifies how each effort to objectify a living species ecosystem fails in the measure of its own pretention. The living nature that is displayed is the exact result of the technical device at its origin. The sound work of the French artist Eric Samakh (born in 1959) is an interesting illustration of the difficulties resulting from the intention to restitute nature's voice in all its complexity. For some twenty-five years, Erik Samakh has been capturing, recording and re-integrating what he perceives as a true artistic material in museum spaces that he installs and diffuses in all places suited to discovery. Whether he patiently recorded the singing of frogs or the rustling of insects, or whether he captured the sun's energy to make flutes sing or fireflies light up, Erik Samakh orchestrates the natural elements in his delicate and poetic structures, somehow invisibly making use of new technologies. Created in situ, his work is often present in parks or nature reserves (the Tijuca forest in Brazil, The International Center for Art and the Scenery of Vassivière, Chaumont-sur-Loire Regional Park, etc.). On the bank of the Saône in France, on the site of the Chemin Nature, Erik Samakh has installed the work *Les Girouettes à crues*; stone blocks placed on a mobile stainless steel axis, which pivot in accordance with the river currents and water levels. It's the sort of work that one feels inclined to play around with and walkers are able to have fun changing its direction, or are welcome to use it as a seat for picnicking on or for fishing from. The artist explains:

> Today I'd call myself a hunter-gatherer. Nature is something, which is intrinsic to my work, something a lot more natural than current ecology, which is more political. My relationship with nature is more primitive. I use new technology because I feel it needs to be adapted to nature. I've chosen to introduce artificial fireflies to the Nature path site for a number of reasons but notably because in nature, fireflies are gradually becoming extinct. Symbolically this extinction confronting fireflies is important and I feel it.
>
> (Samakh, n.d.)

Histories of ecosystems

Presenting the histories of ecosystems, and how they have been integrated for centuries with a sustainable culture of local peoples, informs us today, by contrast, of what is increasingly lost. Such is the historically based project of artists Suzanne Husky and Walter Kim who proposed an interactive site on the history of forests in France. This story is intrinsically tied to the rise of the industrial era, as forests were cut down to fuel the machine age in Western Europe. Viewers are invited via images and information to 'discover the true complexity of the evolution of forests in France'. The site is meant to be a pedagogical artistic tool, both for research and visual based visitors. The underlying history, while seemingly one of ecology, eventually unfolds to a political and historical narrative of the rise of France's naval empire (including ship-building) and ensuing conquest of other populations and geographies around the world. As the forests shrink across the countryside, the French empire, not coincidentally, grows. The artists make a direct visual relationship between the environment, a political regime, and the accumulation of capital and power.

Another artist is also another ecosystem story. Working with the fragile ecologies of the North Atlantic coastal rim, artist Lilian Cooper draws the cliffs and ridges in intricate detail in her ongoing, twenty-year *Coastlines* project (see Figure 6.2). By depicting the effects of rising sea levels and coastal shifts, she is literally documenting artistically the changing context of our planet. As she states, these are the 'locations at the forefront of climate change'. Through her travels, which thus far have covered Norway, Ireland, Scotland, the far southwest of England, Britany, Maritime Quebec (Iles de la Madeleine), Nova Scotia, Newfoundland and Maine, she lives in each community and draws. Out on the cliff faces overlooking the deep ocean, Cooper connects directly with the environment she is documenting in a profound way. Bringing the line drawings back into the gallery setting, the audience is then reunited with the local ecology they know so well, now interpreted through a visitor and memorialised to a certain extent, by the artist's hand. The sites are re-contextualised and attributed as the gallery sets the images in a pristine sphere for contemplation.

Figure 6.2 Lilian Cooper, *Coastlines Lobster Cove Head, Newfoundland, Canada*

Exhibited without frames, the scrolled drawings are pinned to the wall in a visceral format, avoiding any bent toward grandeur or icon. The humbleness of the hands-on quality reproduces a sense of fieldwork, rather than museum artefact. And it is within this context that the artist continues in a long tradition of artist as documentarian of the natural world and witness to history. In this case, she records the decline of our planet along with the rise in sea levels. Whereas this type of research would traditionally be in a science museum or remain in a research laboratory file, Cooper places it in the context of traditional art, thereby unsettling the viewer's expectations of information.

The farm as laboratory

Often focused on wild species, some artworks concern domestic animals. Among the latest examples of artists who are observers and producers of nature descriptions, Eva Galtier (born in France, 1989) made a documentary film of a farm (cattle and dairy). This documentary is presented as a study that describes the farmer's organisation as well as the building, the materials and the processes of production and livestock. The progression of a typical morning allows you to meet and consider this case study. It is thus possible to discern the relationships that develop between the different actors of the operation and, in particular, the relationship between human, animal and machine. A typical day is defined by a few key points: maintaining the area, feeding and milking. Onto this pattern of action, while we are going through the activities of a regular morning, other activities are grafted: from the slaughterhouse, to calving. The filming takes place over one year, allowing the spectator to see the daily organisation but also seasonal farming. This artistic work focusing on agriculture and a farmer's life is present in many artistic projects seeking to honour farming culture, and what it means to care for a domesticated nature. Local and peasant cultures are considered exotic enough to constitute a work of art in themselves. Also focusing on rural spaces as living cultural places, the German artists, Antje Schiffers and Thomas Sprenger (COAL Prize, 2012), have compiled a collection of 25 films from all over Europe, including Austria, the United Kingdom, the Netherlands, Macedonia, Switzerland, Germany and Romania. The farmers' families get a video camera and the artists support them when they are filming, discussing the structure of the film, and talking about possible commentaries ending with the final editing together. 'I like being a farmer and I would like to stay one' deals with questions of self-representation, and wants to give insights into existing and possible economies and social structures. It tries to connect and interweave 'high' and 'low'-culture in the so-called centre and periphery; it preserves images of country life that might disappear in the future. Farmers tend to be 'very local' and do not travel too much; the archive of films made by farmers allows them to connect farmers' voices and ideas on agriculture on a transnational level, though very directly and unfiltered.

An olfactory experience

Martina Florians (COAL Prize, 2012) tries to stage situations in order to allow her public to feel anew what it is to smell and to experience all kinds of associated memories and feelings. Florians (born in 1974, Netherlands), gives a role to the participants' gestures to the extent that they are invited to smell nature. Thus she uses the same participatory techniques as Brandon Ballengée to propose an experience of our ecological settings. The European Herbarium of Scents is a collection of scent descriptions from several areas in Europe. They are collected in collaboration with participants. The participants document the changes in smell of wild plants during a year's cycle in their own subjective way. The scent descriptions are recorded in their native language since it asks for a specific vocabulary to describe a scent. This is a situation of live experience related to our body memories. The various projects of Martina Florians concern olfactory memory and its role in the apprehension of the place. Whether it's the smell of nature or of city, subjective memory is enhanced by sound devices, visual, olfactory. There is thus an aesthetic subject playing with the importance of multi-sensoriality. The idea of a collection, more than of an inventory, is very present in this artwork. However, the intuitive mind, that is, seeking to capture what is impalpable either in terms of physical phenomena or of feelings at work, is the thread of these various installations. Irony is also a strength in the work of Martina Florians. The flexible *Dua Aroma* installation created in 2003 promises a malleable recipe to change the smell of one's faeces. The system consists of a karaoke where one can record one's own recipe whilst producing.

One might argue that the artist's connection to nature has remained the same over time: a deep involvement with her beauty, power, majesty, and sublime spirit. The tradition of the visual arts in the West has celebrated nature within a context of religion, the relationship to the individual, or formal codes of geometry, colour or compositional structures. The arts in indigenous cultures, on the other hand, have never separated themselves into a separate category from the community and environment they live in, be it social (handworks), political (representations of power), religious (sacred objects) or conceptual (dance, music, performance, ritual). Many contexts outside of the 'developed' world have maintained an intrinsic connection to the environment that surrounds them. And in many of these cultures, the creation activity is not an individual act, but is tied to a communal process. With the globalisation of the latter half of the twentieth century, international artists can now travel and share ideas as never before, creating a true global community of exchange. It is remarkable that these works depict the wonders of nature or lament their disappearance or degradation. Yet, they take little notice of the dark aspects of nature that human beings have always fought against to the point of creating cities of the future far from the natural land.

The paradigm shift in art has not necessarily been a change of subject matter, but a change in the grammar. 'What' has been replaced with 'how'. The human relationship to nature will always be one of our most human engagements. With the threat of so much of that very nature now in danger of extinction, an expansion of the context of art practices makes more than sense. It is a dialectic that returns to holistic engagement on every level, broadening definitions of what art is, and where it is, and who if any, is the maker. This removal of the artist as centre point leaves a counterpoint of community and spirit, where activity produces change. Project after project presented in this book builds the case for individuals working locally with global repercussions, not only aesthetically but economically.

Note

1   See www.hass.rpi.edu/pl/hass-events/?objectID=100003791

References

Boetzkes, A., 2010. *The Ethics of Earth Art.* Minneapolis: University of Minnesota Press.
Liebgott, N., 2000. The Representation of Nature in Art. *Naturopa*, 93, 14–16.
Samakh, E., n.d. Interview. Available at: www.lesrivesdesaone-grandlyon.com/designers-and-artists/erik-samakh/

7 An aesthetic of repair

The second chapter in this section is focused on the idea of an artistic way to repair or restore the quality of habitat for animals, plants and human beings either in cities or in rural areas. These practices are creating new art forms and, sometimes, different kinds of living beings. This opens the dialogue to sustainable alternatives to the formerly closed structures of creative endeavour. Let's first go to the cities and see how artists have been dealing with urban spaces. Aside from the fact that the cities have become the environments in which the bulk of this planet's inhabitants dwell – a contemporary dwelling mode – urban environments are also colossal consumers of natural resources both far and near, exporters of their problems and waste, and predators without any real contact with the 'soil and nature' that nurture them. The city is a specific environment; a technical environment in both senses of the term. First, it encompasses the implementation of numerous technologies (as borne out by the success of eco-housing and eco-technologies, amongst others). This is also demonstrated by a certain number of urban and 'city-design' professions. Making cities is an art in itself and architects cannot be held solely responsible for the failures of the modern city. Second, the urban environment is a technical milieu for urbanites – the city may even be considered the ultimate technical milieu. As long ago as 1953, the sociologist Georges Friedman explained that:

By natural milieu, we mean the milieu of pre-machinery civilisations or communities in which man reacts to stimulations emanating mostly from natural elements – earth, water, plants or seasons – or from living beings that include both animals and humans. In this milieu, the various tools comprise the direct extension of the body, adapted to the body, fashioned by the body using processes underpinned by overlapping biological, psychological and social conditioning ... However, by technical milieu, we mean those which have developed in industrialised societies and communities since the beginning of the pre-industrial revolutions, in other words since the end of the eighteenth century in the case of Britain and the beginning of the nineteenth century for the Continent. In this technical milieu, the proportion of stimulations described previously decreases but at the same time, increasingly closes in around man and a complex network of techniques tends towards automatism.

(Friedman, 1953, p. 401; authors' translation)

In brief, from a temporal perspective, the city is a planned moment from a temporal perspective that now needs to be reviewed and the creative differences between urban milieus need to be more comprehensively explained. What is therefore at stake are questions of ecological sharing in the broad sense of the term and a political regime that refers conditions for access back to environmental resources, as well as the future of the contemporary city and a possible urban democracy.

Environmental aesthetics offers subsequently – and perhaps primarily – the possibility of contributing to political debate, following numerous actors and making politics an overflow, an excess of stabilised conditions for 'living together', while drawing upon the ungovernable depths of aesthetic sentiment. It also involves changing the institutions that make voting, debating and public opinion the primary reasons for living together.

However, we need to be aware that within the urban domain there are two vices inherent in the aesthetic dimension: (1) the 'all-aesthetic' and the production of an image-based lifestyle framework (the spectacular, etc.); and (2) the aesthesic, that is the production of a city dominated by sensitive experience and the idea of a pleasant milieu. We need to feel what amounts to an aesthetic commitment in the production of milieus, regardless of the scale concerned. We therefore need to be able to state the conditions for intelligibility of the sustainability processes and the conditions for producing an environmental aesthetic that does not erase human complexity in favour of some spectacular environment.

Among the cases discussed below, artists have found two ways to enable themselves to transform the richness and complexity of urban settlements and respond to environmental issues. They seek, first, to vindicate an invisible nature allowing it to grow in different places, either with seeds that have remained dormant under the bitumen or acknowledging that the unique nature of a specific geographical environment does not have room to express itself. These artists support the change of urban wasteland and fallow lands into wild and natural environments, acting as urban developers. Others play with the idea that to produce food in a constrained environment is to be creative symbolically (do you not grow the life that would be useful to all?), but also technically.

Shaping the flux of the city

More generally, the objective may be to shape a poetic of the city. In the 1950s, this poetics of the city fed the thought of the Marxist philosopher and sociologist Henri Lefebvre and the works of the French artistic avant-garde, including the International Situationist. Both of these reflections define methods of intervention in the city; for situationists, this would be psychogeography. In the mid

1950s, Debord defined psychogeography as a science: 'a study of the exact laws and specific effects of the geographical environment, consciously organised or not, acting directly on the emotions and behaviour of individuals' (Debord, 1955, p. 11–15; authors' translation). This extends the materialist geography, which studies the conditioning of the deployment of life in space by climates and environments, while studying the geographic response of feelings and emotions of individuals. It's an aesthetic way, in the meaning of a science of sensitivity, the subjective relationship of the individual to the environment, and its many factors. This scientific study is performed experimentally because it uses a drift methodology, which is the experimental mode of behaviour linked to the conditions of life in urban societies. This is manifested by a wandering journey through the city, using walking or other modes of transport (notably on the occasion of the transport strike in Paris, in the summer of 1953, drifts were organized by taxi).

These artistic and philosophical currents, focusing on a subversion of everyday life, have great influence on contemporary ecological art. It is therefore interesting to see that the idea of the city as an artwork runs through Lefebvre's thought, especially in the *Proclamation of the Commune* (1965), and *The Right to the City* (1968). The thought of the city as an œuvre is a fundamental step in the development of his critical theory of urban and metaphilosophy. The city will take a crucial place because it is the place of this modernity, torn between human being and nature. While modern technology becomes ubiquitous, it also becomes the place where lives change, due to the distance between humans as well as that of human beings with nature. In this context, psychogeography put out by the International Situationist would valorise the study of situations in order to make them conscious, in the same way that Lefebvre's criticism of sociology claimed to contribute to the transformation of everyday life. To make a science of this subjective and emotional relation of the individual to his environment, the used method of observation is adrift: the protocols are set up from the wandering journey through the city on foot, by taxi, by any other means. Drift is an 'experimental mode of behaviour linked to the conditions of urban society' (Anon., 1958) that requires a schedule and set specific conditions. The results are derived by a rather rapid movement through the city, to experience its various moods that transform neighbourhoods into quarters. The atmosphere must be transcribed to document the psychogeographical study of the city. Several methods have been developed: the stories (the adventure of drift), maps, photographic or film images. The drift does not necessarily seek harmonious places as surprises. Contrasts intensify the experience of the course: it allows one to see the attraction and repulsion areas, what Debord called 'hubs' of the city, his 'passionate objective field' (ibid.).

These historical modes of intervention have allowed a rich interpretation of urban ecology, not just tied to the presence of plant and animal elements of nature in the urban space, but interested in renovating their modes of presence in urban spaces. One pivotal movement of recent years is linked to the relationship of the artist to the professional skills of other fields such as that of the gardener, the landscaper, the developer, the scientist, or the social worker. The artist borrows these techniques, turning them into instruments of an aesthetic revival. The designs, like the use of the map, are the artists' tools in seeking environmental knowledge. It accompanies the landscape and the romantic garden as 'schools of vision' but also the ideal of reconciliation of art and science, theory and practice, involved in the process.

Time landscapes

Ecological artists presented below will take advantage of both traditions that associated with the reappropriation of the city, and the one that is related to ecology, crafting the urban environment. Alan Sonfist's *Time Landscape* is a pioneering work, realised between 1965 and 1978 in New York City. *Time Landscape* was built on a parcel between Soho and Greenwich Village, bringing together all the species of the first plants of the island of Manhattan. Completed in 1970, this work was originally a bank of native seeds from North American spaces. The success of Sonfist's work was to persuade the city planners and technicians not on conventional arguments about public art, but on arguments concerning the urban landscape. The 'Gardens' Department of the City of New York, owner of the work since 1989, up until this moment in time has not critically assessed the effective biodiversity in artworks such as Sonfist's. This work had a great influence on New York City's Parks Department, according to Sue Spaid, which then in connection with the Transportation Department of the city, developed small green spaces such as 'Greenstreet' in Manhattan (Spaid, 2002).

Alan Sonfist's historical approach was to provide the New York City community with a memory of its original biodiversity.

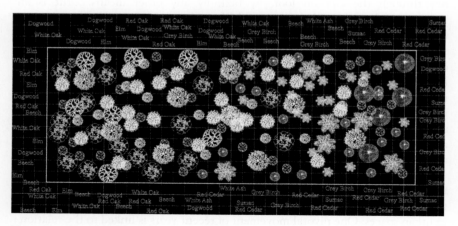

Figure 7.1 Alan Sonfist, *Study, Time Landscape*

Public monuments traditionally have celebrated events in human history – acts of heroism important to the human community. Increasingly, as we come to understand our dependence on nature, the concept of community expands to include non-human elements. Civic monuments, then, should honor and celebrate the life and acts of the total community, the ecosystem, including natural phenomena. Especially within the city, public monuments should recapture and revitalize the history of the natural environment of that location. As in war monuments that record the life and death of soldiers, the life and death of natural phenomena such as rivers, springs and natural outcroppings need to be remembered. Historical documents preserve observations of New York City's natural past. When the first European settlers arrived, they saw the natural practices of the Native Americans. In a city, public art can be a reminder that the city was once a forest and a marsh. Just as some streets are named after trees, street names could be extended to other plants, animals and birds. Areas of the city could be renamed after the predominant natural phenomena that existed there. Since the city is becoming more and more polluted, we could build monuments to the historic air. Museums could be built that would recapture the smells of earth, trees, and vegetation in different seasons and at different historical times, so that people would be able to experience what has been lost. A museum of air sponsored by the United Nations can show different air of different countries. Other projects can reveal the historical geology or terrain. Submerged outcroppings that still exist in the city can be exposed. Glacial rocks can be saved as monuments to a dramatic natural past. The sounds, controlled by the local community, change according to the natural pattern of the animals and the rhythmic sounds return to the city. Natural scents can evoke the past as well. Public monuments embody shared values.

(Alan Sonfist, quoted in Spaid, 2002, p.143)

Hans Haacke's work, like Sonfist's, highlights the unpredictability of life, and opportunities for regeneration. His work is imbued with the idea of time-space continuity, and that everything is part of a landscape continuum of life that the artist can make visible. Besides his *Bowery Seeds* (1970) (see Figure 7.2), Haacke introduced *Seed Catcher* (a 'pool of virgin earth to collect the seeds of nearby forests through wind and animal migration' (Spaid, 2002, p. 90), and implemented it in 1975 as *Pool of Earth* (at Artpark in Lewiston, New York City). The dynamic is thus used to resurrect connectivity and ecological flow. The movement is the opposite of the work entitled *Tabula Rasa*, which sought to get rid of the past to create a new world in the modern era, notably advocated by many architects. Time and memory are the ecologically sensitive dimensions of these art works. But among these dimensions remains a dramatic break between city and countryside that made the city an unloved space in many countries, including in Europe and North America. In fact, the city is not so much an unloved space, than a space produced according to standards that lead to choose species that enter into the urban fabric. These species were not indigenous

Figure 7.2 Hans Haacke, *Bowery Seeds*

species during the modern era, as shown by *Time Landscape*. Today, artists are more cautious regarding invasive species, in other words, modifying the landscape only to benefit its local ecosystems. This issue is the subject of many artistic works quick to denounce urban exclusion mechanisms.

What about invasive species?

Born in 1960 in Brazil, Maria Thereza Alves lives and works in Berlin. Her project is a demonstration for 'multi-horticulturalism'. She is also known as the founder of Brazil's Green Party in Sao Paulo and a former representative of the Workers Party. Relying also upon memory, and the forgotten impact of past technical devices and work organisation, her artwork *Seeds of Change* is a survey based on research of historical ballast sites in European ports (COAL Prize, 2014). For hundreds of years, stones, earth, sand, wood and bricks were used as ballast to stabilise the cargo of merchant ships. Upon arrival in port, the ballast along with seeds that had travelled by accident, were discharged on land or in the sea. These seeds were from any port or region involved in trade with Europe. The seeds in the soil ballast could germinate and grow, contributing to the development of the 'European' landscape. *The Seeds of Change* project is multifaceted, it was exhibited in various configurations to Marseille (2000), Dunkirk (2005), Bristol (2007), Rotterdam (2009).

The *Ballast Seed Project* is establishing a connection between floral history and the port cities' economic and social histories. The dispersal of invasive alien species is directly related to the expansion of trade, goods transport and travel, because the organisms can be transported in boats, containers, cars, floors, etc. Ballast is an intermediate for the influx of invasive and exotic living species showing that the majority of non-native flora do not become naturalised, and that even fewer actually become invasive. Certainly the issue of invasive species is problematic, but few of the species are, compared to the vast majority of species traveling. To be regarded as invasive, species must have an abundant production of seeds, a fast vegetative propagation and growth, a significant capacity of dispersion and a high resistance to disturbances. Their presence causes a removal of the existing fauna and flora and/or significantly reduces the surrounding biodiversity.

From native flora to invasive plants, the demonstration is pungent and problematic. It is therefore necessary to separate what belongs to the invasive and native, a discussion which raises questions on racism issues. Indeed, immigration flow has lately revived the public debate on 'invasive' culture. Whatever the legitimacy of the debates, they raise lively passions, and bring more questions than answers. In *L'éloge du dehors* Liliana Motta, a French artist, also deals with invasive species (COAL Prize, 2013). More than showing them as monstrous, disfiguring localities, she highlights their role in renewing local ecosystems. The artist tries to share her fascination of the adaptation processes that can be developed by a biological individual facing a new environment. Her work documents the perception of this phenomenon by human beings. The study of the botanical family *Polygonums* shows their ability to adapt after their introduction in Europe. Although this plant was introduced there more than a century ago with a single female clone, its genetic diversity, phenotypic plasticity, its polymorphism and its ecological adaptability, allowed it to develop a whole new series of hybrid individuals and to remain in its new territory. The paradox, according to the artist, is that the special environmental qualities of these 'foreign' plants are seen, rather, as a real disaster to the established vegetal organisation, though they could be well used as a contribution to all living beings. This view hides all the benefits that this newcomer can bring, negating any exchange or sharing that could benefit both 'natures/cultures'. New ways of thinking about living beings today gives us the possibility to view these changes with more freedom. To address the issue, to be complete and give this reflection the echo it deserves, a discussion is organised around the concept of the living. Its ability to change is constantly becoming. Large format photo paper prints occupy the space at varying heights, forming a maze in which spectators can walk. This enclosure of lined paper is reinforced by an installation of dried polygonums, giving a cabin appearance to the whole. This work was exhibited in the Musée national des Arts d'Afrique et d'Océanie, formerly the 1932 Musée des Colonies et de la France Extérieure, which was re-baptized in 1990, highlighting the necessity to debate the ecological conditions of immigration.

Feeding the cities

While it is true that the rural-urban link needs to be repaired, and that food provides symbolic care techniques, even urban agriculture's contribution to the feeding of cities remains very problematic. Therefore, urban agriculture adopts the mission of cultural and social transformation without necessarily relating to its, strictly speaking, environmental efficiency. Damien Chivialle, who wants to contribute to urban agriculture, and gives a quick solution to experimentation in urban areas, created a vegetable garden to be installed in public space, the UFU (Urban Farm Unit) (COAL Prize, 2011). It is without land constraints or security. UFU is a farming experiment inside shipping containers. Perched on a container (such as is used in the international shipping trade), the greenhouse is located away from the street. With vulnerable features of a rough and industrial base, it is a paradoxical object that critiques the present urban environment, unable to make a proper place in the living cities. Symbolic, the UFU is also a proposal to residents. This island parked in a parking space will help people to connect with renewed urban roots, to reconnect with the principles of the living or to participate to the circular economy. Reproducible, economical and scalable, the design of the UFU allows duplicate facilities and expands testing in different contexts. Organic fish, fruits and vegetables are produced in the street, avoiding unnecessary travel and providing meaning to food consumption in downtown cities. All prototypes are based on circular agriculture techniques. The objectives of UFU are to find solutions to growing food in polluted and reduced ground. In its blog, UFU interconnects the container initiatives and experiments.

Of a more temporary character than the UFU experiment, *Eathouse* (COAL Prize, 2012) by Atelier Gras (Marjan van Capelle and Arjen de Groot, born 1969 and 1980 respectively, the Netherlands) is a house in a garden that lures visitors with the delicious vegetables, fruits and flowers. This work of art is tenable from April to October. Therefore, the temporality and the re-use of all applied materials applied is a guiding theme in the technical elaboration of *Eathouse*. The system consists of a series of standard vegetable crates filled with growing bags. A growing bag is filled with a unique garden substrate of peat in combination with fertilizer. The plants grow well and have exactly enough food for the first few months. The growing bag takes little space, is exactly tailored to the crates, ready and easy to move. *Eathouse* makes vertical green accessible to everyone, to the outside wall on the balcony or on the roof of your garden shed.

Damien Chivialle and Atelier Gras have a lot in common. Both propose to undertake mediation techniques/objects to feed the city. However, other artists are looking to change cultural behaviours towards nature and body experiences through real work on aesthetics. They create places where one can experience nature otherwise. Classically, the experience refers to the acquisition of knowledge by the experience, and therefore involves the body. It is opposed to the idea of pure and disembodied knowledge. Corporeality is an opening through practice and gestures. It is also a reflection of our culture, of our imagination, our practices and social and political organization. The term 'somatic' refers to the Greek word 'soma' meaning the living body (Thomas, 2004, p. 20). Proposed in 1970 by the philosopher Thomas Hanna to unify a set of physical practices, somatic would be the art and science of synergistic interaction process between awareness, biological functioning and the environment. Appearing at the turn of the twentieth century, pioneers in practices such as Rudolf von Laban or F. Matthias Alexander, experienced a revival in the 1960s (Eddy, 2009). The Feldenkrais practice, for example, enriches the repertoire of similar movements, and accomplishes it through the development of self-awareness through gestures. New ways of experiencing nature in carefully staged situations could be tools of empowerment in the face of current biopolitics. The following artist embodies this attempt to reinvent our cultures of nature.

Amongst the born and bred farmers, Thierry Boutonnier, grew up in his parents' dairy farm in the 1980s, in the southwest of France, but set out to colonise the city (COAL Prize, 2010). As a farm labourer, he financed his studies at the National School of Fine Arts in Lyon before obtaining a degree in the study of pollution. He defines himself as a 'non-specialist' artist who experiments with the entanglement between the economy, society and the environment, to find new political possibilities. In reconciling rural and urban ways of life, he renews the links between city-dwellers and farm animals, as well as between farmers and their cattle. From a temporary farm in urban areas and more specifically in a disadvantaged area of Lyon (France), he tried to reconnect people with domestic animal life through the idea of agricultural production. The artist has created a green building with the people who serve on a forum creating a meeting point around mini ecological projects. During these meetings, he also presented potential projects, which could be developed in the future (see Plate 9).

A friend of Thierry Boutonnier, Olivier Darné lives and works in Saint-Denis (suburban Paris), and also experiments with these links between animals and cities (COAL Prize, 2015). His approach crosses sculptural forms research and issues around cultural, social and urban diversity. He cultivates and harvests honey in urban areas, in a piece called *Concrete Honey*. In 2004, he founded the Collective Poetic Party, and more recently the space Zone Sensitive in Saint-Denis. Since 2009, he developed the Bank of Honey and the Bee savings account, which unites 980 members today. For him, the public space is a playground, and the bee is a medium: the beekeeper artist questions the relationship of man and his environment. Thus, during the summer of 2013, he installed a monumental, utopian hive near the castle in the Domain of Chamarande. Intensive farming using pesticides, practiced particularly on the surrounding fields, produced food and monetary wealth as it destroyed biodiversity, especially bees. The installation *Investing in Heaven* offered visitors the opportunity to turn their money into bees and take part in the restoration of natural environments. It is a 'relational work': it generates in turn a network of interests between the flowers, the bees, the beekeepers and the visitors. The hive is a 'rurban' pollination centre, a place of breeding queen bees and an observatory of local biodiversity.

These last works exemplify the break between rural and urban areas though reconciling them in terms of agricultural production. From a countryside identified as a productive space for city-dwellers, at least since the eighteenth century, to an urban agriculture, there is a huge step that is meant to remind us not to forget the importance of agricultural life with all its specificities. One can go further and ask what does it mean to showcase rural life? At a time when the urban artefact wins and becomes the very principle of social life, how can one understand the idea of the rural among artists? In addition to celebrating the lifestyle, its rhythm, its depths, artists show themselves protectors of living beings, under all their forms, even though they also manipulate them. The city disappears in favour of a habitat system, celebrating the city-nature alliance.

Rural cultivators

On the rural side, there are also numerous experiments, especially amongst a new generation of art-farmers. The Vernand breeding farm, in France, raising cattle and sheep for meat production, developed a system of direct selling from 1989 and carried out a conversion to organic farming in 1992 (COAL Prize, 2013). This farm, which for many years has involved strong relationships with external audiences, also hosts frequent school visits. It now employs two people full time, Isabelle Janin, main operator, and an agricultural worker. A butcher is also a part-time employee to perform the cutting of the meat and participates in its commercialization for the markets. In 2005, the farm was the subject of a joint degree undertaken by brothers Pierre and Rémi Janin, architect and landscape architect respectively, and sons of Isabelle Janin, who is still managing the farm. Since then the goal is to establish an architectural landscape project, reflecting and valuing the primarily agricultural vocation and its forms while having the future plan to open it to new uses. As a result of this degree work, Pierre and Rémi Janin founded the agency Fabriques Architectures Paysages, based on the exploitation site and aiming essentially to carry out projects and studies related to agriculture and rural life. In 2008, and in continuation of this history, the desire to create a cultural event was born. This project was also created by the meeting with some clients, including visual artists, who expressed their desire to use the farm as a subject and intervention focal point.

The collective Polyculture was then created in this direction, bringing together about thirty people, amongst them the site operators, visual artists and other outsiders. It was then decided to formalise a first annual event, taking place over two days at the end of spring, the best time to open the farm (empty buildings, no busy work times just before mowing in June, hay meadows easily accessible, etc.). In May 2009, the first contemporary art cycle was organised, proposing twenty artists to use the farm, its space and its singularities, as support in one way or another of creative and artistic valorisation. The aim was to establish a path defined within the space of farming connecting these different interventions that appropriate different places: buildings, pastures, crops, water points, hayfields, etc. The first event attracted about 1200 persons to the site over a two-day period. Its repetition in 2010 and in 2011 attracted an increased number of visitors, with 1500 and 2000 people respectively. In the contemporary art season, the Vernands intended to open an agricultural area and lead the public to invest emotionally and look at it in a different way. It also aimed to combine a farm in organic agriculture with resolutely contemporary images and forms, valuing the site first as a place of production but also as a fully open space, participating in a dynamic countryside and an extremely urban society. Thus the definition of a new rural space is desired and proposed by affirming its necessary productive vocation associated with the development of agricultural forms with an environmental intelligence, while leading to the creation of a collective voca-tion and shared space. In a context where agriculture gradually appears physically but also culturally isolated, where the notion of production seems blurred, the goal is to try to bring new thinking on agricultural forms and a new definition of their status. The establishment of a cultural approach has appeared to be one of the better ways to ask these questions and to consider the creation of a new open space productive.

The same intelligence guides the creative work of Mathew Moore (Digital Farm Collective), Malin Vrijman and Marlene Lindmark, (artists), and Henric Stigeborn and Maria Lindmark, (farmers) (COAL Prize, 2012). Combining his unique experience as a farmer and artist, Mathew Moore (born 1976, San Jose, lives and works in Phoenix) has created the Digital Farm Collective (DFC). He cultivates his land while campaigning for the revival of agricultural practices. The DFC's mission is to collect and share the extraordinary footage of the most important daily process of agriculture, the growth of our produce. Using time-lapse photography, the process of filming involves all that he grows, and he also invites other farmers to do the same. This footage and the conditions the plant has grown under are compiled and viewed in (on average) a three-minute film.

Figure 7.3 Mathew Moore, *Lifecycles-Nuit Blanche*

The *Living Library* collects videos depicting accelerated growth of food, from seed to harvest, offering interviews to farmers and scientists and presenting practical information on production methods. The project is a true online living library, a unique documentation based on agricultural practices and crops in the world.

Kultivator is an artist collective that initiates and executes projects, exhibitions and workshops. Mathieu and Malin Vrijman and Marlene Lindmark, (artists), and Henric Stigeborn and Maria Lindmark, (farmers), travel and present works in art spaces and elsewhere across Europe, exploring possible crossovers of culture and farming (COAL Prize, 2012). At a site in Öland (Sweden), Kultivator has a residency, exhibition space and a dairy farm with thirty cows plus chickens, ducks, sheep and horses. Since its start in 2005, approximately 80 artists, researchers and farmers have visited and worked on the premises. In addition to this, the artworks produced by Kultivator range from discursive farming projects and eco building experiments to development of smartphone applications. An important aspect of all activities is the exchange of experiences between farmers and artists, traditional and new media, rural and urban cultures. These examples show the territorial turn of the art, not only of a site-specific art, but involvement in a vision of the local economy, broadly defined as ecological and productive, social and fair. Similar sites and projects are springing up across the globe, including ArtMill in the Czech Republic (run by one of the authors), Kravin, also in Central Europe, LaFragua in Spain, The Land Foundation in Thailand, or A.R.E.A. in West Africa. Many of these are artist-run and creating a wide network of exchange and interaction internationally. This supportive aesthetic of local dynamics can go as far as we can see, up to recreating socially, naturally and economically fair movements.

References

Anon., 1958. 'Definitions'. *Internationale situationniste*, 1 (June).

Boetzkes, A., 2010. *The Ethics of Earth Art*. Minneapolis: University of Minnesota Press.

Debord, G., 1955. 'Introduction à une critique de la géographie urbaine'. *Les lèvres nues*, 6, 11–15.

Eddy, M., 2009. 'A Brief History of Somatic Practices and Dance Historical Development of the Field of Somatic Education and its Relationship to Dance'. *Journal of Dance and Somatic Practices*, 1(1), 5–27.

Friedman, G., 1953. *Villes et campagnes: Civilisation urbaine et civilisation rurale en France*. Paris: Armand Colin.

Lefebvre, H., 1965. *La Proclamation de la Commune*. Paris: Gallimard.

Lefebvre, H., 1968–1972. *Le droit a la ville*. Paris: Anthropos.

Spaid, S., 2002. *Ecovention: Current Art to Transform Ecologies*. Cincinnati: Contemporary Arts Center.

Thomas, H., 2004. *Somatics: Reawakening the Mind's Control of Movement, Flexibility, and Health*. Cambirdge, MA: Da Capo Press Inc.

8   The demiurgic gesture

Environmental art therefore raises the question of the status of representation: it is no longer paint nor representing the flesh of reality, but intervening in the same such sequence. Life, therefore, is not unlike a painting to be offered for the admiration of a helpless public, but exemplifies the power to act. Environmental art becomes a demonstration of a power to act when the artist creates a garden, or cultivates potato varieties, or designs a totally ecological bus. It is also called upon to act, while tracing the ways in which such a transformation can operate. Finally, it also maintains a link to action, in that it provides a representation of the latter. Most troubling, in these transformations at the heart of the history of art in recent years, is the will of the artist to confuse the process of artistic creation with biological processes. Life itself could produce art.

The fascination with living metamorphoses is old. However, it is only recently that it has become possible to intervene by the means of genetics on life forms themselves and to transform production. Assigned to geneticists and biologists in general, these changes would be experiments, could be the source of improved agricultural production (GMOs), and finally they could help repair defects and fatal diseases. However, the artist had nothing to do with these developments, though in terms of solutions to problems, justified as such, they did not play with biology. Changes have recently arisen, and artists will will their art to embody the everyday, raising the question of the demiurgic gesture, more Promethean than Orphic, i.e. contemplative or supportive. The latest artistic experiments, based on complex and sophisticated technologies, claim not to be environmental art, not demonstrating commitment in this regard. However, we considered it interesting to give some illustrations in this book. Why?

We have not only sought to account for artists engaged in environmental practices or towards a political ecology, but also artists who show a capacity to act with regard to the latter, changing ecological or biological cycles consciously. The tools developed to accomplish this feat borrow from new technologies, modelling living systems, thus recreating their fascination with it. The various examples will show how the artistic processes are at the heart of the life dynamics, by various methods, which also correspond to different views of life. Engaged with their complexity and systemic nature, many artists today perform work on the edge of ecological engineering, returning to the source of an art near *techné*.

Finally, joining these two currents, the highlighting of living systems and an engineering of the living, artists develop simulation models of living processes, a source of technological marvels.

The wonder of living processes

Andrea Caretto (born 1970, Italy) and Raffaella Spagna (born 1967, Italy) have been working together on a regular basis since 2002, exhibiting in public and private institutions in Italy and abroad (COAL Prize, 2011). These Italian artists use the language of science and rely upon the crafts of different disciplines (biology, anthropology, etc.) to witness the relationship between the human being and his/her natural environment. They, in their respective studies, (landscape architecture and garden art for Raffaella, natural sciences and scientific museology for Andrea), learned many techniques and tools, which they infuse into their passion for collecting, processing, classification and study of natural elements. Their work is located at the crossroads of Arte Povera and art made with organic materials. Since 2002, the Italian duo engage life sciences and offer installations and performances drawn from raw materials: plants (fruits, vegetables, plants, grains, lichens) and minerals (salt, gypsum, water).

Some of these raw materials are transformed into consumable goods. Their installations, being a complex and evolving work experimenting with the relationship of nature in different situations, question the symbolic, organic and economic value of natural resources (*Esculenta Lazzaro*, since 2003; *Recinti (Enclos)* since 2004; *Primary Resources* since 2005). They also collaborate with the research centre IRIS (Interdisciplinary Research Institute on Sustainability) of the University of Turin and Brescia. For them, the term 'environment' is defined as a 'network of relationships between whole elements that make up the system in which we live', meaning that all art is 'environmental' (Blanc and Ramos, 2010, p. 108–9). They are interested in the environment field understood as a relationship between things and a testing of these relations, once their aesthetic hold on the world is permanent. They want to change the perception of things, the basics of the relation with the world, and do not describe themselves as environmental activists. According to them, art should give a perspective, another point of view and also another mode of vision on a subject. If art becomes useful for other people, the communication of its contents is successful (see Plate 10).

For these artists, revealing hidden aspects and giving different reading keys to the world is the main purpose of art. If the work of art works in this sense, it can be very helpful. Their work is characterised by their very strong commitment to process. It is virtually impossible to predict the end of the process and especially its effects. Their project *Pedogenesis* was developed for the Parco d'Arte Vivente (Park of Living Art, PAV) Contemporary Art Centre in Turin. Through this work, organic and inorganic matter come into contact creating metamorphic processes involving the different states of matter: solid, liquid and gas. *Pedogenesis* is a system consisting of two strictly connected installations: the 'Trasmutatore di

Sostanza Organica' (organic matter transformer), an organic matter transformer and the 'OrtoArca' (vegetable garden-ark), objects that function as catalysers for broad-spectrum relations among people, places and matter. The 'Trasmutatore di Sostanza Organica' is a sort of composter consisting of a ring-shaped tunnel greenhouse made of zinc-coated iron where a group of citizens from the surrounding area leave their organic waste. People participating in the project receive some food and a new biodegradable bag for organic waste for each bag of organic waste left in the transformer. In this way, food and organic waste are put on the same level since both are made of the same mutating matter. The transformation from organic waste to compost takes place in the transformer; later the compost will be used to fertilize the soil of the 'OrtoArca', a tunnel greenhouse made of zinc-coated iron and turned upside down, delimiting a garden and a public area where people can rest on benches. The tunnel greenhouse is a very common element of the rural landscape in the Pianura Padana. This structure excludes the external environment, creating an induced microclimate, however, when turned upside down, the tunnel greenhouse becomes a sort of big crib sunk in the earth, ready to welcome whatever comes from the outside.

The portion of land delimited by the 'OrtoArca', which hangs in balance between public and private dimension, was assigned to a small group of citizens from Turin through a public lottery called 'Estrazione del Lotto'. Over 80 people, including several groups of young people, participated in this public contest. The winner of the draw had the opportunity to cultivate, for at least two years, this piece of land to produce food. However, anybody can visit the 'OrtoArca' since it is situated in a public area within the PAV. Visitors can actually sit on the benches located in the 'OrtoArca', close to the cultivated area; after more than two years, it is still active today. The artists conclude:

> absolutely all areas contaminate and feed on each other. The mineral becomes plant, carnivorous plants. The rhizome joined the hypertext while being rooted in the archaic system of growth and cycle. The complexity of our system is ridiculous, both technically and developmentally, to try to replicate a small piece of the natural system. That is disproportionate. The strength of this work lies in its precariousness, instability, this tenuous balance that allows the operation of the entire cycle. We have the illusion that science can control everything. In the first experiments on the genome, it was thought that once mastered, we could understand everything and simply reap the benefits of these mechanisms. But this is an illusion, as things are not simple. The supposed knowledge is a good starting point for our reflection; methods and interpretations are the heart of our investigations. The scientist says things are impossible to see because we live from a system inherited from the Newtonian 18th century. We must work in a new dimension and a reassessed system of analysis and representation.
>
> (Blanc and Ramos, 2010, p.108; authors' translation)

Bio-art: 'Artists-in-Labs'

Moving forward and not only implementing works of art in various places, artists have been designing whole environments. What link can be made between direct involvement in and on living environments, and artificially recreated nature? The main assumption is that of a universal 'treat', in other words we have become accustomed to certain basics (Sloterdijk, 2014). The human species naturally seeks comfort, beyond everything except perhaps basic survival. So we tend to recreate whole environments such as cities on the basis of human scale. This technological tendency refers to a tension between groups of artists in the field of environment: on one hand there are the rebel artists rejecting the technological order, evoking the accompaniment of nature, rather than unveiling its mysteries thanks to sciences; on the other hand, some artists transform the common usage of biotechnology as an artistic challenge. We wish briefly to address this second current, often in opposition to the first, treating the more nostalgic and backward looking ideologists, to the extent that those artists, who might be interested in geo-engineering, highlight the creation of environments beyond the remediation, restoration or any process to lessen the damage done to the earth.

In 2002, during the festival 'Art Outsiders', Eduardo Kac (born 1962, Rio de Janeiro) presented *Genesis*, a highly symbolic and relatively complex installation that reveals the use of biotechnology in the field of art. It is not his first transgenic work; the genetically modified rabbit *GFP Bunny* was a breathtaking work, creating a buzz in the art world. To create *Genesis*, Eduardo Kac translated into Morse a verse from the book of Genesis, where God's order to man is to control the living: 'that men dominate the fish of the sea, birds of the air and every living thing that moves on the earth.' The artist then converted Morse code in DNA pairs before getting the synthetic gene he has, finally, integrated into a bacterium. Spectators of the show, like those connected via a web interface, could then turn on or off the ultraviolet lamp located above the Petri dish creating control of the container of the bacteria. The participating public could increase or decrease the rate of mutation of the bacteria carriers of the divine order and thus partially control the transformation of the biblical verse. 'The ability to alter that sentence carried a symbolic role: it means that we do not accept its original meaning, and new meanings emerge when we try to change' says Eduardo Kac.[1] This romantic work sublimes the expression of genes at the expense of recent scientific research, showing that gene expression is restricted, especially the reaction norm. Thus, a thrifty gene can produce a puny phenotype under the influence of an environment that thwarts the expression of the genome. This is the standard reaction. Phenotypic plasticity differs from the standard reaction: there, from the same genotype various descendants follow. With phenotypic plasticity, the characteristics of plants and animals vary depending on their environment. This phenotypic plasticity clearly contradicts the 'genetic information theory', at least its most neo-Darwinian principle of genetic determinism: a gene should always produce the same character. In addition, these acquired traits can be passed on hereditarily, supported by epigenetic mechanisms (Lodé, 2011).

Less embedded in the engineering of living organisms, and much more involved with the use of new technologies to find innovative ways to represent nature, artists have been tackling the idea of 'herbaria' and virtual gardens. Miguel Chevalier's (born in 1959, France) different virtual art creations, *Ultra Natures*, *Other Natures* and *Sur-Natures*, have their starting point in the observation of the plant world and its transposition in the digital universe. The process of growing seeds, which expand and then die, is governed by a computer program that allows them to constantly innovate. *Second Nature*, installed in Place Arvieux in Marseille in 2010, has been designed in collaboration with the architect-designer Charles Bové. This work combines the real and the virtual. It consists of an 18m high, orange-coloured sculpture that reminds us of the shape of shells. At nightfall, a monumental generative virtual garden of 28m by 14m, is projected onto the facade of the building. This garden is inspired by the Mediterranean flora and changes with the seasons. These virtual plants are autonomous, are given birth uncertainly, bloom and die all the time. This virtual garden is interactive. As visitors pass in front of the sculpture, plants bend, turn on themselves.[2]

Dandelions, created by Edmond Couchot and Michel Bret (professors and co-founders of training Arts and Technologies of Image at the University Paris 8) was presented at the exhibition 'Natural/Digital' organised in Paris with Numeriscausa and Biche de Bère Gallery and Terre Active.[3] In this interactive work, nine umbels of dandelion are gently scattered by a virtual breeze corresponding to the actual breath of the viewer visible on the screen (in reality, these images are the result of an interaction between the virtual object – dandelions – residing in the computer, and a foreign element, outside, the breath of the audience); the seeds are then off, flying and falling slowly. New umbels form again ready to undergo the breath of a new interaction. Some people do not understand right away that this is a simulation and think that the images are already registered. It is not. These images are the result of an interaction between the virtual object – dandelions – residing in the computer, and a foreign element, outside the viewer's breath. No dandelion, no movement in the virtual space of the computer, and eventually no pictures are evidenced outside this real breath instigator.

Other artists-researchers have the potential to disrupt virtual plant environments through technological devices. Diana Domingues (born 1947, Brazil), who is the head of the research group Artecno, presented the work *Terrarium* that explores the notion of artificial life (at the Art Outsiders festival, 2005). The public participates in the creation and development of an ecosystem by creating, through an interface, virtual snakes. Many settings, ranging from thermal management to that of virtual food affect velocity, or life momentum of the reptiles. Diana Domingues explains that:

> Interactive technologies are changing our notion of space, distance and time, of the natural and the artificial. In our post-biological era, there is no doubt that the human condition is reinforced by interfaces and complex feedbacks within artificial systems.[4]

A protein is an amino acid chain. Each amino acid emits a vibration when it binds to a developing protein, which the physicist Joel Sternheimer compared to notes of the musical scale by transposing them into the audible range for humans. Thus was born the principle of protéodies: a sequence of specific notes could act on amino acids, so on proteins and therefore on the structure of the living. Karen Houle, a philosopher, and Karine Bonneval, a visual artist born in 1970 in France, have partnered to create a project of 'listening living rooms' on four specific sites in the Guelph campus, in Ontario, Canada. It revolves around four plant specimens chosen for their special relationship with humans. Reconstructing the 'song of proteins' of each plant selected, tree or plant, the song became audible to humans (COAL Prize, 2012). They do the same with the result of human proteins, diffusing to vegetation. The idea here is not to use the quantum song for healing purposes, or for its therapeutic aspects, but to reconstruct the normal sequence of a tree or a human being, and create a common listening experience. It was called *Chambres d'écoute du vivant*. The experiment is to communicate with the living, not through language but by a system of sensory waves. Four specimens of plants were chosen, their amino acid composition was determined by the geneticist Tara Narwani, and sound equivalences were drawn and created by physicist musicians. Physicist composers Pauline Oliveros and Paul Steenhuisen composed musical suites corresponding to the selected plant specimens and humans. They seek to create a resonance in both directions of communication: human to other living beings, and those beings on humans. This project is still thriving, but this time concerns gas (CO_2) exchanges: Karine Bonneval works with the scientific Claire Damesin, on the principle of a human and a plant matter in an insulating chamber. The film, shot in specific technical conditions that detect gas leaks, highlights views of the breath of a tree.

Carolina Pino Ahumada, who studied in Chile and in New York, addresses the digital technology from a critical perspective. Her work combines elements of both art and science in projects operating in cities and involving inhabitants.

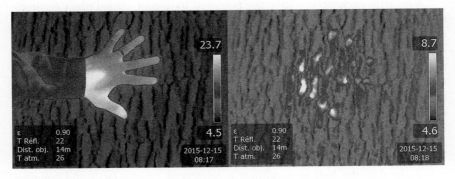

Figure 8.1 Karine Bonneval Houle, *Chambres d'ecoute du vivant, cam thermique*

Ahumada developed *INHABIT-mycotechnology* as an urban physic system of organic Shiitake mushroom farming that can be monitored, harvested and consumed by means of electronics, social networks and civic participation (COAL Prize, 2011) (see Plate 11). The modules can be replicated to build a physical and virtual network. Based on the concepts of lump and parasite, a wooden module 'appears' from a building in the city, with an interior space that allows light conditions, humidity and ventilation for growing Shiitake mushrooms. These fungi can be grown from an organic substrate, as the waste of the building. Within the module there is a video camera that records the culture growth over the Internet. There are also light, humidity, ventilation and temperature sensors that collect data and translate it to text messages on Twitter. Via Twitter, people will be advised on the growth and harvesting of the fungi and they can assist physically with the module, to observe, and consume them.

With the advent of social networking and online do-it-yourself sites, human behaviour patterns have ranged obviously and inevitably, toward a path of knowledge and acquisition of specific, practical tools, according to personal interests. These trends are generating new ways of acquiring knowledge and ways of relating. The structures in social networks are generative and work only if they act as a group, (mass), able to mobilise in pursuit of some idea that will trespass from group to group, gaining strength in relation to a given context. Human networks, like vegetable or animal or fungi, are living networks that in order to survive get together and face almost the same problems in order to survive: they must fight each other, compete to mate, they must invade new territories. In this sense, we generate strategies linking different fields of knowledge such as science, technology and art in a type of collaborative work, bringing new responses. *INHABIT-mycotechnology* attempts to implement electronic and digital technology to serve a specific community (humans). Here the use of transitional space, such as a window, opens the physical world and connects it to the online space of free access, that could potentially connect us with other species (in this case, fungi).

Notes

1   See www.ekac.org
2   See www.miguel-chevalier.com/fr
3   See www.arborescence.org/rubrique4.html
4   See www.nouveauxmedias.net/artOut.html

References

Blanc, N. and Ramos, J., 2010. *Ecoplasties: Art et environnement*. Paris: Manuella.
Lodé, T., 2011. *La Biodiversité amoureuse: Sexe et évolution*. Paris: Odile Jacob.
Sloterdijk, P., 2014. *Globes: Spheres Volume II: Macrospherology–Bubbles: Spheres Volume I: Microspherology*. Los Angeles: Semiotext(e), Tra Edition.

Part IV

The actors of the art-ecosystem

Environmental issues and the dialogue around sustainable development raise the question of the practical nature of our actions: we must act directly on the environment. Indeed, the pragmatist turning towards action in western societies affects both forms of consciousness and political commitment as well as social relations and practices of everyday life (Blanc and Emelianoff, 2008). Artists and the arts emerge in this context in close relation to the mobilisation of civil society and are seeking to lever their power to shape and develop many 'situated alternatives' or 'micro-utopias'. Artists develop a renewed attention to landscapes, places and ways that human societies have of investing in them. They create a critique and a way of doing in these landscapes that give 'territorial arts' a new vocabulary. These artists are deploying solutions and ways to dramatise their interventions or collective actions (when acting with grass-roots or civil society organisations) that involve an aesthetic know-how. They are often at odds with the terms of government actions or institutions oriented towards 'conventional' forms of development.

It is in the loopholes, cracks and interstices that many of the artists represented in this book have responded freely to opportunities to create change in whatever way is available, because this freedom is what is expected of them in Western societies impeded by stiffened codifications. They are not engineers, but sometimes put themselves in the shoes of engineers, or in the role of farmers or inventors, precisely to overcome these obstacles or borrow and divert already developed expertise. Between the local and global scales, sometimes without significantly developing the problematic link between these local actions and global solutions required by the magnitude of environmental problems, that these artists work. We can draw roughly three polarities. A first pole takes into account the artists involved in the communities. A second pole refers to artists who work with developers and with the cartographers' tools. A third concerns the artists working with scientists from the disciplines of life and physical sciences.

Some artists choose to offer their services to local communities with the idea of a social invention of art (see, for example, *Fallen Fruits*, a project where the artist collects fallen fruits in suburban gardens to redistribute them to poorer neighborhoods). Others seek to raise local awareness, contributing to the destiny of a democratic collective, such as Sitesize in Barcelona, who transform the metropolitan landscape and make it the site of their installations and interventions.

Finally, some artists choose recycled forms as meaningful vectors in ecological contexts. Are they doing so for the quality of memory-laden materials? Do they genuinely care about the depletion of natural resources? Or are they most of all after the beauty of inventing and transforming one form into another? All of the above may be true, but it remains to be noted that artists showing the way to successful recycling also indicate potential pathways for the disenfranchised to reinvent their everyday life. The artist Dan Peterman, who worked beside the university in an African-American neighbourhood of Chicago, put his studio into a collective place of bike recycling, etc.

Artists working with planners or redefining their activity to make the city their playground use hybrid techniques such as mapping, interviewing, field recording, intervening at construction sites or sidewalk libraries. Their work uses territorial geographies in order to show a utopian ecology or to contribute to the cities' development. Sometimes artists who are anchored in the transformation of local regions and communities turn themselves into – or collaborate with – geographers, planners and social scientists.

Other artists are linked to biologists, ecologists, chemists or physical scientists and aim to transform their biophysical materiality. The link is often technical; art and science are exploiting each other through collaborative projects. It can be a deeper link, science and art interpenetrating in terms of method, but also because both have the desire to produce new forms. Either the artist approaches the scientist (chemist, biologist, physicist, oceanographer, ecologist, etc.) or the scientist is an artist on Sundays (Einstein probably being one of the most famous examples). Although there is a long tradition of artists and scientists working together, such collaborations are considered common practice today.

A first chapter (Chapter 9) will address how artists will rely on civil society organisations, far from getting support from the economic world in order to push towards environmental commitment. If some artists are contemporary, we nonetheless found it useful to highlight the artists' participation in the struggle against totalitarian regimes in the Eastern Europe during the 1980s. A second chapter (Chapter 10) will address the issue of how artists, as creative individuals, are able to change lifestyles, and contribute to a more localized production. The last chapter of this part (Chapter 11) is about how artists have developed objects and forms in collaboration with scientists, engineers or designers, allowing them to integrate their ecological ideas, a scientific reality and the creation of an object such as a habitat for non-human species. In the latter case, it is of course important how these species will live with the created object or even transform it into a new habitat. Public art is changing and becoming very demanding insofar as marine animals or birds have in fact become the primary audience (as it is known that the aesthetic component of animals and habitats, for example, play in inter-specific exchanges).

References

Blanc, N. and Emelianoff, C., 2008. *L'investissement habitant des lieux et milieux de vie: une condition du renouvellement urbain ? Etude européenne et prospective (France, Pays-Bas, Allemagne, Russie)*, Paris: PUCA, Université du Maine.

9 Making new local economic cycles

Artist as player and catalyser of civil society

We might consider visual art history as corrupted at this point in time, having been subsumed into the capitalist market economy, void of checks and balances, and certainly transparency. As playwright-president Vaclav Havel wrote: 'In the world of today – enveloped by a global, essentially materialistic and widely self-jeopardizing civilization – one of the ways of combatting all the escalating dangers consists in the systematic creation of a universal civil society'.[1] The art world now consists of gallerists turned museum-directors and collectors buying art as investment. So while there are a few organisations working internationally to support artists and keep the 'separation of powers' (California Lawyers for the Arts, for example), traditional creative arts have little legal recompense; and rarely the finances to afford help. Therefore, it is no coincidence that many artists who are engaged in environmental art are simultaneously working with communities and building strong civil organisations to facilitate their projects, with an end goal of eventually effecting policy (such as Annie Leonard's Story of Stuff organization, 5 Gyres Institute, or Plastic Pollution Coalition). The two go hand in hand. One goal is not just enabling the other. The connection of the two allows a symbiotic relationship of civil society to the health of the planet, the two being mutually beneficial. This is not only true in purely ecological terms, but in terms of the jurisdiction, contemplation and activity needed by any local or global group to actually create change inherent in non-governmental groups that participate both within and outside of the central government of any nation. These mobilisations involving civil society and artists have various shapes, depending on the society at the heart of which they grow, and their creation mode. Whether it is a response to a totalitarian system or a struggle against capitalism and its impacts, or even an aid to movements of resistance to urban development, artists and civil society invent a representation of events, which leads to an answer. Environmentalist artists suggest alternatives in terms of environmental micro-utopias. Sometimes, rather than simply responding to a series of environmental problems, artists in a collaborative and interdisciplinary approach, not only invent works of art but life forms that call for unprecedented aesthetic modalities and new representations. The first paragraphs will be devoted to contemporary examples while at the end of the chapter we highlight the artists' contribution to the late 20th century Czechoslovak struggle against the totalitarian regime.

Global organisations and activism

Visualising the impact of climate change has been one of the challenges for both artists and policy makers, environmentalists and activists. The ubiquitous polar bear on a melting arctic iceberg has run its course as far as messaging loss of habitat, global warming and rising sea levels. The eco-activist group 350.org has consistently used art as a way to message the public in fun, colourful and upbeat ways. Their website (http://art.350.org/get-involved/make-your-own-art) is a virtual 'how-to' on art-activism, with categories for suggestions of art at climate-change meetings: 'murals, Aerial Art, Land Art, Street Art, 350 Concerts…' etc., all aimed for the largest outreach to the widest audience, particularly leaning towards the spectacular to garner press.

Dr Wangari Maathai, the Nobel Laureate and environmental activist who changed the ecology and politics of her native Kenya from the 1970s until her untimely death in 2011, set a standard for environmental activism that creates social and political change around the world.[2] Maathai's genius was in creating civil society out of existing local groups, starting with the women. When women would meet to do chores together, go farming, walk for water, Maathai would insert a time for education on forest ecosystems. She and her colleagues would travel from village to village, handing out saplings to plant, with instructions on

Figure 9.1 Wangari Maathai, U.N. Safe Planet Campaign Launch, U.N. Climate Conference, Bali, Indonesia

how to do it correctly so the plants would thrive. They explained the importance of the ecology of the rainforest, how without the trees, there is no more firewood, and women and girls will need to walk further and further each year in search of wood to burn in the stoves. The caveat was that each woman who received the saplings to plant, was responsible for starting her own group and continuing the process of education and passing on the knowledge. In this way, Dr Maathai created a movement that not only eventually changed the ecosystem of the Kenyan highlands, which were in danger of desertification by the clearing of the trees, but also a civil society. As the women gathered each month, they would discuss politics and their situations. The Green Belt Movement eventually led to political protests in Nairobi, and the overturn of the regime. In the African tradition, Wangari Maathai was a wonderful storyteller, and it is the medium of story, an ancient art form, that spread the message of an eco-revolution across the country. It is no small detail that this protest and change was instigated, propagated and delivered by women.

Later, as her fame increased internationally, she used her position to speak out on many environmental issues, from plastic pollution and plastic bags (that in African countries capture water and create a malaria problem), to deforestation. At the first United Nations Body Burden Forum in Bali, Indonesia in 2010, Dr. Maathai helped to raise awareness on invisible chemicals that are affecting every human being on the planet. Named 'Body Burden', these toxins are now in our bodies at birth, and increase with our consumption of pesticides in our food, toxic chemicals used for fire retardants in our beds, or the very water we drink now polluted from the ground up. In conjunction with specific United Nations conferences or exhibitions around the world, there is increasing attention paid to non-governmental organisations and local organisations that work within the specific cultural context and on the ground. They are aware of specific local environmental problems that a large global organisation may not yet be informed of. Since Rio+20, NGOs have created active international dialogues and loose organisations that share list serves and newsletters (such as CIVICUS, ngo-mgunga), which, thanks to the internet, have brought small rural organizations from around the world together online.

Plastic pollution, perhaps the most visible of the pollutants, and yet filled with invisible persistent organic pollutants (POPs), has spurred one of the more straightforward campaigns, since most people come into daily contact with the bags, plastic bottles and other one-use plastics that are now endemic on our planet. Artist Chris Jordan's now famous photographs of the albatross carcasses on Midway atoll, one of the most isolated places on the planet, and home to the breeding birds, demonstrates an instance of environmental art making a specific message of intent, vis-à-vis education and inspiration. The amount of plastic in the birds' bellies, which eventually starves them to death in their overstuffing of toxic plastics, is a horrifying vision that strikes the viewer immediately and forever. These untouched images, – no Photoshop or interference was used to manipulate them – have travelled the world and raised awareness on the issues of plastic in our oceans in a very accessible (and fairly inexpensive) medium:

Figure 9.2 Chris Jordan, "What Will Be" exhibition, Universidad Technologica de Cancun, Quintana Roo, Mexico, at the U.N.F.C.C. (Climate Conference)

photography. Jordan has been extremely generous in lending out these images of Midway to schools, exhibitions, lectures, magazine reproductions and digital forms, in the name of 'getting the message out'.

> There is no time to lose. This is the challenge of all time. Addressing it will take collective political will. That is why we need an institutional mecha-nism, a geographical information system, and equitable governance structures to channel resources efficiently and to ensure transparency and accountability.[3]

The recognition by the United Nations of the importance of culture creators has been a long time coming, despite UNESCO's founding in 1945. It was not until the 2013 conference in Hangzhou, China, entitled 'Culture: Key to Sustainable Development' that some true focus on the act of making art, creating, was recog-nised as key to fostering the imagination that is critical to problem solving and confronting our interrelated human dilemmas encompassing social justice, poverty eradication and protection of the environment. This conference was unique in that it was striving to put 'Culture' into the broader interpretation of a sustainable life, emphasising the process of creating culture, and not just the resulting 'thing'. It is an emphasis on the way that culture is made instead of what it becomes. This is a very important shift for both a vision of sustainable education and sustainable development as a whole across the globe, as it puts emphasis on local and indigenous culture as well as a truly sustainable model of fostering creativity.

This top-heavy model of recognition of the arts has nothing to do, really, with what artists are creating in local environments, except for the fact that when governments accept the validity of creativity and civic groups in the larger process of founding solutions, there can potentially be a smoother collaboration and higher success rate for shared goals. Artists today use the environment as their medium, the society as their palette and anything from social media to architecture as the brush. In an effort to document and record the outcomes and effects of how culture transforms the social and natural environment, ('indicators'), more artists are turning to scientific models of research and documentation.

Civics 101: food, waste, and the lesson of the bees

French artist Stephan Shankland (visual artist, lecturer at the National School of Architecture in Nantes, France), with his collaborative team TRANS305 Raum, spent several months researching the recycling of rubble at a building site in the southeastern suburbs of Paris, Avenue de Verdun in Ivry-sur-Seine. *Marble of Here* (COAL Prize, 2011) invited stakeholders from various walks of public life: politicians, artists, designers, teachers, city professionals, etc. to contribute to the process over a two-year period (see Plate 12). School children, who learned on-site about the history of the place at the demolition spot, which covered two centuries of French history, were then invited to help cast the debris into 'core samples'. The waste material was therefore cast into a new, locally produced, raw material. This material was then transformed into the facade of the Atelier/TRANS305, installed at the site of the Ministry of Finance. The transformation of a polluting 'nothing' (waste) into an aesthetically enhanced new architectural 'something'/structure, built and managed by artists, is complete. The involvement of local players in the production enhances the responsibility to the future by all actors, especially the school children who have learned to recycle and recreate in a socially cohesive experiment.

The Beehive Design Collective, based in Maine, has similar civil and aesthetic effects on environmental education, conservation and preservation. It operates via large-format images, posters and other educational visuals about 'big issues' like globalisation, free-trade policy, biodiversity degradation and monoculture. Deeply committed to social change and environmental justice issues, this NGO (of mostly women) uses brilliantly executed graphics to demystify complicated ecological devastation. In a project entitled 'the True Cost of Coal' in particular, they express their deep engagement with civil society:

> We are committed to confronting the root causes of climate change and defending forest ecosystems, waterways, and land-based livelihoods by using

collaboratively-made, anti-copyright visual education tools to support grass-roots-led organizing in opposition to coal extraction and combustion in the Appalachian region of the USA.[4]

Like the bees they are named after, the collective travels extensively across the country, lecturing, visualising, sharing information with schools and communities. The strong visual aspect of their presentation is engaging and fun. Working with other grassroots groups fighting against 'Big Coal' companies, the collective inspired, as they say, both 'critical reflection and strategic action'.

There are generally seven agreed upon strategies for NGO operations, which can be broadly interpreted as a foundation for functioning civil society. In her popular book *A Handbook of NGO Governance* (Wyatt, 2004) – now translated into over twenty languages – Dr Marilyn Wyatt sets up some basic principles for civil groups. These can be almost directly carried over into the work of today's eco-artist/activists, and come out of broad democratic traditions. The artist must first and foremost be accountable and responsive to the community and practice 'good governance', which involves the separation of governance and management. Like NGOs, eco-artists are generally mission-based, always promote the highest professional and ethical standards, and exercise responsible resource management and mobilisation. Translated, this might mean that an artist creating a piece on honeybees is not going to spray his/her lawn with Round-Up. Or more broadly, make sure that a work on an urban garden is inclusive of all residents and not just some.

This desire by artists today, and the main focus in this book, is on the phenomenal movement of an art that is experiential, communicative and relational. The 'spectacular' representation of art history is left behind in an engaging experiment with a living social environment.

Forty-three-year-old American artist Theaster Gates embodies this current with transformational social activities that cross the borders of community redevelopment, pottery, music, economics, real estate, environmental restoration and installation art. Based in Chicago, he has transformed numerous buildings in the traditional black slums of Chicago's South Side, from near demolition sites, to thriving communities with artist residencies, creative cottage industries, book clubs and restaurants. Celebrating the African American neighbourhoods by what he describes as 'reimaging the possibilities of the "black space"' (Austen, 2013), Gates' art is a living example of civil society being born in a formerly psychologically, economically and socially abandoned place. His artwork is what he refers to as 'a kind of ecology of opportunity'. He is creating systems that are democratic, and not only socially engaged, but transformative on every level. The artist's renovation of a long-abandoned historical bank building in Chicago, further expanded the political implications of complete social change when Gates started selling pieces of the interior marble from the nearly dilapidated site, into chunks of art for sale, starting at $5000 each. These works eventually paid for the renovation of the building, and the artist's creation of his own 'stock market', based on the predicted increase in value of said 'sculptures' over time.

Collectors invest in Mr Gates as they would in the stock market, and the artist in turn is creating a parallel economy that benefits the local community (see Plate 13). He therefore brilliantly sets up his own separation of economic power, whose transparency is a living lesson in altruism.

Contemporary civil society, be it post-totalitarian or a 200-year-old democracy, must still exercise good governance as a form of accountability (Wyatt, 2004). These are the checks and balances, the transparency, the 'sharing of decision-making authority so that power and resources don't accumulate in the hands of a single individual or group' (ibid., p.14). Artists who have chosen to work outside of the mainstream gallery/museum economy or at least minimally, are reinventing a new form that is imagining a knowledge base outside of visual representation.

Two women in London decided to build a community garden in East London in 2009. Karen Guthrie and Nina Pope envisioned a space in the centre of the city that would not only give the local community food, but would harken back to the great civic parks during their opulent time in British history (see Figure 9.3). Awarded a space in the derelict Abbey Gardens, the two artists called the project 'public art', and so it was. Initially planned to last for a three-year period, the garden is still thriving today, thanks to community activities and the claiming of the space by the neighbourhood. It has become part of the genii loci, which was one of the artists' main goals, besides mere food production. Like Gates in Chicago, the artists transformed a former derelict space into a living, thriving ecosystem, self-creating its own rules and future (see Plate 14).

Mobilising society in closed, post-totalitarian countries, or lands without a democratic history presents special challenges. And artistic activity in such places is also necessarily specific to that particular cultural context and history. And yet, even with a lack of civil society, artists in former Soviet-bloc countries or China, for example, have been able to create environmental public art works that defy a repressive regime and build the structures necessary for 'good governance' in the sense of shared community, and human society.

In 1982, Czech artist Ivan Kafka (born 1952) built a step-like structure, thirty meters high, from recycled bundles of paper waste, bound for the incinerator. As part of the underground exhibit 'Dvorek' (Morganova, 2014), it was a risky installation under a political system that punished non-conformist artists with heavy prison sentences. The 'steps', symbolically lead to 'nowhere', a comment on the life of the Czechoslovak citizen, yet remained formally tied to the tightly formalist Donald Judd school in the West. Kafka's work however, remained full of 'meaning', despite a visual remembrance of minimalism's formalism. For within this cultural context, recycled paper has history. Pre-eco art, paper has been recycled for re-use in poorer countries for decades. In 1976, when Czech author Bohumil Hrabal wrote his novel *Příliš hlučná samota* (*Too Loud a Solitude*), it was censored (Hrabal, 1990). The main character, a sad, none-too-bright paper crusher can never throw away the astounding books he collects each night that are sent to be shredded, and he amasses not only a huge library of rare manuscripts and books, but becomes a collector of knowledge. Hanta is trapped in his

Figure 9.3 Guthrie/Pope, *What Will the Harvest Be?*

love of books, which he is forced to destroy to maintain his job. The paradigm is very Czech, and part of the political context of that period in totalitarian Czechoslovakia. Kafka's 'Steps', while creating a call to recycle waste, perform on a much deeper level of interaction with the audience that is both universal and local.

1989: a case study

During the totalitarian regime in the former Soviet-bloc countries of Central and Eastern Europe, civil society was not only forbidden to exist but was punishable by law, as an 'enemy of the state'. Any artist or citizen caught or even accused of organising outside of the central government's all-pervasive eye (Orwell's 'Big Brother'), would be punished. Police tactics were brutal; families of those that fled were persecuted, phones were tapped, relatives disappeared, children were forced to attend trade schools instead of having a chance to study at university, intellectuals and professors became window-washers to keep food on the table. The consequences of being a dissident under a totalitarian regime were and still are formidable. But, as the poet/playwright/president Vaclav Havel pointed out in his pivotal essay of 1978, the 'Power of the Powerless', the alternative to abdicating civil freedom in the 'low-rent' version of a political system (a totalitarian state), is the equivalence of a living death:

Of course, one pays dearly for this low-rent home: the price is abdication of one's own reason, conscience, and responsibility, for an essential aspect of this ideology is the consignment of reason and conscience to a higher authority. The principle involved here is that the center of power is identical with the center of truth. It is true of course that, all this aside, ideology no longer has any great influence on people, at least within our bloc (with the possible exception of Russia, where the serf mentality, with its blind, fatalistic respect for rulers and its automatic acceptance of all their claims, is still dominant and combined with a superpower patriotism which traditionally places the interests of empire higher than the interests of humanity).

(Havel, 1985, p.2)

The beauty of Havel's prose and the message behind it – of hope for overturning the communist regime in Czechoslovakia and the Eastern bloc – was written by an artist. In the essay, he uses metaphors, simple and poignant, comparing the actions in everyday lives of people as tools of revolt through ordinary movements. When he calls for grocery store clerks to refuse to exhibit the ubiquitous propaganda posters of the Party of that era, that would proclaim 'Workers of the world, unite!', he is calling for an individual act of civil disobedience. As all businesses from the greengrocer to the brewer to the baker were required to follow the Party line, there were certain public displays that they had to abide by, or face severe consequences.

So how was the writing of a playwright able to help overturn a totalitarian state? How is the artist in general able to effect change in civil society? In studying the actions of artists in the former Soviet-bloc countries (Poland, Czechoslovakia, Hungary, Yugoslavia, Romania, Bulgaria), prior to the fall of the Berlin Wall in 1989, we can better understand the role of today's artists who embrace environmental issues as the core to a rebellion against a larger systemic destruction of human rights: the inherit right to breath clean air, have access to drinking water, stand on firm soil and eat food that is not poisoned. The so-called 'Artist's' Revolution or 'Velvet' Revolution of 1989 in Czechoslovakia is a case in point of the metaphorical power of art's potential for social change. More than just intellectual arguments or scientific documentation of the situations, art potentially creates a shared aesthetic dimension that allows for deep and cathartic redefining of the social regime.

During the 'worker's state' of countries under communism, the relationship to work was obligatory and fanatically documented each day with spying on co-workers to undermine their place in the hierarchy, the infamous 'time-clocks' to be punched in each day, and unexcused absences taken as an affront to the state. The historical situation in Czechoslovakia was particularly harsh, due to the huge (and inefficient) bureaucracy, left over from the Hapsburg Empire of the previous 400 years. Prague had long been the bureaucratic capital of the Hapsburg empire, next to Vienna, and continued into the post-communist era, with the Czech Republic having the most office workers per capita than any other country in the EU, and yet is still, in fact, a 'democracy without democrats'.[5]

In 1981, an artist in Prague decided to confront the individual with an immediate decision and call to action. He arranged an installation of one thousand wooden sticks, the size of kebab skewers that were placed systematically within and between the cobblestones of a small street in the Neruda district of Prague, just below the Castle (since the ninth century the historical and symbolic head of the Czech government and latterly the modern presidency). As the unknowing citizens of Jansky Street opened their front doors to go to work the next morning, they were confronted with the decision to stay home and not ruin the beautiful arrangement of sticks (art), or walk across the courtyard and destroy the piece. Ivan Kafka's seminal work of defiance against the regime, called *Definition*, asked the local population to take a stand, one way or the other, to define their existence. In doing so, he created a critical dialogue around the totalitarian state, and made it ordinary. He gave the power of decision-making back to the populace, now complacent, fearful, exhausted and damaged under a hard-line political system since 1948. Kafka, like many artists of his generation from the Eastern bloc, created works of art that gave a frame for the dream of civil society to again flourish, via discourse, open thought, and action.

Collective activity, unlike the organised 'collectivization' of society under socialism was a way to create 'parallel structures' to the existing state-run systems. So that even while borders were closed and passports confiscated, the underground kept an alternative culture alive and thriving. Music was smuggled in on cassette tapes from Los Angeles, samizdat literature copied on Xerox machines in the night when a 'friend' with a key to an office would let one have access, were smuggled out, and artists made works that were ephemeral because they could be quickly disassembled before the police would come to break up an exhibition. The land art and earth art works of pre-1989 Czechoslovakia, while aware of the trends in the West, were also deeply rooted in a local history and culture. The culture of communism demanded the works were not in galleries, so they went out to the hops fields and the barns in the countryside, the forests and fields outside of Prague, and farther away from harassment and discovery by the authorities. Artists formed collectives for protection and more anonymity. 'Alternative' became the status quo for contemporary artists working with any sort of political, social, or aesthetic critique. The strength of these groups 'TvrdoHlavi' (the HardHeads), '12 : 15', Jazz Section, B.K.S., etc. was critical in helping to bring down the government in 1989. These cultural collectives exist into the twenty-first century throughout much of Central Europe, focusing on artist-run galleries, organic farms, artist residencies and the re-purposing of rural and urban architectures.[6]

Artists in former Czechoslovakia and other Soviet-bloc countries took their art out to nature not only as flight from persecution, but also, as mentioned elsewhere, reflecting a deep connection to the rural landscape and forests of the countryside. Performative works, temporal sites and ephemeral materials were the basis for much of the underground art happening from 1969 (Prague Spring) until 1989, when the Berlin Wall fell. Pioneers like Kafka, Thomas Ruller, Zorka Ságlová, Jiři Kovanda, Miloš Šejn and Margita Titlová-Ylovský (see Figure 9.4),

Figure 9.4 Margita Titlova-Ylovsky, *Movement of Tree and Body*

created earthworks and installations that are only recorded in photographs and oral histories. This return to nature grew out of what the critic Pavlína Morganová calls a 'breakthrough to the everyday' (Morganova, 2014).

As we begin the twenty-first century with more cultures expanding, migrating, intermingling and marrying than ever before, there are bound to be clashes. And while one can only hope that the resulting violence is not permanent, the role of civil society and local engagement will be tested beyond imagination as our neighbourhoods and countries welcome in new languages and colours of existence. Human imagination and creativity, is now called upon as a last natural resource to remember how to live on our planet in harmony with one another. Artists, organised into collectives, NGOs, neighbourhoods and other alternative communities, in the cities and in rural environments, are working to create something effective. This is neither the Socialist Realism of a centralised government, nor another top-heavy mandate. Environmental art-activists are generally working locally and from the ground up, embracing the rules of community, good governance, ethics and sound management. And it is regenerating how we imagine art.

Notes

1   And he continues with:

> In my opinion, the state in the next century – in the intrinsic interest of a rapidly growing humankind – should visibly transform itself from a mystic embodiment of national ambitions and a cult-like object into a civil administration unit, and it should get used to the necessity of delegating many of its powers either to the levels below it, that is, to organisms of civil society, or to those above it, that is, to the transnational or global – and thus actually civic – communities and organizations. (Speech given at 'Václav Havel's Civil Society Symposium', Macalester College, Minneapolis, 26 April 1999. Available at: www.vaclavhavel.cz/show-trans.php?cat=projevy&val=106_aj_projevy.html&typ=HTML)

2   See www.safepla.net/videos.html#prof_maathai.
3   Wangari Maathai, at the Assembly High Level Meeting on Climate Change, New York, 2009.
4   The Beehive Collective proposal for COAL Prize, 2011.
5   This unstable political environment has contributed to the fact the Czech Republic is the only EU member which still does not have a civil service law that would depoliticize the state bureaucracy. That, in turn, has led to very poor performance by the country, as well as corruption, in processing European funds.
(Pehe, 2014)
6   In the Czech Republic alone there is Meet Factory, ArtMill (since 2004), Kravina, the Plasy Monastery and Čimelice in the 1990's, Mělnik, Karlin Studios and Futura residency to name a few.

References

Austen, B., 2013. 'Chicago's Opportunity Artist'. *The New York Times*, 20 December.

Havel, V., 1985. 'The Power of the Powerless'. In J. Keane, ed. *The Power of the Powerless: Citizens Against the State in Central-Eastern Europe*. New York: M. E. Sharpe.

Hrabal, B., 1990. *Too Loud a Solitude*. San Diego: Harcourt Brace.

Morganova, P., 2014. *Czech Action Art, Happenings, Actions, Events, Land Art, Body Art and Performance Art Behind the Iron Curtain*. Prague: Karolinum Press, Charles University.

Pehe, J., 2014. 'The Czech Republic and the EU: Democracy Without Democrats'. *The Huffington Post*, 10 August.

Wyatt, M., 2004. *A Handbook of NGO Governance*, Budapest: European Center for Not-for-Profit Law.

10 Creative individuals

Local production, lifestyle and Robinson Crusoe

If one wishes to push the comparison, it may be best to think of present-day localism as 'Small Is Beautiful 2.0', this time with an economic base in a pre-existing economic class and with greater concern for independent ownership than for appropriate technology. Even that qualified comparison should not be pushed too far, because the class basis of present-day localism is considerably different from that of 'small is beautiful' economics, which remained rooted in a vision of building appropriated organisations and technologies for the world's working class and poor people (Hess, 2009, p. 50).

E. F. Schumacher's *Small is Beautiful* of 1973 (Schumacher, 1989), made popular the concept (new to many in the Western world), that the planet's resources were limited. It became one of the most influential books of the post-World War II world (*Times Literary Supplement*, 1995, p.39). An economist by trade, Schumacher raised important themes that have influenced today's environmental justice thinking as well as the environmental movement in general: finite natural resources should not be consumed at the risk of future generations being left without. The push towards localism, which has become also a political, and ethical effort as well as economical, stems from this time period.

Many contemporary artists have embraced this philosophy as both an environmental philosophy as well as conceptual. With the rise of the art market economy that is based on the capitalist model, today's generation of artists are increasingly frustrated at the 'one per cent' structure that effects the gallery/museum system much as it does the world economy in general; very few artists 'rise to the top' to become stars/rich, or are even able to afford a basic standard of living. Even worse, younger artists are now often saddled with the ubiquitous student loans from prestigious and not so prestigious art schools. We might say that embracing local production is a 'return' to a simpler system of production, but it is also a very contemporary and progressive consciousness in the eco art movement.

The current art of the environment almost always is sustainable. By that, we mean that it is non-toxic, often working with organic systems and materials, found or re-cycled objects, no objects at all, and/or 'ready-made' sites. The material is more often than not the context: the neighbourhood, the community, the ocean, a forest. With the end of modernism, followed by post-postmodernism, art has moved into what Malcom Miles terms an 'expanded field' (Miles, 2014, p. 13; quoting Rosalind Krauss, 1979).

A Parisian frame, no longer golden

> The idea of modernity would like there to be only one meaning and direction in history, whereas the temporality specific to the aesthetic regime of the arts is a co-presence of heterogeneous temporalities.
>
> (Rancière, 2000)

Contemporary art-making practice, if we can even call it that anymore, engages Rancière's 'heterogeneous temporalities' in a way that was unthinkable even forty years ago, during the modern era in the West. Yet these cross-disciplinary, localised, ecologically involved works have reverberation on indigenous cultural practices, which have, in some cases, survived intact into the twenty-first century.

The 'Urban Orchard' in London, designed by Heather Ring (see Plate 15), created a new environment in the centre of the city, transforming an empty lot into a thriving community centre that provided, food, recreation, interaction, beauty and thought. Over 100 volunteers worked over the course of one summer to create the transformation.

> As much of the build as possible was developed to incorporate contributions from the local and volunteer community. We had council office workers digging trenches, lawyers shovelling gravel, a web designer rolling turf, a school cook building apple crates, firemen painting blueberries and an accountant who made copious amounts of tea. Materials came from far and wide. Carillion [construction sponsor] would often bring stacks of pallets for our perusal and use, and our junk man, Mo, who ran a 'green' waste disposal company, Junk, etc., would drop off doors and sinks, old work tops and white boards, floor boards and more pallets. Anything left on site was fair game for appropriation.[1]

While a tangible garden brought in BBQs, dancing troupes, book clubs and a senior centre over time, the results are intangible. The effects on the community – the aestheticised space, the production of organic food, the songs made – are temporal. This particular garden was eventually pulled up and given away in pieces to neighbours. It was a performance, a happening, an event. The artist, Ring, and her many volunteers created a space in time, an experience, which is the foundation for transformative works (Dewey, 1980). Is it art?

There is perhaps a radical element inherent in the arts that current environmental works embrace. Definitely non-corporate, many of the garden projects are a direct response to the loss of bio-diversity, the take-over of seed production with GMOs, chemical fertilisation without consent by the consumer, and the general lack of governmental protection from hazardous food production practices. Urban land production has risen in populated cities, often spurred by artists' groups. 'The purpose of these gardens is not the production of food only, but also the creation of relations of people among each other and relations between people and their environment' (from the artists COAL proposal).

The project by Asa Sonjasdotter (Norway), 'High Diversity' (COAL Prize, 2014) planned for the heart of Paris, includes planting twelve different varieties of potatoes that were grown at the time of great famine in France during the eighteenth and nineteenth centuries. The artist quotes the historical significance of the potato, which as we all know came from the Americas and helped to bring Europe out of famine. She gives a detailed historical account of the potato's specific history in France, how it was originally banned, then finally welcomed for its vitamin content, ease of growth and economic durability. The vegetable has been associated with the commoner and heroic endurance since these times, (it needs no special tools to harvest except one's bare hands) when it survived the global climate changes of 1783 during a volcanic eruption in Iceland that caused weather conditions unfavourable to the common wheat crop. It was grown in the Jardin de Tuileries during the French Commune, cites Sonjasdotter (see Plate 16).

By contextualising the potato as associated with democracy, feminism (the first cookbook written by a woman, *La Cuisinière Republicaine* by Mme Merigot, was dedicated uniquely to the preparation of potatoes and published in Paris in 1794) the commoner, heroes (the Revolution) and good health, Sonjasdotter paints a picture around the project. She, the artist, creates a frame around an 'ordinary' thing, and makes it something else. Added to the history and glamour of the potato are the current political EU regulatory restrictions, which we learn in the proposal, includes the ban of all twelve varieties of these historical roots, due to the globalised monoculture now common in the EU and in the USA. As industrialised farming was implemented with the food shortages after the Second World War, local breeding techniques were lost and eventually banned, in favour of higher yield, state-authorised National Variety List, which maintains strict genetic compositions for production in the European Union.

'The notion of *terroir* is typical for French farming culture ... Many old potato varieties that were discarded from the modernization programs, were saved by farmers and re-vitalized for cultivation' (artists COAL proposal). Many of these varieties are now the gourmet brands smuggled into gourmet restaurants, and treasured by connoisseurs of good cuisine. Sonjasdotter frames the local farmers as heroes, for rebelling against mono-agriculture (which, by the way, requires massive amounts of pesticides and chemicals, as we know), and the lowly potato is raised to object of admiration. She has placed her proposed potato gardens at historically sensitive and loaded neighbourhoods around Paris: Le Jardin des Plantes, where Antoine-Augustin Parmentier was forbidden to grow potato plants by the Royal Physicians during the regime of Louis XVI; Le Jardin des Tuileries, where potatoes were grown during both Paris Communes to feed the population of Paris; La Ferme de Marconville in Villers-Saint-Barthélemy, which is one of the pioneering organic producers in Île-de-France today, etc. thereby completing the frame around the garden into a geo-political work of art leading into environmental justice issues. The fact that these potatoes are 'outlawed' by the European Union, makes them rather subversive and the project becomes politicised. More importantly, the audience is engaged with the gardens in a transformative way. Community is built, as in other urban gardens, activities take place, the site is changed. Sonjasdotter brings us to a thinking place, about history, empire, power, resources and place, in the *way* she framed the potato gardens in Paris. We see them differently when we understand her text.

Stepping back for a moment to the frame, one is reminded that history is in fact only a *story*, with an author who is perceived as black or white, male or female. In this way, framing has everything to do with politics, power and value. Which is why modernism was so determined to let go of the physical frame completely. With the rise of democracy in Europe, after a long period of empire, the gilded furniture and decorative flourishes of aristocratic European design streamlined with modernism's simultaneous embrace of 'civil society'. In looking at a work by Moravian artist Tomaš Ruller (an active dissident artist who later went on to found the New Media Atelier at Brno's Art Academy) from 2004, entitled *Chimera* (see Plate 17), referencing French Impressionist painting, which itself was looking at the world in a new way, the viewer becomes active subject of the environment, as well as the work of art. The artist created two live video screens for *Chimera* for the exchange exhibition 'Dialogue: Prague/Los Angeles, Certain Traces' (2004) held in Prague and Los Angeles.[2] The scenes were of the river Moldau in the heart of Prague, at a vantage point near the Smetana House, looking back across the river at the Museum Kampa, where the work was then shown in the gallery.

The other image was the park in front of the Frank Lloyd Wright Hollyhock House and gallery in Los Angeles (Barnsdall Art Park). Both scenes are bucolic in the nineteenth-century style of landscape painting, made so even more by the blurry focus of the video camera, (via some wax smeared on the video screen), the classic framing (gilded wood), and balanced composition. All elements, form, colour, texture, light, balance, subject matter, relate back to the impressionist structure of art.

Yet Ruller created the works in live time, with live video plays, cleverly recording the viewer from outside and afar. It takes the museum-goer some time to realise the trick, for movement is nearly non-existent. The light is obviously new technology, but it seemingly could be a projected painting. It is not until a tree slightly blows in the breeze or a ripple on the water swells, that one notices it is 'real'. This play with sensory perception, history and the frame bring many layers of understanding to the work. The artist, as the title indicates, questions the history of painting and representation. He plays in Plato's Cave, asking the viewer where reality lies. In re-creating faux landscapes of the late nineteenth century, when modernism was first questioning how we see the world, Ruller is not only re-addressing the closed society of that 'bourgeois' state, but also how they viewed nature. In bringing the scene into 'real time', he breaks the mysticism of modernism's world-view, of landscape that is outside of us. And in turning the camera back at the viewer, he places contemporary wo/man squarely into the picture, both as voyeur and as actor in the public scene that is alive and free. The public becomes the subject matter, involving them in the creation of the art piece. They are demonstrating democracy on a fine, sunny day, walking about in their Sunday clothes in a banal demonstration of freedom. When the piece was shown in Prague (2004), it was an exhibition to mark the fifteenth anniversary of the Velvet Revolution. In other words, fifteen years ago such a bucolic walk would not have been possible, as there were water cannons in the street shooting at demonstrators in that spot. Thus the context of the space, historically, ecologically, socially and politically, creates the work and gives it value.

Schumacher's second thesis in *Small is Beautiful* (Schumacher, 1989) regarded limited resources and the distribution, protection and use of such. Crucial to much of the environmental art today, as we have seen in this book, is the recognition of these limited resources, (water, food, soil, clean air, etc.), and the re-creation of micro-labs for growing food, engaging community and education. Yet there is another aspect to this 'return to nature' which might be a romanticised primitivism or noble savage lifestyle that harkens to Rachel Carson's *Silent Spring* (1962) that spurred the organic food movement and inspired much of the current Eco/Gaia discussion. There might be a survival instinct in the eco art projects that propose an alternative lifestyle 'away from the city's roar'.

Literally going 'underground', the artist team of Anna Romanenko and Björn Kühn, have proposed the installation *Phantom* under the streets of Paris. Their materials are bio-filters (rocks) framed in bronze casings made into the form of chandeliers. The COAL prize theme of 2014 was 'Paris', and the artists chose the literary (and now musical) theme of *Phantom of the Opera*, the haunting story of the man who lived in the subterranean pools and sewers beneath the Paris Opera House, as portrayed in Leroux's 1910 novel. The artists decided on the chandelier as a metaphor of the ruling class that extracts and uses natural resources. Chandeliers were a symbol of aristocracy in Europe; 'old bourgeois representational values' said the artists (artists' COAL proposal). The traditional 'glass' of chandeliers, now replaced with bio-filter stones that actually cleanse the air and environment, turn the economical–historical balance upside down. What was once a symbol of the 'consumer economy', becomes an object of repairing that damaged system. The fragile balance of the ecosystem earth is deeply distorted. Pollution, CO_2 and the exploitation of natural resources are the key concepts of the ecological apocalypse to come. They have replaced many mythological narratives that used to define our libidinal economies with our environment.

Post-modern lumps of coal

In December 2015, the global focus (COP21 in Paris) was to cut carbon emissions from the environment in order to curb global warming to the ambitious two degree Celsius by 2050. Many nations signed on to the 1.5 limit, although that number seems even more fantastical as time marches on and the UNFCCC 'agreements' in Paris turned into an even bigger disappointment than

Copenhagen. The absence of many NGO (grass roots) and Indigenous People's voices at the agreements (due in large part to the terrorist attacks in Paris shortly before the conference began), left decisions on how much fossil fuel to keep in the earth largely up to those governments whose economies depend on fossil fuels. While recent studies have shown that there are alternative and supporting solutions to climate change besides carbon reductions (Ramanathan and Press, 2015), most environmentalist groups are still focusing on the bigger issues of carbon off-setting and emissions (whose fate, unfortunately, is held mainly in the hands of global corporations and governments). There is hope, of course, in individuals and organisations working to educate the public.

To call attention to the problem, Dr Dara Montag has created his project named 'CHAR' that produces charcoal, packages it and sells it to individuals, as a symbolic example of keeping carbon in the ground, or in the burned wood, or a carbon neutral state of pyrolysis. In creating charcoal, carbon is not released into the atmosphere, and remains 'locked' into the material. This is a reproduction of the natural process in a forest or field, when natural fires occur. Indigenous people in the Amazonian rainforest regularly covered large areas of the forest with this biochar, which improves the soil and takes carbon out of the atmosphere. Montag lectures and performs around the distribution of bags of the RANE-CHAR project, which are documented on a website showing geographical locations of various CHAR 'burials' around the world. His 'artist multiples' of the brown paper-bagged and aesthetically designed lumps of coal, are also a wry comment on the art-world distribution and marketing of art objects.

Jacques Cousteau meets Robinson Crusoe

As sea levels rise at an increasingly alarming rate, lowlands are flooded and small island nations are crying out to tell us they are disappearing, we begin to collectively think of our relationship with the sea in a different, intrinsic way.

With coastlands being swallowed into the ocean and river people losing their homes, our species, being survivalists, dream of new inventions to get ourselves to higher ground, a new country, another planet, or, embrace the change and build underwater domiciles. Jules Verne captured the imagination of a generation with his underwater/middle earth/flight-filled worlds, as did Cousteau, who brought cameras to the sea and opened up a new world to the public one hundred years later. Daniel Defoe's novel of 1719, *Robinson Crusoe*, was not the first story to be told of a stranded individual in a dangerous, foreign land who overcame obstacles and survived. Crusoe's cunning and adventures were thrilling and romantic (since he lived to tell the tale), and appeal to our sense of triumph over nature and the 'hostile natives' of a remote island in the middle of an imaginary sea. The myth is epic, and indeed goes back to ancient history in the dramas of the Labyrinth, Perseus, Odysseus, or Noah's ark. Escaping natural disasters, migrations or floods, are as old as time and thus our creativity in building homes in foreign places is perhaps in the human DNA.

The Portuguese artist Miguel Palma (born 1964) has presented the 'Six Feet Above Water' project, which literally creates a new living structure able to float above water. Based on similar structures from around the world (particularly in Southeast Asia and Africa) he uses local materials (bamboo, wood, plumbing pipes) to build a hut-like feature that is able to stay above sea level (for now), and is run on an electric motor. Another bamboo tree house, but more functional, was created by Suwan Laimanee. Long straddling the art world and indigenous world of his native Thailand, Laimanee studied and later worked with Michaelangelo Pistoletto in Europe, bridging the performative spirituality of his Buddhism with gallery exhibitions and installations that included massage (the ancient Nuad Phaen Bo-ran), Ayurvedic medicine, food, prayer, or a street art piece of his own t-shirts designs claiming 'Thai rice is for Thais: NO GMO's!' His 'Bamboo Tree House' (COAL Prize, 2007) is a totally self-contained living space, complete with 'swimming pool', biogas, proposed solar panels and a self-contained garden – in short, everything the artist needs to be self-sufficient.

Yet, within this idyll of an off-the-grid sustainable habitat, is the artist's desire for connection to community vis-à-vis his project. 'An important part of the construction and living process was knowledge exchange and interaction with the local community' (artist's COAL proposal). He goes on to give the examples of receiving help from a local builder with his bathroom and teaching the plumber how to use concrete for stabilizing the bamboo structure. The local people have in turn taught Laimanee how to forage for immense varieties of mushrooms in the forest, which he calls his 'supermarket'. This give and take between artist and community offers new ways of living in the local environment, each benefiting from the knowledge shared, with the added benefit of artists then taking the projects out into the world to multiply in the form of art.

Compare this utopian idyll with the often playful work of the New York-based Czech art team, Krystina and Marek Milde. Working at the junction of domestic nature and urban wilderness, the artists create furniture pieces from forest woodlands, make soup gardens in the streets of New York, and otherwise illuminate the human condition, now removed from our once innate environment, but forever striving to somehow return:

> The site-specific installation *In-Tree-Net* made with trees and branches hung from the ceiling resemble pipes and wires of engineering systems that bring vital functions into the building. Trees and their complex interconnection present in the ecosystem of the woods are here reduced to a rigid model of a machine representing the mechanistic approach towards Nature. Pipes that in industrial settings are usually exposed while the architecture in civil buildings usually attempts to meticulously cover in order to create an intact environment. In the *In-Tree-Net* the pipes become alive pointing at the environmental dependency of the seemingly independent interior environment. *In-Tree-Net* critically approaches culturally conditioned understanding of nature, which produces the perspective that nature as such has borders, beginning and end, similar to the architecture and urbanism. Nature here is

Figure 10.1 Lucy Davis, *Teak Road project* (Ranjang Jati: The Teak Bed that Got Four
Humans from Singapore to Travel to Muna Island, Southeast Sulawesi and
Back Again)

an element that penetrates not only the walls, but also crosses artificial
borders, that divide landscape without a context, cutting through the mountains and rivers. In the *In-Tree-Net* the organic systems represent an idea of
bringing nature closer and the way of its estranged perception, implying a
reconnection of a fragmented environment to a whole.

Figure 10.2 Lucy Davis, *Ranjang Jati: Bedprint & DNA*

Another artistic process for understanding local ecological systems is to define and document their history. *Teak Road (Jalan Jati)* by Singapore artist Lucy Davis, produced this art and ecology project 'on Trees, human, wood and DNA' by tracing the route of one bed, originally built in the 1950s (see Figure 10.1). Davis treats the tree as historical agent of information as well as cultural collateral: mythologically, metaphorically and ecologically. Using current DNA tracking technology applied to timber, she is able to locate the exact forest that the wood was milled from, around which she then creates a narrative that traces 'micro and macro arbo-realities, or arboreal relationships and influences in Southeast Asia' (COAL Prize, 2011). The physical work has been shown in museums and exhibition spaces across Europe and Southeast Asia, in the form of photographs, film and music. While Davis seems to be the lead visual artist on the work, there is actually a large team of scientists and artists collaborating under the name of Migrant Ecologies. Tracing the story of wood, one so particular to the world's rainforests, brings a local ecology, a specific domesticated functional object (bed) to the larger implications of the destruction of the earth's rainforests.

Stories of individuals make a work 'real' to many audiences. It is in the local that we find the universal. And so when Anglo-Guyanese artist Jason D'Caires Taylor started building underwater sculpture gardens to help offset the human impact on coral reefs from tourism, he began casting the figures of local residents from his home studio off the beach of a small fishing town in the Yucatan of Mexico. Located just a few miles south of the overdeveloped tourist 'ghetto' of Cancun, which lies in the ancient Mayan region of Quintana Roo, the area is noted for its crystal azure seas and clear diving waters, the resort grew quickly in the 1970s–1980s. The World Bank funded the resort, which as of 2010 had over 80,000 tourist beds. The sleepy village of fishing huts and mangrove forests, stretching out before the second longest coral reef in the world, is now an 'ecological disaster that never should have happened' say experts.[3] Within twenty years of the building of the resort, over eighty per cent of the coral reefs are now dead or dying. Human waste, agricultural runoff (after mangrove forest destruction), polluted waters from the hotels and golf course chemicals draining into the ocean have all but destroyed the environment that tourists are paying to visit.

D'Caires Taylor comes from a diving background, as well as an academic art education at the London School of Art. He grew up diving the reefs in Malaysia, an experience that has informed his work as an artist-scientist and environmental activist. In 2009, after another similar project in the Bahamas, working with local authorities, D'Caires Taylor co-founded the Museo Subacua tico de Arte, an ambitious underwater sculpture 'garden' placed in two locations off the coast of Cancun. The museum, covering over 420m² of seabed is in the Cancun Marine Park, one of the most visited seas in the world. The artist's ambition is two-fold: to attract divers and tourists away from the natural reefs now being destroyed by visitors, as well as to create new artificial reefs with his carefully placed and specially designed cement sculptures that are breeding new marine ecosystems to life. His materials are specially designed to help breed new corals; adventurous art-lovers and divers are able to see the process of progressively rich colours and textures grow and form into living sculptures as the corals grow.

The sculptures themselves vary in size and design, but can weigh up to a ton each. *Silent Evolution* (2012) was created using body casts of local residents from the fishing village near the artist's studio, just south of the Cancun resort.[4] Each face tells a story, has a history, and when placed under water, creates a new history and life. The faces are so realistic and individualised, that one is able to trace ethnic characteristics, even under water. The rich diversity of Mexico's Caribbean coast – African, Cuban, Mestizo, Asian, Mayan, European – is reflected in the life-size figures, now silenced and frozen in time. Due to the casting technique the models must close their eyes while the plaster casts are made so that all 400 of the statues seem to be holding their breath until another era dawns. And indeed, D'Caires Taylor's wish is that his work will inspire a new generation to steward our oceans and work quickly to repair the damage this generation has done.

Notes

1   Kendall, T. 'Shed Morphosis' in the artist's COAL proposal.
2   Curated by B. Benish and S. Brock, see: www.art-dialogue.org
3   Barbara Bramble, adviser to the National Wildlife Federation in Washington, DC, quoted in Vidal, 2010.
4   From the artist's website: www.underwatersculpture.com/sculptures/the-silent-evolution

References

Carlson, R., 1962. *Silent Spring*. Boston: Houghton Mifflin.

Dewey, J., 1980. *Art as Experience*. 22nd edn. New York: Perigee Books.

Hess, D. J., 2009. *Localist Movements in a Global Economy: Sustainability, Justice and Urban Development in the United States*. London: MIT Press.

Miles, M., 2014. *Eco-Aesthetics: Art, Literature and Architecture in a Period of Climate Change*. London: Bloomsbury.

Ramanathan, V. and Press, D., 2015. 'The Other Pollutants', *Los Angeles Times*, 28 December, opinion section.

Rancière, J., 2000. *The Politics of Aesthetics: The Distribution of the Sensible*. London: Bloomsbury.

Schumacher, F. E., 1989. *Small Is Beautiful: Economics as if People Mattered*. 2nd edn. New York: Harper Perennial.

The Times Literary Supplement, 1995. 'The Hundred Most Influential Books Since the War'. *The Times Literary Supplement*, 6 October, 39.

Vidal, J., 2010. 'Cancun: From Mangrove Paradise to Polluted Mega-Spraw'. *The Guardian*, 9 December.

11 Macro to micro

Artists as scientists, engineers and designers

If artists borrow from science, they do not refer only to the life sciences, although this is often the case for those artists attracted to ecology. Many artists will seize tools and the vocabulary of local development, dealing with the space sciences. The development tools, such as the use of the map, are how the artists utilise knowledge of an environment woven with materials, shapes and linguistic representations. They involve the landscape and the romantic garden as 'schools of vision', but also with the ideal of reconciliation of art and science, theory and practice. This reconciliation is precisely the slogan of artistic engagement in the nineteenth century, under what in France was in the form of 'social art' as opposed to 'pure art'. This movement, engaging art towards a social critique in the nineteenth century, was worldwide from Mexico to Russia, as political systems were broken down and changing.

Without delving into the details of this story, some points may illuminate tensions experienced by contemporary artists engaged in ecology. We know, for example, that Greek and Latin have a term (*ars* or *techne*) to describe technical and artistic activities. The Renaissance provoked their separation to allow the artist to be emancipated from the status of the artisan, from the 'mechanical arts', and thus raised it to the rank of 'liberal arts'. The Enlightenment cemented the break, separating 'fine arts' and knowledge (science and letters). It is this last separation, completing the first by a greater abstraction and greater specialisation of components of any form of work, that had the most serious consequences on the social status of artistic function. Artist-thinkers, such as Francisco Goya, were already questioning this separation of 'reason' from 'imagination', as is evidenced in the controversial 43rd *Capricho, El Sueno de la razon produce monstruos* (*The Sleep of Reason Produces Monsters*, 1799) (see Figure 11.1). This iconic series, but especially the 43rd, sets up a critique of the Enlightenment in Europe, and in particular Goya's Spain of that time, which shortly thereafter supported the horrors of the Inquisition. In this sense, the work is an early precursor to the debate on the dangers of separating art from science.

Some thinkers, among them Claude de Saint Simon (1760–1825), will try to think of the usefulness of art emphasising its educational function. This trend is still present among ecologists, where art retains the simple role of propaganda of an underlying ideology. Progressive politics are not always art. The interest of the

Figure 11.1 Francisco de Goya, *El sueño de la razon produce monstruos (The Sleep of Reason Produces Monsters)*

Saint-Simonian episode is also to valorise the issue on the ground of the developing city more than natural or rural settings. The architect and urban planner have inherited the prerogatives of social art. The demiurgic power conferred to the designer today is a direct result of this desire to join the beautiful and the useful. It is precisely in the name of the alliance of art and knowledge, so predominantly thought of as rationality, that these historical figures can still fascinate artists and their audiences.

György Kepes

This fascination is particularly expressed in the avant-garde of the early twentieth century, reappearing in some post-war attempts of an alliance between 'artist and scholar'. However, it was not until the 1960s that artists inspired by the methods, materials and preoccupations of science and engineering will attempt to deal explicitly with the environment. They began to address pressing environmental and political issues in the 1960s–1970s. This vision of the environment and the role of artists can be summarised by the path of György Kepes (1906–2001). At first a painter, he opted for design and joined the New Bauhaus in Chicago in 1937, and then founded the Center for Advanced Visual Studies (CAVS) in 1967 at Massachusetts Institute of Technology. He specifically took the challenge of the relationship between art and science in the realm of environmental issues. He curated and edited publications, from *Arts of the Environment* (1972) to *The New Landscape in Art and Science* (1956), which assembled a range of artists and practitioners, from artist Robert Smithson to cybernetician Jay Forrester. In the essay 'Art and Ecological Consciousness', he writes: 'Environmental homeostasis on a global scale is now necessary to survival' (Kepes, 1972, p. 6). According to him, creative imagination, and artistic sensitivity will help us all to 'register and reject what is toxic and find what is useful and meaningful in our lives.' Kepes' path of artistic commitment and the alliance of art and science demonstrates an awakening of consciousness and research for solutions. However, Kepes expresses a somewhat dated vision of ecology referring to the famous formula of astronaut William Anders about the earth photographed from the Apollo shuttle, 'a fragile Christmas tree ball, blue-green, that we should handle with care' (Kepes, 1972, p. 6). A 'depoliticized and organismic' approach is expressed here, obscuring local distinctions including social-political ones.

Environmental art and science

In contrast, American artists became pioneers in this field, investing ecological problems and linking art and science in very new ways. Among the leading pioneers of the eco art movement, the collaborative team of Newton and Helen Mayer Harrison (born 1932 and 1929 respectively), often referred to simply as 'the Harrisons', have worked for over forty years. They did some early work that is still considered avant-garde. 'It is not surprising that a very few artists are beginning to become involved with growth and harvest cycles of nature' wrote Jack Burnham in 1974:

> Newton Harrison is one of the most intuitive and perceptive artists to move beyond the concerns of recent Ecological Art. His career in this respect is revealing. In the 1950s he began as a sculptor, turned to painting in the 1960s, and by the late sixties moved into Technological art with a series of glow discharge tubes. These provoked several proposals directed towards

creating atmospheric effects at high altitudes. Two years ago, Harrison produced a compost-earth pasture for the Boston Museum's 'Elements of art' exhibition and a Brine Shrimp Farm for the Los Angeles County Museum's 'Art and Technology' project. The notion of Ecological Art was well established before these projects. What distinguishes Harrison's attempts is a desire to question and record his own interactions and to construct systems involving a complex hierarchy of organisms.

(Burnham, 1974, p. 163)[1]

The German artist, Hans Haacke, mentioned earlier in this book, uses a word system for things that are not systems in terms of perception, but are physical, biological or social entities. He believes this to be more real than perceptual titillations. Much of his work since the 1970s has a clear ecological dimension. *Bowery Seeds* (1970), a circular area of earth open to receive airborne seeds, proposed for the buildings of the German Ministries of Education, Science and Justice in 1973–4, represents a clear alternative to a rigid political structure. For Haacke, this area constitutes an enclave of unpredictable and free development. The installation *Rhine-Water Purification Plant* (1972, Museum Haus Lange, Krefeld) is also emblematic of this trend.[2] To highlight the fragility of the ecosystem, an artistic device purifies the polluted water of the Rhine in the gallery space and gives it back to the garden outside. A basin with goldfish is placed before a window overlooking a wooded landscape, highlighting the confrontation of two ecosystems: a 'natural' space, whose invisible pollution is revealed by the technical museum installation and its specific ecosystem. Haacke borrows from general science the notion of systems, which deals with the effectiveness of organisational structure, in which the conversion of information, energy and/or material is involved. The fact remains that *Rhine-Water Purification Plant* is as much a model and a symbolic object questioning the boundaries of art and its exhibition, as it is what remains in the gallery.

In Europe, there is no such similar infrastructure as the US system of arts funding projects in situ, for example the Land Reclamation and the National Endowment for the Arts (National Arts Fund). The latter organization awarded a grant of $10,000 for the first *Revival Field* to Mel Chin (born 1951, US), *Revival Field I: Pig's Eye Landfill*, developed between 1990 and 1993 in collaboration with the scientist Rufus Chaney on the polluted site in St Paul, Minnesota. Planted for three seasons, the phytoremediation field is strictly circumscribed by a circle in a square crossed by two diagonals, evoking the idea that the earth is a regeneration target. Since phytoremediation is supposed to become a highly profitable business, various *Revival Fields* were successful: they allowed scientists to collect data as well as to raise awareness about hyper-accumulating plants. However, from the outset, the status of such a practice was questioned: the National Endowment for the Arts did not continue funding beyond the first proposal, claiming that it was not art. The artist argued the case by comparing the process of absorption of heavy metals by plants to the hollow where acid etches the metal plate, but on a grander global scale. For Chin, this project can also be likened to

Figure 11.2 Mel Chin, *Revival Field Maquette*

a sculpture with materials that have so far never been experienced (biochemistry and agriculture).

Similar to Chin's attempt to use art as both artefact to document pollution as well as activity to call attention to hidden environmental issues, Los Angeles artist Kim Abeles (born 1951) was pioneering techniques to view smog. Beginning in the early 1990s Abeles would place dinner plates on her downtown Los Angeles roof, and let the smog create images from cut stencils of portraits of US presidents placed on them (see Plate 18). As a cutting simulacra of the gold-plated presidential plates in the White House, the artist wrote in gold lettering around the portraits various quotes from each man, regarding his environmental or business declarations. The particulate matter of the dirty air created stunning images after several days, leaving a readable trace of the dirty sky on each plate. Abeles' public works, sometimes grand-scale installations, such as her floating forty foot 'body' made of trash, often recirculate scientific facts and spotlight the public's access to information or lack thereof. Her environmental commitment has been steadfast over a forty-year career, earning her the prestigious Guggenheim award in 2014.

Tropes to incite curiosity

Jennifer Wightman (born 1973) is a Cornell University Research Associate specialising in greenhouse gas inventories and life cycle analysis of agronomic systems (COAL Prize, 2014). Her art practice began in 2002 and employs scientific tropes to incite curiosity of ecological phenomena. Informed by her scientific inquiry, Wightman's art poetically articulates the incongruities between our current economic growth paradigm (conceptually unlimited) and our emerging notion of sustainability (limited by finite resources). Her work captures a visual language of embodied form moving through cycles of destruction and creation within a finite landscape. She works on city portraits, such as New York City, with mud, water, endogenous bacteria, eggs, newspaper, chalk, steel, glass, silicone as a medium. She builds steel and glass frames to hold mud and water from polluted waterways to create evolving portraits of New York City. Each frame includes mud from one of the following: Hudson River (PCBs), Gowanus Canal (heavy metals), Deadhorse Bay (exposed landfill), East River (raw sewage) or Newtown Creek (oil spill). Bacteria photosynthesize pigments and create a transformed colourfield as defined by the physical and chemical conditions of each water/mud sample. As one species exhausts its preferred resources and dies out, another species thrives on the waste products of its predecessor. Transition of colour indicates ecological succession of micro-fauna colonising New York City.

Viewers of the sculptures or the documentary photographs will witness infinite growth in a finite ecosystem. These living paintings frame an unfolding drama of changing relationships in a finite molecular landscape. Each organism thrives

Figure 11.3 Wightman, studio shot of the Hudson River, Newtown Creek, and Gowan's Canal

upon available resources building higher order structures such as pigment. As the individuals reproduce, seemingly invisible micro-organisms synthesise species-specific dots of colour pointing to the construction of community. The species expands until it exhausts its preferred resources and is surrounded by its waste products; the colony plateaus. However, these 'waste' products become the resources of a successor. Here, in the micro-landscape, 'resource' and 'waste' are interchangeable and a viewer can witness this transition in resource use by a shift in colour. The living organisms manufacturing the pigments are simultaneously the subject and substance of this 'painterly' objectification – both object and medium, both a work of art itself and a working of auto-poiesis. The landscape is literal. Construction and deconstruction of molecular building blocks produce an ongoing dis/integration of form. Therefore there is not one landscape, but a series of real time/space negotiations performed by bacteria within a frame of finite natural resources. The transition of colour signals an ecological reflexivity between the industry of a biological body and its environment that might inform our own ecological rationality. How do we, a cultural mosaic of seven billion individuals begin to come to terms with a convention of infinite economic growth within a finite planet? The ecological industry of bacteria acting as both figure and field serves as a point of departure for thinking of an ecological rationality within our own landscape.

Sculpture underwater

If Wightman highlights aspects of living systems, using her scientific background as a tool, Nicolas Floc'h (born in 1972) in France performs a reflection conducted in conjunction with researchers on the forms and structures designed by engineers, watching them from the perspective of the sculptor and without losing sight of their biological function (COAL Prize, 2013). These productive structures are designed to become marine reefs, similar to the work of d'Caires Taylor. The first job is to establish a classification of different types of existing artificial reefs in the world, constituting a relational database in volume and as an installation. A second task is to establish a second database on the behaviour of different species of fish inside and even around the reefs, and thus study their way of living.

This is to acquire sufficient knowledge of subsea architecture and biological function based on existing scientific studies to be able to think of biologically effective forms. In the end, this establishes a corpus of images enabling us to see the families of a reef situation, in other words, modes of colonization by plants and animals. The goal is to design and build sculptural reefs whose shapes meet the scientific and formal information gathered. These sculptures are not necessarily submerged and they have a dual function: the exhibition space as a sculpture and marine areas as ecologically functional reefs.

Celia Gregory, an English artist (born in 1961), also creates underwater installations (COAL Prize, 2012). With others she is a working example of how in collaboration with science, marine management and coral gardening a localised

Figure 11.4 Nicolas Floc'h, Structure productive, récif artificiel – 23m, Japon

coral reef ecosystem can be brought back to thriving fish and coral nurseries. Her sculptures and mosaics are set within the context of eco tourism. She aims to assist in the changing of our relationship to the seas as a role of stewardship. Her first scientific collaboration is with BioRock® a coral restoration method, which uses a safe low voltage electrical current to accrete natural limestone from sea water onto steel structures of any size or shape. This BioRock® process creates a layer of calcium carbonate over the metal; the same natural material that coral skeletons are made from. The structures are transplanted with broken, immature and unattached corals that are collected from the surrounding reefs. Damaged coral reefs form large areas of rubble beds, which are constantly shifting which stops the corals' ability to fix and find a permanent home in which to mature. Fish move in to the new structures and the form grows into a living reef, a marine ecosystem. The BioRock® process speeds up the growth of the coral and aids in their survival during bleaching. The nurseries provide sanctuaries for corals and fish that can then repopulate the surrounding reefs. During 2011 the *Coral Goddess* designed by Celia Gregory was installed, inspired by the local Indonesian culture, using BioRock®, as a nursery for fish and coral (see Plate 19). These works, involving a fascination with living systems, are moving towards a 'life engineering' based on the best intentions. Dealing with the ordinary, the artist works with a creativity that is directed towards eco-design and green engineering in search of solutions.

Survival

Thus, contemporary artists not only work with scientists, but with engineers and designers. On one hand, design can be a means of speculating how things could be – speculative design. This form of design thrives on imagination and aims to open up new perspectives on what are sometimes called 'wicked problems', to create spaces for discussion and debate about alternative ways of being, and to inspire and encourage people's imaginations to flow freely. Design speculations can act as a catalyst for collectively redefining our relationship to reality.

On the other hand, what is done in the field of engineering harkens back to extracting a problem from a complex society or situation, then describing it in terms of Newtonian mechanics and finally embedding the solution back again into a complex society. Therefore, we not only need other 'business' models but also other 'social' models for engineers to find new ways to inscribe themselves in society: not only the corporate engineer but also other types of contracts with society. It does not imply that solutions will have to be less clever and less complex. We can see, for example, in agriculture that new methods such as permaculture are no less complex and incorporate the challenge to find other ways to relate to the living, while keeping lots of skills and 'soft' technologies. There is a need for a new kind of engineer, which is the kind of person we find in permaculture. And actually we find there a unique mixture of engineers and artists. When we go back to the common root of the two – the 'art' or the craft – this evolution of artistic achievements echoes innovative design practices. Conceptual design refers to the importance of ideas in setting up situated alternatives. The space of artistic creation becomes a testing ground for ideas and ideals. Ideality then suggests the real. Lewitt states in his *Sentences on Conceptual Art* (Lewitt, 1969), ideas are works of art. For many, this has become the core feature of a conceptual artwork. Environmental art shows the need to make these ideas concrete, even if it is not necessary that they be.

Elodie Stephan is a good example of an environmental designer seeking to bring significant environmental experience and awareness to the public (COAL Prize 2013). Detached from the productive dimension, her design is dealing with a given context: recycling systems and phenomena from nature or human being. She worked as a project manager for a bus project with Imperial Missions Signage for public and cultural facilities (Ateliers Jean Nouvel, Renzo Piano, Koz architects, et al.). Sometime later, she founded her own environmental design studio while pursuing collaborations with various workshops: Bus-imperial (an environmental workshop specialising in signage design), Teresa Toïka (creative agency multiform) Wanja Ledowski Studio (visual Designer), Zeppelin Agency (landscape) and KPDP Agency (exhibition, architecture and interior architecture design). The artist developed an artistic approach combining a scientific dimension, interaction and/or pedagogy.

Originally conceived as part of a prospective contest on urban lighting (receiving the special mention 'originality' award in a competition organised by the CLU Foundation Philips Lumec, 'l'humanité mise en lumière', 2011), the project *Survivances* highlights the role of a family of bioluminescent insects, bringing hope and vectors of a strong symbolic meaning as the 'carriers' of light. Research around bioluminescence advances promising and exciting applications: bioluminescent trees illuminating the streets (University of Cambridge, Price Competition IGEM 2010), ambient lighting contributing to a better life in our homes (Bio light, Microbial program Home Philips) or industrial pieces inspired by the marine snail Hinea brasiliana, for lighting future cars (Scripps Institute of Oceanography).

While these potential applications are emerging in laboratories, the actual possibility of bioluminescence is disappearing. The firefly regresses and is vanishing. Disappearing in cities since the 1990s, fireflies have fled urban pollution. In the imaginary prospective alliances between cities and nature, *Survivances* proposes to discover and re-introduce this family of bioluminescent insects into the heart of the cities, as a material-glow to develop technically and economically. The project aims to sustain breeding fireflies to disseminate the singularity of this species in publicly presenting its light 'power'. By publicising its life cycle and unveiling its intense light emissions at the mating period, the project aims to develop a conservation tool – for learning – of a species now disappearing. Through each step of the project, the cycle of the insects' story will be told illuminating the complexity and beauty of the species.

Birds and beehives

Showing a deep care for the life of other living beings as exemplified by Lynn Hull's work, who put her sculptural forms at the service of wildlife, Eileen Hutton, an American artist whose work is environmentally based, has been working with biologists and other scientists and projecting the animals' needs, integrating their work into layers of natural life. This is not exceptional, but tends to be processed through technical design. Eileen Hutton is a visual (Irish) artist, whose investigations into ecosystems have identified the critical role that both birds, in terms of seed dispersal and pest control, and honeybees, as principal pollinators, play (COAL Prize 2012). Her work is realised through the building of artificial habitats and through beekeeping. Within nesting boxes and beehives, she creates sculptures in collaboration with honeybees and small birds. She has built a series of 25 nesting boxes for great and blue tits, which provide artificial habitats for the birds in County Clare, Ireland in the hopes of bolstering their population within this region. The boxes are built in the shape of a hexagon, a shape found throughout the natural world: in snowflakes, basalt formations, honeycomb and in DNA structures to name a few. At the end of the nesting season, the hexagonally shaped nests must be removed so that the birds will return the following season. The result is evidence of a mutually beneficial relationship and a collaborative arts practice. The work is a model for engaged and informed interaction with the environment.

The question is not asked, however: what does it mean to protect the living? It is the artist's intention to collaborate artistically with other priority species also, such as the earthworm. Earthworms can play a variety of important roles in agro-ecosystems. Earthworms are responsible for soil development, recycling organic matter and they form a vital component within many food webs. Their feeding and burrowing activities incorporate organic residues and amendments into the soil, enhancing decomposition, humus formation, nutrient cycling and soil structural development. When earthworms tunnel through the soil and create their tiny tunnels they can provide channels for air and water carrying nutrients to circulate more freely.

Additionally, earthworm droppings, called castings, are rich in nitrogen, calcium, magnesium and phosphorus, which are necessary nutrients for a healthy, thriving ecosystem. Studies have also shown that every year on an acre of average cultivated land 16,000 pounds of soil pass through the digestive systems of earthworms and end up above the soil. In the long run, healthy high quality soils will be the key to a sustainable environment and thus ourselves. Hutton states that 'In actuality, the soil is a reservoir of biological diversity that likely exceeds that of aboveground ecosystems' (artist's COAL proposal).

The fascination for earthworms refers back to the work of Charles Darwin, published for the first time in *The Formation of Vegetable Mould through the Action of Worms, with Observations on Their Habits* (Darwin, 1881) and which was a publishing success and contributed greatly to the development of soil science. Darwin devoted much of his text to 'lifestyle worms'. He describes their constitution and qualities of their habitat, shows that they are mainly nocturnal, they travel long distances and they can live underwater. He details the experiences that show that earthworms – who have no eyes – can distinguish between light and darkness and, according to his hypothesis, through their innate reflexes they can quickly retreat into their holes when they are heavily lit. Darwin thinks that it is amazing that the whole mass of the surface humus is passed through the body of worms, and still reverts every few years. He admires the fact that more than the plough, one of the oldest instruments of agriculture, these creatures, so rudimentarily organised, have played such an important role in the history of the earth.

Beyond just documenting the habits and habitats of earthworms, the work of Eileen Hutton is documenting a knowledge system:

> More now than ever, there are ethical environmental implications associated with the creation of art. I believe that artists today must be aware of the impact their art and arts practices have on the environment. To date, my practice has aimed to generate a reciprocal relationship with the natural environment. I am deeply committed, through the process of creating art, to discovering sustainable and ecologically beneficial solutions that may serve as models for engaged and informed interaction with the environment.
>
> (Artist's COAL proposal)

The plastic pollution battle

There is a new connection of artists, scientists and exploratory missions, engaged in documentation and research of the environment, particularly in our oceans. Increasingly in the media and available to the general public, is one of the more evident battles perhaps, because it *is* visible to the human eye and thus has aesthetic consequence: that of plastic pollution. Not only visible, plastic pollution plays a significant role on marine life and the health of all living beings. Artists around the world have so embraced this challenge that an entire new genre of 'plastic pollution artists' has sprung up. In the 1980s, British artist Tony Cragg (born 1949, Liverpool) began to collect flotsam and jetsam from the shores of Sussex, England, which turned into his first wall and floor installations of found plastics. In re-contextualizing the trash, the viewer was confronted with a variety of questions: where was it from? What was its purpose? Why was it no longer of use? Would it ever biodegrade or recycle? How was human consumption effecting our shores and seas? His 1982 work *Red Bottle*, comprised of only red plastic objects and bits, recreated the form of the plastic bottle; one of the more ubiquitous objects of trash found in the environment, enlarged (108 × 33 × 3 inches) on the wall as a mosaic. The viewer is invited to think about one-use plastic objects and our habits of consumption, while enjoying the beauty of manufactured objects turned into art (see Plate 20). This re-contextualization of garbage has spawned a global movement of 'plastic trash' art, stemming from Dada, Surrealism and the Californian post-war Assemblage movement. And as our waste issues have increased to epic proportions globally, so has the genre blossomed.

A few years later, in 1997, Captain Charles Moore was sailing back to California from Hawaii, and 'discovered' a giant sea of plastic, later dubbed 'the Great Pacific Garbage Patch' and described by the press as a floating island the size of Texas, in the North Pacific. Moore's pioneering research on the *Algalita*, his sailing vessel, opened up the study of plastic pollution that now, twenty years later, is a quickly growing field of marine science. We now know that these waste products at sea are possibly contributing to the uptake of toxins from the petroleum based materials of plastics into the food chain via the fish that live in that environment. Our ocean health, meaning the species living in it, as well a human health, is now jeopardised by these products containing polycarbonates, polystyrenes, PETE, LDPE, HDPE, polypropylene and foamed plastics, that do not photosynthesise nor ever bio-degrade. Interestingly enough, the press reports on the Garbage Patch in the Pacific were not scientific, nor accurate: the gyres are full of plastic indeed, but it is more like a 'soup' than a solid mass. Current research has an even more frightening hypothesis: that the plastics are actually sinking and forming huge mountains on the ocean's floor, disrupting the marine ecosystem in such drastic measures that we cannot fathom yet the consequences. Nonetheless, the visualisation of a floating garbage island captured the public's attention, making not only headlines but political and environmental results: California recently passed a Ban the Bag bill, making the sale of plastic bags in grocery stores illegal. This policy coup took years of action by many NGO and environmental lobbying groups, but in the end it was the citizens of the state who supported it.

Belgian artist Martin Van den Eyrde (born 1977) was invited by the 5 Gyres Institute, one of the leading global plastic pollution research organisations, to sail on their research vessel, the *Sea Dragon*, on an expedition across the Atlantic in February 2010. Under the guidance of Dr Markus Erikson and Captain Charles Moore, they collected almost 400 kilos of plastic in specially designed 'manta-ray' trawls designed by Dr Erikson that collect the micro-plastics for later lab analysis. The larger pieces were salvaged by Van den Eyrde, and once back to shore were documented, then melted down into a 2 × 3 × 2 meter installation. This work, named *Plastic Reef* (see Plate 21) is a growing testimony to the alarming growth of plastic pollution in the ocean. He continues to add to it at each exhibition venue, as it travels around the world. Like the ocean itself and the pollution crisis therein, the artwork is not static. It grows with each installation site and the international travel of the artist. On an earlier trip to the Hawaiian Islands, the artist became aware of the connection of dying coral reefs, ocean acidification, and climate change in part caused by coal emissions pouring into the air but also petroleum-(oil) based economies in general. Working with volunteer environmental groups such as B.E.A.C.H., Van den Eyrde collected five boxes of plastic on one beach clean-up. These were shipped to his studio in Amsterdam where he melted it down to an approximately 1 × 2m mound, the beginnings of *Plastic Reef*.

In displacing the waste from its ocean 'trash-can' habitat, and recycling it back into a pristine, white-cube gallery situation, the viewer is taken aback by the sheer quantity of the plastic that has been compressed into a sculptural glob, and thus transformed. The object is re-contextualised to have an emotional and intellectual effect on the viewer. If it remained floating in the sea, the plastics are seemingly overwhelmed by the vastness of the ocean, and thus made inconsequential regarding life-threatening pollution. Condensed and viewed as a colourful toxic lump, the viewer becomes aware in a different way. By this artistic gesture the artist is not only changing the context of the exhibition site/venue, he has also re-contextualised the artistic process. By engaging the community and public around him – from the crew of the *Sea Dragon* (5 Gyres Institute and their sister organization Pangaea always invite a mixed group of scientists, artists, and general public on board their research/educational voyages), to the public appearances and press conferences at each port, to the local volunteer beach clean-up teams – Van den Eryde has committed to challenging the status quo around him. His process is engaging and not isolated. Collecting tons of waste involves a crew of people, and this creates a dialogue.

In fact, the technology to create melted plastic bricks has been developing steadily over the past decade. They are used for housing materials and a wide variety of construction purposes, perhaps most successfully as an alternative to asphalt in roads. A plastic monoblock technology was patented in 2002 by Indian Chemistry Professor R. Vasudevan, in Madurai. These monoblocks are strong enough to hold 300 tons of weight and a major benefit is it checks water penetration. These blocks can stand firm even if an elephant is standing on top of them, he claimed, adding, it can be used in building construction (Anon, 2012).

The uses are endless for sustainable architecture and public infrastructures. Another seemingly indomitable alternative for building material is bamboo. The fastest growing wood on the planet, it also sequesters carbon dioxide at an excellent rate, creating 35 per cent more oxygen than a forest of trees the same size. Once the miracle plant for sustainable forestry practices, it has now come under criticism due to the uncommon amounts of pesticides used to grow it, and the ensuing toxic chemicals used in the processing phase of the bamboo, which are contaminating the surrounding environs. Other environmental issues surround the once admired bamboo, including loss of animal habitat, and polluted rivers surrounding the forests, which therein contaminate water tables. At the same time, over-harvesting has contributed to the destruction of nearly half the bamboo species in existence. Artist Jon Wyatt, a British self-taught photographer born in 1975, quotes that 'every six seconds fifteen acres of the planet are deforested'; he takes the name of his piece *Bamboo (Six Seconds)* from this fact.[3] Shot

Figure 11.5 Jon Wyatt, *Bamboo (Six Seconds)*

in a bamboo forest in Anhui Province, China, the film and photo stills create an ambiguous monologue of forest scenes, overlaid and cut every six seconds. The beauty of the black and white imagery, in both the film and the accompanying still photos in large format, is both inspiring and frightening. Are we seeing a glimpse of the forests disappearing? Or is this the rich recreation of carbon jungles that can re-oxidize the planet, and produce sustainable alternatives to hardwoods for building, for textiles and even oil? The artist keeps the context of the scenes open-ended, thereby leaving the viewer room to ponder the dilemma of forestry and the bamboo 'solution'. Is it sustainable?

Notes

1   Burnham's outdated discourse of the Harrisons' work points out the huge changes in the last half a century in interpretation in art criticism. Helen and Newton Harrison were in fact one of the earliest male/female teams to give credit to the female part-ner. And Helen's contribution to the partnership was vital to its poetic and aesthetic existence. Since that time period, several male partners acknowledged the equal contribution of their partner, such as Bruce Nauman and Susan Rothenberg, Christo and Jeanne-Claude.
2   Hans Haacke, *Condensation Box*, 1965.
3   Notes from the artists' COAL proposal, 2011.

References

Anon., 2012. 'Chennai Professor R Vasudevan Invents Plastic Monoblock Technology'. *The Economic Times*, 3 January.

Burnham, J., 1974. *Great Western Salt Works: Essays on the Meaning of Post-Formalist art.* New York: G. Braziller.

Darwin, C., 1881. *The Formation of Vegetable Mould, through the Action of Worms, with Observations on their Habits.* London: John Murray.

Kepes, G., 1956. *The New Landscape in Art and Science.* Chicago: Paul Theobald.

Kepes, G., 1972. *Arts of the Environment.* New York: George Braziller.

Lewitt, S., 1969. 'Sentences on Conceptual Art.' *Art-Language*, 1, 11–12.

Part V

Re-embedding forms

A transformed public

This portion of the book will address the historical, and possibly deceptive, possibility of an 'elimination' of the art object as its own end and how the ensuing artwork is brought to the public. Stemming from its Dada roots with ironic overtones, up until the modernist works of Robert Smithson's *Spiral Jetty* viewed as an environmental artwork, the paradigm shift over the past three to four decades is outlined (Chapter 12). With the postmodern refusal to accept permanence of artworks, valorising the experience that uses the art object as a medium to intensify emotions and feelings, the public (and market) are put into new roles. Now artists' practices without permanent material objects can be valued creating a new audience. This reversal is even stronger with environmental art sometimes being elaborated as an ecological process (Chapter 13). More and more environmental artworks are processes without traces except for their documentation (photographs, videos, books, etc.). Therefore, as relational aesthetics claims, the public is called into the artistic game, more and more. Moving from a passive audience to an appreciative public, experiential, performative practices (pro/con) lead to an interrogation of the very notion of what is public. Can non-human be considered as a public? What is an environmental community? There are many definitions of 'community'. Whereas community in the United States or in England can be synonymous with geographical community, in France and in many European countries, it refers to a national and political community. The artist contributes, often at the request of local authorities through calls for projects, to build an environmental community that would mean a community with strong ties to its aesthetic environment, through the development of relationships at the same time sensitive, human, environmental, but also social and political. And who are the community leaders and participants involved? We won't respond to all these issues, but will try to clarify how and why the environmental artist works with the public (Chapter 14).

12 Deception
Dada to Smithson

The evolution of Dada, first described by Roman Jakobson in 1921 in an essay of the same name, embraces the 'destabilization of identity' of the modern era.[1] Migrations and immigrations, war and political upheaval coincided with the developing theories in relativity in philosophy and physics. Western man was unloosed from his empirical roots that over the course of centuries had been built on growth, capital and the exploitation of natural resources and human enslavement. Marcel Duchamp's *Fountain* (1917), perhaps the most renowned of his 'Readymades', presented not only a critique of mass consumption and manufacturing that obliterated the individualism of craft, but also challenged the viewer's perception of reality itself within changing contexts. In their 'traveling mode' Duchamp's reclaimed everyday objects became 'art' because he claimed it so, and with each reincarnation of their display, different exhibition sites, different forms (such as photography), they took on new meaning.

Ubu's belly

The poetic Dada performances at Cabaret Voltaire in Zurich also reflected the outbreak of the First World War in Europe. But earlier, in 1896, Paris held forth the revolutionary theatre piece by Alfred Jarry, which has been called the earliest precurser to modernism. *Ubu Roi* (*King Ubu*), was a satirical, nihilistic performance that opened and closed in one day at the Théâtre de l'Œuvre (Jarry, 1997). Not just in its burlesque critique of cultural norms and conventions, but also in its form, the work was precedent to the Theatre of the Absurd and what would become Dada. Jarry explains his term 'pataphysics' as the underlying theory behind *Ubu Roi*. It is 'the science of the realm beyond metaphysics', of 'imaginary solutions'.

The First World War marked the end of the modern world as Europe knew it during the nineteenth century. In a reaction to rising nationalism, artists 'gave-up' their nationalities, immigrating to new countries (America, Brazil, Mexico) and creating new identities in the new cultures. Duchamp's great work of this period, his *Boîte-en-valise*, which miniaturised his entire work up to that point into a suitcase, sums up the status of a migrant/emigre: there is memory, but identity must be created anew, symbolised by the size of a suitcase. Art not only left

Figure 12.1 Alfred Jarry, *King Ubu Roi*, "*Véritable portrait de Monsieur Ubu*", Paris, Éditions du Mercure de France, 1896

the museum pedestal, jumped down the staircase nude, and went out the door; it joined the thousands and thousands of other people fleeing the life they once knew for something else, unknown. The existentialism of these wandering objects, while breaking away from their past, unfettered, opened up the possibility of embracing only the essence of the idea behind them, based solely on its relationships to its surroundings.

And, not coincidentally, that concept was un-gendered. Duchamp's works, most particularly the gender ambivalence of Rrose Sélavy, *LHOOQ* (1919) or the challenges of his final great work, *Etant donnes* (*Given: 1. The Waterfall, 2. The Illuminating Gas*, 1946–66) were opening the way of an art released of its modernist patriarchy. As Amelia Jones points out 'this tendency of the modern subject to search for an origin by which he/she can legitimate himself as subject is dependent on his opposing himself to an other' (cited in Demos, 2007, p. 2). As an emigre, Duchamp himself became the 'other'. As did many of the French and European artists fleeing the wars to America and beyond.

As the artist's gaze framed the context that the object was experienced in, the genii loci, sense of place, took on new meaning. Just as Dada could turn a grocery list into a poem, postmodern artists turned mountains into sculpture. What was experienced in the surrounding environment became the subject, and the object, the viewer her/him self. The pivotal Earth works and land art of the 1960s and 1970s set the stage for environmental art of today, as it questioned what surrounds human beings. But this genealogy is still in keeping with the development of environmental art, which eventually grew out of and in reaction to land art which had become in the following years, ambivalent, and problematic for the reasons discussed earlier. But the American experience was very different to the existentialism of European emigre artists such as Duchamp.

While Robert Smithson's *Spiral Jetty* (1970, Utah) is often cited as the cornerstone of the land art or Earth works movement in the United States, there were synchronistic works happening around the world based in nature, from South America to Central Europe. The feminist critique of Smithson's and other male artists who moved and in fact destroyed or altered the earth as they created, embodies a rejection of aggressive methods of art practice that in fact damage the very ecosystem they are engaged with. The comparison to a white, male-dominated art world and the power structures behind that economy is not lost in the comparison. *Spiral Jetty* is continually changing as the environment affects the water levels. Submerged for 30 years, it re-appeared in a drought in 2001, and then again more recently and frequently as global warming brings on more drought conditions.

Many less evasive works of environmental art were performed and installed in Central Europe during the Soviet era of closed borders, where devastation of the natural environment was occurring at a fast pace (see Chapter 20). Work by Ivan Kafka (born 1952), which laid out fallen leaves in geometric patterns in a local park in Prague (see Plate 22),[2] or the series of iron-cubed silhouettes surrounding random sites in nature – a tree, a hill, a forest – that framed a site in minimalist echoes of geometric precision.[3] As a Czech, Kafka works very specifically within his own cultural heritage, and while appreciated abroad (he represented his country at the Venice Biennale in 1997), he is the forefront of artists who are using 'indigenous' and local history to create specific works that resonate with their surroundings. The conceptual beginnings of Smithson's spiral are historical keys for artists working today in environmental art, while his later, now famous monumental work, loses the impulse of the early ecology concepts. If we look at the *Monuments of Passaic* series of photographs (1967) that decontextualized an existing site, were performative in definition, and critical of the political structures, then we can garner a much stronger thread to follow into today's eco-works than what later turned into land art. In the early pieces, Smithson was much closer to Mendieta, Hess and other artists working with the ethereal and transformational, rather than historical grandiosity of dominating, oversized earthworks.

Spirals

Robert Smithson came to Rozel Point, (the Great Salt Lake), as a foreigner. The story goes that it took a lot of convincing to get the bulldozer driver to spend six days pushing around sand and rock on the lake bed. The artist seemed suspicious to the locals, the absolute antithesis of community based eco-artist work today. But he was at home in the American landscape of large-scale and bountiful presence. 'I like landscapes that suggest pre-history', the artist stated before creating this monumental work.[4] In an era of 'progress' and modernism, this could understandably be a challenging concept to embrace, yet there are Modernist precedents, in Picasso's influence from African masks to Paul Gauguin's romantic return to Polynesian 'paradise' (Rora Tonga, Tahiti) in the early twentieth century. But Smithson and the other land artists of the 1970s were not romanticists, their contribution was in the ability to re-frame an existing site into a moving experience – later labelled and packaged, but nonetheless, art. Smithson's determination to give the viewer a primordial experience was paramount. In an interview from 1971, Smithson explained how the visitor's experience of space shifts as one walks through the work: a 'constriction or concentration exists within the inner coils ... whereas on the outer edge you're kind of thrown out, you're aware of the horizons and how they echo through the Jetty' (Baker, 2005, p. 158).

This ritualistic walk of the space echoes ancient land forms built as religious or ritualistic encounters with nature and self, from the Minoan labyrinths to Celtic and Scandinavian stone circles, to Egyptian and Mayan circles. The cosmological references are universal on nearly every continent, tied into the solstice and natural rhythms of the sun and moon. Smithson was not unaware of these transcendental references when he built *Spiral Jetty*. While the influences of the seminal land art piece could be many, there has been reference by the artist to his New Jersey home and landscapes, his reading of Nabokov's autobiography, *Speak Memory*, and most importantly, a visit to his aging paediatrician and neighbour in 1959, at the age of twenty-four. Smithson's childhood doctor, as is now well documented, happened to be the American poet William Carlos Williams.

Williams' struggle in the epic poem 'Paterson', which engages local vernacular, and was a direct reaction to the ennui of T. S. Eliot's *Wasteland* following the First World War, influenced the young Smithson. In a photographic essay for *ArtForum* in December 1967, Smithson's piece *The Monuments of Passaic*, recreates the spiralling roads and landscapes of his birthplace, in what he later called "'a kind of appendix" to Mr. Williams' famous poem, "Paterson"' (Schwendender, 2014).

That zero panorama seemed to contain ruins in reverse, that is, all the new construction that would eventually be built. This is the opposite of the 'romantic ruin' because the buildings don't fall into ruin after they are built but rather rise into ruin before they are built. This anti-romantic mise-en-scène suggests the discredited idea of time and many other 'out of date' things. But the suburbs exist without a rational past and without the 'big events' of history. A Utopia minus a bottom, a place where the machines are idle, and the sun has turned to glass, and a place where the Passaic Concrete Plant (253 River Drive) does a good business in STONE, BITUMOUS, SAND, and CEMENT (Sante, 1998).

ROBERT SMITHSON / JAMES COHAN GALLERY

Figure 12.2 Robert Smithson, *The Fountain Monument, Bird's Eye View,* MONUMENTS OF PASSAIC

The American artist's embrace of the local landscape of his New Jersey child-hood, complete with derelict factories and abandoned cement plants, while rooted in the absurdity, social rebellion and not a little irony based on an inher-ent critique of the status quo of Dada, was also a celebration of decline. And, we might say, capitalism: 'they rise into ruin before they are built' (Smithson, 1996, p. 298). The inherent environmentalism and understanding of the earth's destruction by industrialisation in Smithson's essay and photographs, echoes his mentor William Carlos Williams.

In situating himself directly into the landscape from which he came, Smithson exemplifies the postmodern break from a subject/object dialectic, inherent in modernism. This is even more so evident in the land art works of female artists such as Mary Miss or Ana Mendieta. *Spiral Jetty* is therefore an installation on the cusp of a postmodernism that bore today's environmental art movement. Smithson's attempt to connect to the transcendental nature of the great western desert was not romantic, but the complete abnegation of the object stemming from Dada's revolutionary stance, and the shadow of King Ubu's belly.

Monolithic stones of anthracit coal

The political and social agendas attached to art that left the galleries in the last decades is not hidden by any means. When we examine the meta-structures of commerce and economics, they are inextensively tied to consumption, labour, waste and natural resources. Social justice is tied to environmental justice. So when artists like Robert Flottemesch create installations in 'the capital cities of all twelve of the world's largest economies' (COAL Prize, 2011), it has a direct relationship to King Ubu's irreverent fattened belly with the spiral circling on top of it. As the Theatre of the Absurd mocked all that was known in the 'Age of Enlightenment', artists today are increasingly critiquing the economic struc-tures that have brought the planet to the brink of disaster. Flottemesch's proposal for monolithic 'stones' of Anthracite coal, to be placed in rings in each capital remembers the ancient structures of Stonehenge and other ancient sites, much like Smithson's. Each coal cube 'depicts an individual citizen's annual fossil fuel consumption' (artist's COAL proposal). Concentric paving blocks that radiate out from the stone centre, act as spatial measuring recorders of each nation's population. The artist proposes an educational element within the circles – a solar-powered kiosk that provides a live web-feed of the other locations around the world (China, the US, South Korea, Mexico, Italy, India, Japan, China, Germany, Russia, the UK, France, Brazil and Italy) along with other pertinent information on energy use. To make his point clearer, the monolith installations are placed in the centre of each city, near the major governmental bodies such as the parliament building or the capital building, etc.

Like *Spiral Jetty*, the works have an archaic feel to them, made of dark coal as ancient as the earth herself. Flottemesch's work is also placed in concentric circles, or spirals, encouraging the viewer to walk, to experience and to think. This tantric, hypnotic-inducing motion is another harkening to ancient times of meditation and ritual. But the similarity ends there, as *High Energy* (Flottemesch) is situated in the centre of commerce, government and the city. What the viewer comes to understand in this installation is not only what one consumer uses, but the ratio of consumption to population. Thus the viewer learns that China or India, with the largest populations, use actually less energy per capita than the so-called 'developed' countries of the United Kingdom or France, for instance. The balance of power, translated into energy consumption, is visually translated and embedded in the audience's 'walk' through the work.

The artist's drawings for the work are ironically similar to Smithson's preparatory drawings for *Spiral Jetty*, as well as the much earlier *Monuments of Passaic*, influenced admittedly by Smithson's meeting with Donald Judd's work. The minimalist perspective of cubes, geometric circles, spiralling out, has a resonance in both artists' fascination with gemstones and mineralogy. Just as Smithson's essay was a groundbreaking split from the gallery exhibition space (photo essay/travel log/philosophical tract which later influenced so many other postmodern artist/writers such as Mike Kelley), it also changed the artist's expertise, allowing him to work as writer and/or philosopher, but more often with other professionals. And 'it was also a poignant meditation on time and entropy (one of his favourite terms) in postindustrial suburbia' (Schwendender, 2014).

If we now turn from history to the present, it is clear that the context has changed completely in favour of an ecological crisis of great magnitude. As the planet spins out of order and sea levels rise to displace more and more populations daily, entropy is an ever recurrent theme in contemporary environmental works. *L'Enfant accroupi*, proposed by French artist Robin Godde (born 1984, Nancy) (COAL Prize, 2011) presents just this theme. A simple figure is placed in the ancient city centre in Strasbourg, where the river meets the stepped banks under the bridge. His youthful body gracefully bends to touch the water. We have the science to know that this sculpture will be submerged within a few decades, perhaps sooner. But for now, if installed, it will be a marker in time of rising sea levels, much like *Spiral Jetty* (unbeknownst to Smithson) has become a marker of the increasing droughts in the western United States. At times the work is completely submerged, only to appear 30 years later as it was created. Whether Godde's sculpture would be as fortunate to reappear one day remains to be seen. But the artist's intent, to visualise climate change and the consequences of passing time, embraces the entropic theme of Dada, and early earthworks such as *Spiral Jetty*.

A lake at the Halles

Two artists, mentioned earlier in the book, who have long worked with engaging and transforming local ecosystems, from a micro to macro level, long before the words 'climate change' were even in our vocabulary, are Helen and Newton Harrison. Sometimes called the founders of environmental art, their projects embrace entire cities and regions of the planet, river systems and forests from China to Europe to California, (where they are based now as Professors Emeritus at the University of California, Santa Cruz). For the COAL Prize 2014, they submitted a proposal to create a lake at Les Halles in the heart of Paris (which was actually an idea originating in the 1970s). The absurdity of a new lake of that size in the heart of an ancient city is Dadaesque. Yet the science behind it, as with all of the Harrison's work is sound.

The piece proposes to create a new ecosystem that would enhance and heal the surrounding area. These are 'collaborative designs that offer possible geopolitical solutions to ecological problems' (Lebowitz, 2009). Like the Les Halles project in Paris, which addresses the ancient location of a marketplace, now lost to the public, each work confronts the larger politicised location, making a new form that is sustainable and ecologically sound. The hypothesis being that this creates a socially just environment also. In the attention to local history and context, the Harrisons bring science to art, re-contextualising the former to convince the public and/or government officials. By and large, their works heal the local environment, bringing a more balanced ecosystem, which is not immune to the larger geo-political structure(s) that surround it. The genius of the Harrisons' forty-year oeuvre in environmental art, is that they are managing a larger systematic change from the ground up, empowering local communities to have responsibility for their natural environment, which is ultimately always connected to capital in some way. Born in the US, but at home in many geographical locations in the world where they have worked on watershed and eco-systems regeneration, they embody Demos' 'reconsideration of Duchamp's practice, wherein expatriate existence and deracinated aesthetic structure also coincide' (Demos, 2007, p. 79). Because, in fact the future of human existence will be that of migration and immigration, as climate now shifts the earth's ecosystem dramatically each month (International Organisation for Migration, 2008).[5]

Will not the sense of 'local' take on new meaning as neighbourhoods shift demographics and borders open and close and immigrants flood into new territories? Artists without a country, foreigners on new soil and carrying only memory of culture recreate the local context without nationalistic baggage, nor the encumbrance of local history. Like the early Dadaists, who were reacting against the patriotic nihilism leading up to the First World War, contemporary environmental artists are using local spaces to react against the corporatisation of public life. And as more and more 'foreign' artists work in new neighbourhoods and communities across the planet, their work re-contextualises the local histories in light of each individual/s collective experience.

Like Smithson's journey to the dry salt beds of Utah to create *Spiral Jetty*, the outsider artists' vision upon entering a new space helps to rename what, in fact, is local.

Notes

1   What animated this system and determined its reaction to the culture of relativity, for Jacobson, was a confrontation with foreignness, according to which, difference

would be either neutralised by its reduction to the familiar, or consigned to a condition of denigrated alterity (Demos, 2007, p. 77).

2   Lesní koberec pro náhodného houbaře VI (*Forest Carpet for a chance Mushroomer*) (1986).

3   Vymezení - Kmeny (tmavé) (1979), dural, les, sníh, 320 x 320 x 320 cm.

4   Quoted from Dia Art Foundation www.diaart.org/sites/page/59/2155

5   Professor Myers' estimate of 200 million climate migrants by 2050 has become the accepted figure—cited in respected publications from the IPCC to the Stern Review on the Economics of Climate Change representing a ten-fold increase over today's entire documented refugee and internally displaced populations. To put the number in perspective it would mean that by 2050 one in every 45 people in the world will have been displaced by climate change' (Migration, 2008).

References

Anon., 2014. '"Robert Smithson's New Jersey" at the Montclair Museum.' *The New Yorker*, 7 March.

Baker, K., 2005. 'Talking with Robert Smithson'. In K. Kelly and L. Cooke, eds. *Robert Smithson:* Spiral Jetty. Berkeley: University of California Press.

Demos, T., 2007. *The Exiles of Marcel Duchamp*. Cambridge, MA: MIT Press.

Jarry, A., 1997. *The Ubu Plays*. London: Nick Hern Books Ltd.

Jones, A., 1994. *The En-gendering of Marcel Duchamp*. Cambridge: Cambridge University Press.

Lebowitz, C., 2009. 'Review at Ronald Feldman Gallery'. *Art in America*, 4 May.

International Organisation for Migration, 2008. IOM *journal: Migration Research Series*, Geneva: International Organisation for Migration.

Sante, L., 1998. 'Robert Smithson: *The Monuments of Passaic*, 1967: (Art Photographer; Passaic River in New Jersey)'. *Artforum International*, 36(10).

Schwendender, M., 2014. 'New Jersey Images, Unbound by Galleries'. *New York Times*, 7 March.

Smithson, R., 1996. 'Conversation in Salt Lake City. In J. Flam, ed. *Robert Smithson: Collected Writings*. Berkeley: University of California Press, p. 298.

13 Taking it seriously and the refusal to accept permanence

Performative and process artworks emerged from a synthesis of a movement away from the art object as well as an increasing involvement with nature and natural processes, which included the human body, sexuality, its ability for improvisation and serendipity, and other non-traditional materials not used in Western art since ancient times. In the words of Ana Mendieta: 'My art is grounded on the belief in one universal energy which runs through everything … from insect to man, from man to specter, from specter to plant, from plant to galaxy' (O'Hagan, 2013). Often rooted in indigenous rituals, shamanic rituals, or other actions inspired or born of traditional cultures that did not separate object and subject as 'art', the occidental art world shifted from Minimalism to a more anonymous abstraction that was movement and ephemeral. The focus on activity, presence, and improvisation can be traced to Dada of a generation earlier. Works of the 1960s were political and social, staging the way for today's environmental artists whose projects engage community and embrace nature in a social sphere.

'Post-minimalism', a term coined by the critic Robert Pincus-Witten in a 1971 essay (Pincus-Witten, 1971), defined a point in time, which helped expand what artists were doing as they left not only the 'object', but embraced processes like growth, decay and decomposition as acts of art. The Whitney Museum of Art in New York had presented the exhibition 'Anti-Illusion: Procedures & Materials' (1969) which echoed the artist Robert Morris' show of the same year, '9 in a Warehouse'.[1]

One of the young artists in that show was an emigre from Cuba, Ana Mendieta. This iconoclast artist, influenced by her early college years in Iowa by visiting artists such as Hans Haackeand Vito Acconci, was also, like Duchamp, an emigre. Her story is now well documented, but the abrupt emigration from her native Cuba, to the brutality of Catholic reform school in the American Midwest at the age of twelve, puts Duchamp's immigration to the US into a different perspective. Her early works dealt with rituals in blood. Passages of time of the female body, which include blood are not only monthly menses but violence towards the body. Her photos and performances encoded how the body interacts and IS nature. And even more radical: female. Her self-portraits embraced her Cuban homeland in an innate retrieval of all she had lost through immigration.

More than a personal narrative, Mendieta opened up the landscape for a connection to the earth that was tragic, ancient and reverent.

She came out of the feminist movement as much as Cuba. In the 1970s, blood was being reclaimed as a feminine – and a feminist – material in art. Her early Earth works, particularly those made in Mexico, are made even more potent for being made by a woman in that time period. Ruby B. Rich, feminist critic and writer, on her friend Mendieta said:

> People place her in the Earth Works tradition of Robert Smithson or Richard Long, but when a woman engages with the earth it is a very different statement. Her body was her art and she placed it in the ground. In doing so, she was trying to ground herself in the earth but also reconnect with the earth that she was standing on even if it was not Cuba.
>
> (O'Hagan, 2013)

Figure 13.1 Ana Mendieta, *Guanaroca (Esculturas Rupestres)*, Siloutes series

As Amanda Boetzkes has pointed out (Boetzkes, 2010), Mendieta's work is often compared to the work of British artist Andy Goldsworthy or American Dennis Oppenheim's early earth/body performative works. But there is a fundamental break from the conceptual strategy of such artists, and it is that of the emotive and indigenous. When Mendieta was finally able to return to Latin America in the 1970s, she created her 'Silueta Series' in Mexico. She would lay down in the earth and photograph her body in it, surrounded by water, or pigment, flowers or later fire, documenting the traces of the female form in the land. These 'Earth-Body-Sculptures' as she called them brought her home. 'This obsessive act of reasserting my ties with the earth is really the reactivation of primeval beliefs ... [in] an omnipresent female force, the after-image of being encompassed within the womb' (Barreras del Rio and Perreault, 1988, p. 10).

The fusion of her Cuban homeland, where Afro-Cuban rituals are often immersed in the Santeria religion, is contemporary for the time, as well as ritualistic and time-based. Mendieta embraced the manifesto of the German artist Hans Haacke (whom she met as a student in Iowa) from the mid 1960s:

> Make something which experiences, reacts to its environment, changes, is non stable ... Make something sensitive to light and temperature changes, that is subject to air currents and depends in its functioning, on the forces of gravity ... Make something that lives in time and makes the 'spectator' experience time ... Articulate something natural.
>
> (Burnham, 1967, p. 8)

Space and light

The California Space and Light school, as we mentioned earlier in this book, also came out of post-minimalism of the 1960s, embracing natural phenomena in a more ethereal way that focused on light. Even large earth works such as James Turrell's *Roden Crater*, are engaging the experience of light and atmosphere that is a process piece of sorts. In this sense, not unlike Mendieta, Turrell's masterwork in the Painted Desert in Northern Arizona, is recreating the ritualistic connection of man to nature as we continually discover the movement of the sun, stars and the awesomeness of space around us. Formed from a dormant volcano crater, shaped from the earth, this monumental sculpture is a work in progress that will transform the viewer into an alternate reality from the urban or even surrounding natural landscape. 'Indeed it is more akin to the communally developed sites of ancient Incas, than to the conceptions of any individual one can think of in modern times'.[2] Like the ritual sites of indigenous peoples around the planet, where the jungle has now overtaken the site with time, or the sea levels have risen and erased the past, Turrell's work will pass back to the desert in time. Yet the audience will take away the experience, which is processional.

Such ritual spaces are symbolic reestablishments of the ancient umbilicus, which, in myths worldwide, once connected heaven and earth. The connection is renewed symbolically for the purposes of the tribe or, more specifically, of that caste or party in the tribe whose special interests are ritually represented. Since this is a space where access to higher metaphysical realms is made to seem available, it must be sheltered from the appearance of change and time. In Paleolithic times the ultra-space filled with painting and sculpture seems to have served the ends for magical restitution to the biomass; afterlife beliefs and rituals may have been involved also (O'Doherty, 1976, pp. 8–9).

As Brian O'Doherty goes on to describe in this seminal book (*Inside the The White Cube*), modernism tried to keep spaces heroic and religious, an ode to the social structures of form, object, dimension and contained space. The classic white-walled, empty rooms of the 'new century' (twentieth), brought the reference and sanctity of traditional religion with all its boundaries and rules, even though abstracted, yet still 'appealing to supposedly transcendental modes of presence and power' (ibid., p. 11). Even Robert Irwin's now infamous Venice Beach installation, *One Wall Removed* (1980), in which the complete facade of a former storefront was covered in a scrim that transmuted the deep Southern California beach light, was a pioneering Light and Space work. Yet even still, Irwin was working with a permanent structure (the building), albeit bathed in impermanent and ever-changing light. His transitional concepts were revolutionary in opening up art to serendipity, improvisation, entropy and instability, as well as non-objectification. As Turrell later explained, 'We don't normally look at light, we're generally looking at something light reveals' (Vartanian, 2013).

The revelations of art working with natural, organic or often transitory materials, such as light, grass, cloth or other soft malleable materials, came at a time when women were just beginning to be recognised as professionals, both in the work field and in the art world. The influences of domestic practices and processes were dominant in much of women (and male) artists' work of this time. The Women's Building, founded by Judy Chicago and Miriam Shapiro in Los Angeles in 1973, was a hotbed for such works, producing performative pieces and feminist works by Chicago, Shapiro, Cheri Gaulki, Kate Millet and Ann Phillips to name a few of the hundreds of women who passed through those liberating doors.

It does matter

In New York, the young German immigrant Eva Hesse was already experimenting with cast resin, cloth, latex and other emotionally expressive materials. The sense of impermanence, which the non-objects of post-minimalist environmental works create, have grown out of the pioneering departures from modernism during the fruitful era of the 1960s civil rights and feminist movements of the Western world. Hesse, not unlike Duchamp, or Mendieta, was a foreigner in a new country full of contradictions: a democracy built on a slave system and genocide, an increasing economic divide between the rich and poor, a creative hotbed of other immigrants and artists working closely in New York City or Los Angeles, and a loss of all that was 'home' in that mix. Displacement can also be freeing, and for these artists it allowed for the complete reinvention of their art via materials. In a time dominated by the daily threat of nuclear attacks during the Cold War as the East/West axis of power threatened to unglue all semblance of humanity, artists like Hesse let go of stable materials and the promise of immortality, future fame. The eventual disintegration of the object was left to time and nature. Hesse's famous quote, towards the end of her short life, sums up the feeling of the time, 'I am not sure what my stand on lasting really is', she said shortly before her death at the age of 34. 'Life doesn't last; art doesn't last. It doesn't matter' (Sooke, 2009).

The word 'matter', which Hesse uses in the colloquial expression to mean 'that which has meaning or consequence' is etymologically symbolic in her statement, which indeed references the 'letting go' of the physical substance which had until that time, been art. What later came to be called 'process art' was in fact embracing the natural processes of decay and de-materialisation, that happens in natural ecosystems. 'Matter' stems from the Latin *materia*, the 'substance from which something is made', 'also 'hard inner wood of a tree' (source also of Portuguese madeira 'wood'), from mater 'origin, source, mother'. Matter, is in fact that which decays, and artists working with biological life systems are embracing these natural cycles not as just a moment in time, such as the Dutch still lifes of the seventeenth century, but as a continually changing and dynamic process. The medium of painting forced the viewer's experience to be of just one sense: the visual. The contemplative engagement (and it was, of course, only for the wealthy classes to enjoy) of the Vanitas genre during the European Renaissance was therefore limited to a finite proportion of the population and but one of the five senses of the body.

A massive hemlock tree fell in a forest outside of Seattle in 1996. Artist Mark Dion (born 1961, US) had been searching for just a tree, not completely decayed, still maintaining its own ecosystem, in order to transfer it to his installation in conjunction with the Seattle Art Museum. Named *Neukom Vivarium*, Dion recreated an artificial greenhouse, complete with water misting systems, climate control, light, etc., to duplicate nature as much as possible, in order to allow the public the experience of a human-created 'forest' (see Plate 23). The tree, as the artist says, is the 'superstar', even though it is dying. He compares the work to a life-support system, made available to an audience that would not ordinarily witness this death in its full glory of blossoming mushrooms, lichen, insects, and decaying timber as the tree biodegrades and becomes, once again matter (mother earth).

> I think that one of the important things about this work is that it's really not an intensely positive, back-to-nature kind of experience. In some ways, this project is an abomination. We're taking a tree that is an ecosystem – a dead tree, but a living system – and we are re-contextualizing it and taking it to another site. We're putting it in a sort of Sleeping Beauty coffin, a greenhouse we're building around it. And we're pumping it up with a life support system – an incredibly complex system of air, humidity, water, and soil enhancement – to keep it going. All those things are substituting what

nature does, emphasizing how, once that's gone, it's incredibly difficult, expensive, and technological to approximate that system – to take this tree and to build the next generation of forests on it. So, this piece is in some way perverse. It shows that, despite all of our technology and money, when we destroy a natural system, it's virtually impossible to get it back. In a sense, we're building a failure.[3]

Dion places himself firmly in the school of the American Hudson River landscape painters, who valued the majesty and awesomeness of nature and the great wilderness that was still then untouched by human destruction. And, while he is indebted to earth artists like Smithson and Irwin, he, like most of the artists we talk about in this book, is engaged in a political discourse that is layered throughout the work. We might say the systems of scientific knowledge that were incorporated into artworks of the latter half of the twentieth century, (contemporary environmental science, systems analysis, etc.) have, in the twenty-first century engaged in specific and pointed political science as well. This includes a political discourse that is dependent upon a social contract: the citizen is encouraged to be involved in the process of direct democracy via the full experience of the artwork. It is no longer only visual, but in many cases such as *Niokum Vivarium*, engulfs the visitor in a sensual bath of sound, touch, and aural as well as visual experience. Many artists working today also add the fifth sense of taste (Rikrit, Food House, etc.), to the mix for a complete haberdashery of physical events when visiting the artwork.

Soil remediation

American artist A. Laurie Palmer in Chicago works 'with theoretical and material explorations of matter's active nature as it asserts itself on different scales and in different speeds'. Utilising soil remediation techniques, she is exploring mineral extraction sites across the US. This process-oriented scientific exploration yields surprises and unexpected results. Like many process-oriented artists, Palmer documents her work as part of the visual diary of the activity, which in turn then becomes the 'evidence' of the work. Like Mendieta, Smithson, Judd, Beuys, Naumann or Ruscha, the photographs of the process are often the only remnants of the work.

Another American artist coming out of Chicago working with soil remediation is Frances Whitehead.[4] *Slow Clean-Up, Civic Experiments with Phytoremediation* (2008–12) was originally situated on a former gas station in a residential neighbourhood, still leaking toxins into the air and leeching into the ground. Set up as a model-system that could be duplicated around the country *Slow* brought not only potential environmental cleansers to the site, but engaged local community.

Designed for abandoned gas stations, the legacy of the automobile culture, the sites are prevalent throughout the urban landscape. These designed civic experiments contribute to the aesthetics and revitalisation of the sites, while simultaneously adding value at every stage of development by creating educational opportunities along with habitat, reduced heat islanding and carbon sequestration.[5]

Whitehead's process of gathering information on the site, its toxin levels, its social history, the weather and soil samples, its role in the former neighbourhood, etc., is creating a system of knowledge and ephemera which she then places into a structure for change. Building gardens and planting native plants able to detoxify the polluted ground, finding caretakers and stewards of the site willing to invest back into the neighbourhood, all contribute to her 'medium', which is not only about the final product of a 'clean' site. While a goal is to eventually return the earth to a place where the water table will not be contaminated, there is a collective activity in place that places human events and interactions in the realm of another organic system, much like the rain water cycles or the organic compost of the garden. There is an open-endedness to systems in nature, either with or without a human involvement, and the serendipity of the synthesis of actions is not unlike the drip paintings of Jackson Pollock.

The uncertainty and insubstantiality of the outcomes in these works is the very magic of art projects such as Whitehead's. Community gardens, urban renewal projects, installations in nature where the wind blows and the flowers rot is part of the recipe for making ecological art, as the key medium in nature herself, ever-changing, growing, dying. There is an inherent social contract in much of the art working with the environment, and a commitment therein to social change.

This is what happens with artistic inventions such as Lucy Orta's collective clothes, which are used both as a 'home' and as a form of collective bond, in order to create 'lasting connections between groups and individuals' (Rancière, 2009, p. 77).

The work of the Ortas, Lucy and Jorge, has for over two decades embraced art and social change, with a deep commitment to the environment and climate change issues. Their Antarctica series (see Plate 8), which originated from a trip there in 2007, comprised of 50 dome-like structures on the ice that could theoretically be domiciles, and were swathed in flags from countries across the planet. The pseudo-'village' embodies the dream of a peaceful and healthy climate of habitation, where all the world resides in a utopian (albeit frozen) wonderland. The installation is only half of the work (documented in photographs and later exhibited internationally). The on-going social action is:

> The Antarctic World Passport Delivery Bureau, a travelling installation recently presented at the Nansen Initiative Global Consultation in Geneva and at the Grand Palais in Paris during the COP21 UN Climate Summit. Visitors to the Antarctica World Passport Delivery Bureau, an architectural assemblage made from reclaimed materials, receive a uniquely numbered Antarctica World Passport, and in exchange pledge to support the project's principles: to take action against the disastrous effects of global warming and strive for peace.[6]

Works such as the Ortas' has pushed the very definition of what art is and can be. While their Antarctica installation is moving, it is the performative, action, process aspect of the 'Antarctica World Passport Delivery Bureau' that gives the piece it social impact, with over 55,000 'passports' printed and distributed since 2008, encouraging holders of such to promise to 'to take action against the disastrous effects of global warming and strive for peace'. The 'village' erected on the sheets of ice has disappeared, but the utopian idea of global community may remain with viewers.

Notes

1   '9 at Leo Castelli' (1968) Anselmo, Bollinger, Hesse, Kaltenbach, Nauman, Saret, Serra, Sonnier, Zorio, 4–28 December, 1968.
2   From the artist's website: http://rodencrater.com/about/
3   Interview with the artist in Art21: www.art21.org/texts/mark-dion/interview-mark-dion-neukom-vivarium
4   Frances Whitehead submitted to COAL Prize in 2015 a project about green sentinels.
5   Frances Whitehead, http://franceswhitehead.com/what-we-do/slow-clean-up-civic-experiments
6   Press release for the Jane Lombard Gallery, exhibition Lucy+Jorge Orta, 14 January–20 February, 2016. The Ortas submitted to the COAL Prize in 2011 a project called *Amazonia*.

References

Barreras del Rio, P. and Perreault, J., 1988. *Ana Mendieta: A Retrospective*. New York: The New Museum of Contemporary Art.
Boetzkes, A., 2010. *The Ethics of Earth Art*. Minneapolis: University of Minnesota Press.
Burnham, J., 1967. *Hans Haacke, Wind and Water Sculpture*. Evanston: Northwestern University Press.
O'Doherty, B., 1976. *Inside the White Cube: The Ideology of the Gallery Space*. Santa Monica, San Francisco: Lapis Press.
O'Hagan, S., 2013. 'Ana Mendieta: Death of an Artist Foretold in Blood'. *The Guardian*, 21 September.
Pincus-Witten, R., 1971. 'Eva Hesse: Post-Minimalism into Sublime'. *Artforum*, 10(3).
Rancière, J., 2009. *The Emancipated Spectator*. London: Verso.
Sooke, A., 2009. 'Eva Hesse: her Dark Materials'. *The Telegraph*, 4 August.
Vartanian, H., 2013. Exclusive Video: James Turrell Talks About Working with Light. *Art21*, 8 May.

14 Passive audience/acting public

One step further is necessary. Does the passage from the art object to the aesthetic process mean a better involvement of the public? Indeed, when the artist focuses on the process, it has often been associated with the increasing role given to the audience. It is not always the case. In spite of numerous theoretical works tending to revise the opposition of creation and reception, common practices still tend to oppose both, the creation designated as an activity and the reception as pure passivity. Indeed, the vision of the 'public' is often oriented in this direction: a passive receiver of a production (artistic, architectural, urban, technical). This vision is also strong in the world of evaluation and, more broadly, in the domain of environmental action.

Given this way of thinking regarding the process of formation, it is important to emphasise that the receptive process is also an active process and thus re-creative or creative. Indeed, any reception is also construed as an interpretation, and every interpretation is, by the meaning it attributes, a production. More fundamentally, the shape is not only an object/event, or only a creation or interpretation thereof by a subject, it is the system formed by the interaction of the three poles – of the manufacturer, the objects/events and the receptor/interpreter – so a system that incorporates a multiplicity of actors/producers and kind of knowledge. Artistic forms are thus not only the source or the result, but the crystallisation of a process of mediation and are setting possible dialogues between different inhabited environmental interpretation systems and its agents and its players. They are collective productions, common and 'negotiated'. The 'public' is as much a producer of forms as the other agents and territorial stakeholders, be they urban, natural, peri-urban or rural.

This positioning allows us to avoid the usual divisions, from an analytical entry by the actors and producers of shapes, their systems of thought, the mobilised knowledge, etc. These political divisions separate categories of actors: for example one that is in charge, and he who suffers; the latter being the historical subject, namely that which is placed below the action, the latter supposedly producing him as such. Returning to this order of things, and transforming the viewer into a producer has philosophical and political implications beyond the artistic act, which even changes its essence and plays on its political role. Thus the participation of the viewer into the artistic act, the transformation of its role in the creation or production of the work, refers to a deeper sense of political upheaval.

A new public

Politics could be viewed as the art of administering herds, this time human ones. It is not just the production of emancipated, democratic subjects, but also building the space and the capacity for personal actions. The production of the subject and of the political subject falls under aesthetical self-knowledge, feelings being the foundations of the plurality of ways of doing, of ways of being, and of the capacity to be moved, in short, subjects of nature. It is therefore important to look back onto this cleavage in the light of ecological or environmental art.

What can we learn from these artistic works? First, environmental art borrows from political ecology its chain of subjects and objects transforming their agentivity, the animal and the food, the planet and the world.

Second, what interests us is not so much what the artist produces as the number of subjects who find themselves within the realm of artistic action. The viewer, in that context, often is a producer of ecological meaning, either because he/she is accused of participating to destroy the planet or because he/she is invited to participate in its repair. The philosophy certainly has gradually built a subject behind the action. According to other philosophers, it is possible to analyse the subject as the provisional result of the action. The construction of the latter is the effect of a process established sociologically to address these new developments. As to artistic developments, the artwork is opened to the point that contemporary art includes popular items. The public is invited to contribute as being part of his learning and in the optic of the democratisation of taste and culture. Relational aesthetics invites the public to participate in the design and execution of works (Bourriaud, 1998). Conversely, art plays a role in human relationships or in its fabric as an aesthetically admirable element. Joseph Beuys in his time deemed the 'Social Sculpture' as a notoriously contemporary aesthetic project.[1] To expand, we focus on building a 'positionality' or the construction by the artist. Also, in the context of developments associated with a sustainable culture of 'positionality' or a located perspective that restores their limits to people and things, without, however, allowing that focus to interrupt their capacities to resonate with each other. Especially since the environment is a collective production.

Sustainability +++

What are the conceptions of the audience and implicit theories of communication involved in this change of perspective, the transfer of an aesthetic theory of art to the environment? The work of art is part of a double temporality. It is an object of the physical universe and is indeed the product of a past completed and definitive process. In this it resembles indeed the artefacts and to all the embodiments of the art, and it belongs to a temporality of the world. But it also participates in a temporality that 'is not defined by the continued existence of something in time and space, but by the constant capacity for a sense to be updated, and even enriched as it is discovered by a receiver' (Doguet, 2007, p. 52 [authors' translation]). The work of art as an object resulting from intentional intersubjective construction is not only a linguistic message: it is distinguished precisely by its double relation to space and time. This object is sustainable in the sense that one can give it to this word, it is, and remains available for reception; and then, it is important to desubstantialise the artwork. This thesis makes art a privileged media of the meeting with others. It means recognising the relevance of aesthetics to enrich the public debate. As was previously stated, aesthetic criticism once extended to the environment, testing the ability to give an aesthetic meaning to our surroundings, shows a meaning that we communicate and that can be shared by people who live there. Indeed, the aesthetic problem now seeks both the view of nature as well as the creation of artificial environments, and therefore calls in to question its reception. If something like a democratisation of art is possible, it is first, Jean-Paul Doguet says, 'the work of legislators and especially educators, of all those who directly run social organisations, and secondarily that of technicians and artists' (ibid., p. 253). In order to understand, judge and appreciate the works of art as fully meeting their status as objects of communication, and not reducing them to mere conveyors of messages, it is necessary that everyone can link them to sensory experiences regardless of the contingencies of birth and of money. Perhaps we should also think of it for the built environment. Let us give a few examples.

De Runde stories

In the north-east of Holland, near the town of Emmen, is a small stream called De Runde. *Was Getekend to Runde* is a project that aims to revitalise a dead landscape. Industrial agriculture and 25 years of peat extraction (during the last four centuries) for urban energy has depleted the soil and completely dried up the original marsh. There are only two hundred hectares of what was a swamp 100km long and from 5–40km wide. The land-restoration re-allotment project of the former peat colonies of Emmer was commissioned to improve the possibilities of experiencing the hidden treasures of this landscape. The artist's proposal was to revive the most important hidden treasure: water welling up from the ground (see Plate 24). This special water has the power to enable nature to recreate variation and a sense of security in the open, barren land, now wasted by industrial agriculture. Not that the original Runde would be copied from historical maps, but a course would be set, based on stories of the inhabitants of the area, and finding a way through cultural obstacles. Though it took a long time, the original idea proved to be strong enough to take the plans into reality, mainly thanks to the faith and stubbornness of many inhabitants who demanded that the plans should go through, and thanks to local nature organisations who understood the ecological and economical power hidden in the idea of a 'new Runde'. The drawings by Dutch artist Jeroen van Westen from the locals' souvenirs, contribute to a joint construction of this landscape architecture project (van Westen, 2007). Jeroen van Westen worked with some of the inhabitants to redefine the landscape; sketchbook in hand, he strove to represent the links and forms of the De Runde Stream from their memories. In contrast to realistic drawings, these abstract visual forms have generated a river landscape. The collaborative approach involving people and drawing techniques showed the need for landscape projection to successfully achieve a representation of the site's future. The method he used is based on people's stories; the new stream will host the agritourism revitalisation of this former bog landscape. The audience is comprised of two groups, the 'excluded', (the inhabitants and people more generally affected by these problems), and on the other hand the gallery and the local government people who represent the companies involved in the realisation of the works of these artists. Finally, there is a general art public.

For the artist, the specificity of the Netherlands is that people understand that nature is based on cultural conditions. There is no wild landscape or area that is not partly human. In a landscape, changing places means changing views, and changing the relationships between objects, colours, etc. The artist knows this well, and realised that it was possible to relate the concept of signature to both stories of people dwelling locally and to the 'hidden treasure' (water) as described in the reports accompanying the landscaping project. If he could understand the local stories and the value these local people gave to objects, 'localities' in the landscape, he could appreciate them and mark them as positive or negative energies. Kandinsky said that a straight line is a link between two points on a neutral territory. This line will be bent towards positive points of attraction and depart from repulsive energy. To create these curved lines, he had to make sure that people shared their experience, intimate knowledge of the landscape, a landscape which they were no longer proud of.

Initially, the adventure was to invite the inhabitants of the five villages to a symposium about their landscape. A leaflet was made introducing the idea of landscape: their landscape as a work of art, awaiting a signature giving it life; a stream that would be created through their stories. *Was Getekend to Runde* is a project in which the artist becomes a chooser and collector of stories, stories that are used to make a stream, De Runde, which in turn becomes a creator. The artist anchors as many stories as possible, discovering sources of new stories, new possibilities. The conditional design is to search for creativities. We must transform our relationship to nature: from one of control to that of a creative relationship carrying possibilities, eventualities. It is an invitation to change.

This project revalues the experience of residents by transforming life stories into patterns that polarise the stream design. The drawing then becomes almost a participation tool. Indeed, it also incorporates the planning logic. *Was Getekend to Runde* is part of a wider programme of land restructuring. The government at the national level finances these programmes to conserve agricultural activity that supports rural areas while developing tourism based on the consumer landscape.

Dare-Dare

Even those traditionally without a voice, can be at the centre of an environmental artistic construction. The experiment of the artistic collective Dare-Dare was analysed by the art historian and geographer Suzanne Paquet (2009). She studied the role of artists in the transformation of public space, particularly the urban public square, which produce new forms, new situations and new relationships between people.

She analyses two public squares. One is Place Jean-Paul Riopelle, created in 2004 in the new international district of Montreal. It uses public art, in this case the *Jout*, a beautiful fountain designed by the artist Jean-Paul Riopelle, spitting flames and smoke as well as water. As an addition to the representation of public places, these operate as symbolic figures or emblems of the city. Some distance from this place is the recently renovated Viger Square, also built around a work of art. The *Agora*, a public square sculpture by Charles Daudelin was conceived as equipment for the use of the citizens. This site now has an 'undesirable' image because the homeless have transformed it in a dwelling place. Its destruction was planned before a group of artists, Dare-Dare, moved there to experiment directly within the public domain. The restitution of the experience of the homeless by the Dare-Dare artists helps reintegrate them into the community. The experiment attracts the curious and art lovers.

With these two examples, a public space defined by developers based on its formal image is opposed to alternative public spaces shaped by the action of these artists and enriched by a relational intake. The intervention of artists in these 'commons' allows the fluidification of a public space. It represents a new modality of a democratic breath. These performances express the reconquest of political freedom opposed to the hardened public space. These art actions reanimate dead public policies (crystallised in laws, institutions, normative equipment, urban and architectural memorials) to give it an experimental and pragmatic dimension. Ephemeral and mobile forms of relational art performance revitalise public space that had been monumentalised, crystallised and staid. The economy that characterises the artists' intervention provides the maximum effect.

The work of Dare-Dare draws our attention to the plasticity of forms reflecting their turbulent life. It exudes a true picture of the political life of forms such as the *Agora*, a public square monument in Montreal. It becomes a hardened form, monumentalized initially and then marginalized by its exclusive ownership by the homeless and the residential developments of the area. This place was threatened with demolition until the action of a group of artists (Dare-Dare) (re) animates this 'tired' form for a time that then allows renewed support of relationships within a diverse local community.

The Experimental Building

Many artists, in addition to engaging the participation of the public in their work, propose to create micro-political places, or perhaps what could be considered as micro-utopias. All the levers to relocate lives, and territories, are ways to revolt against the increasing financial abstraction of a globalized productivism, and to avoid societies becoming the mere tools of a capitalist logic. Finally, the community food projects boosting local production, alternative clinic networks, local currency creations, repair shops and exchange and recycling networks are involved in the expansion of these new principles of coexistence.

Dan Peterman (born 1960, US) is an artist combining innovative strategies of local engagement and activism, with national and international exhibitions, projects and installations. Among his diverse projects, Peterman explores networks of recycled, or discarded materials frequently producing starkly minimal works that function interchangeably as stockpiles, sculpture, functional objects, and critiques of environmental oversight and neglect. Peterman is a founder and current board member of the Experimental Station, an innovative Chicago-based incubator of small-scale enterprise and cultural projects. The Experimental Building, for example, is a utopian place in the sense that its function - its operation – is not predetermined by a project, but takes the liberty of local integration, exchanging with the environment. This project was not the result of a demiurgic gesture, quite the contrary. Dan Peterman was initially simply involved in local life in this huge brick building in a black, university neighbourhood that was at the time quite derelict. When Peterman was a student at the University of Chicago, the Building functioned as a recycling centre and was known to hold just about any object. Peterman felt attracted by what was going on, this rich and chaotic existence of specific objects with no destination other than the one that people would see in them. Inside the building were many companies and small-scale commercial adventures. Most of these companies, such as a book and clothing exchange, a bakery, gardens and a bike shop, had neither energy nor money to continue. Their histories were still inside the building, and were part of a rich local social life. Peterman took the opportunity of this moment, comparing it to the Christiana neighbourhood in Copenhagen. This vision and how the Building was resurrected was inspired by 1960s culture. Environmental concerns were a part of this, but not totally. Most people working in the Building at that time had become friends and work colleagues. Therefore, the artist installed objects and activities to continue supporting the Building, and seized the opportunity to develop social, environmental and artistic adventures.

The question for the artist is not, on the contrary, to assign a collective and militant social project. The question would be to ask how to act in a state of a given culture and not to sit back passively. Members of the Experimental Building Resources Center have challenged Peterman to put to the test the ideas and act accordingly. Years ago, the Resources Center had one of the largest fleets of used VW buses anywhere outside of the Third World. And they were engaged in a seasoned practice of recycling, with a very simple ecological mission. The goal took into account the social complexity across both the University of Chicago and the intensively disinvested neighbourhood of Woodlawn, in addition to environmental activism. The Resource Center provided a model of

Figure 14.1 Dan Peterman, *Plastic Bones*, post-consumer reprocessed plastic, 76 bags,
    40lb each

employment for people who had fallen through other social safety nets. Dan
Peterman deliberately creates a political posture and an ethical position: his is an
art that is experimenting with a future humanity.

Recycling is a way of drawing sustainability:

> I'm interested in finding ways to float propositions that can be very utopian.
> Beginning with simple exchanges of things. The bike shop is a good exam-
> ple of trying to build a small economy. The shop provides tools, resources,
> positive social contacts between adults and young people, a safe place, and
> job training for kids who are sorely lacking constructive things to do – and
> it's fueled by old bikes donated from apartment building basements. So that
> kind of basic economy can become a really complex sort of thing – it is
> wildly utopian in terms of it gathering all the loose ends of society and then
> getting the most you possibly can out of it all.
>
> (Wang, 2004)

Dan Peterman's well-known investigations of recycling systems and material
waste were given their just due in 'Plastic Economies,' the first major US survey
of this Chicago-based artist. Employing a practice that is highly localized to

address environmental issues of global magnitude, drawing upon social and collective energy and activity, Peterman has crafted a unique vision and aesthetic centred on alternative processes of use and reuse.

Capabilities, an aesthetic process

In these experiments, the aesthetic agents (artists, landscape architects, city-dwellers) recreate the experience of inhabitants to legitimise them and to debate their boundaries. Drawing inspiration from these examples, we make the following hypothesis: to involve the people in public policy, we should be able to give shape to their sensitive experience for it to become admissible and be put in to a debate. For this, we could use the knowledge base of artists, novelists, landscapers, designers... and use the common forms of representation and enunciation (atmospheres, landscapes, stories, images, etc.). This hypothesis is doubled with three recommendations.

The first is about participatory aesthetics. The environmental experience of the citizen has to be the base of the participatory process. This presupposes the existence of a transmission chain: the designers and implementers of policy must pay attention to transmit the experiential elements for it to be communicated to the other participants of the procedure. This is the condition from which public debate will be structured vis-à-vis sensitivity and aesthetics. This process covers new issues: the rich riparian ties that bind the lives of its inhabitants to their territories; how important these riparian links are for locals; the terms of evolution of these riparian links in a consistent way meets the expectations of residents.

The second recommendation is for the mixing of forms and media transmission to restitute the richness of aesthetic experience. This will combine the dwellers' stories with landscape and atmosphere to mix the visual, narrative and audio media providing an escape from the grip of the visual (in landscape) as well from the primacy of the written word (in the story) that would weaken the rendering. Visual artists, novelists, theatre people, are expected to play a central role in the making of the political forms, but should not be appointed representatives of the people, per se. A better scenario is probably as a mediator, the guarantor of the proper functioning of the transmission of the chain of forms.

The development of an aesthetic education for all could therefore be a guarantee of aesthetic democracy. It is therefore to provide residents with aesthetic criteria as well as the ability to develop them. Thus the participatory aesthetic could therefore be accompanied by various workshops: writing workshops residents with a writer, a composer with music workshops, dance workshops, etc.

The third recommendation is to imagine participation procedures that can include emotional and sensitive elements. The experience of citizens is an aesthetic experience in the strongest sense of the word. Today, this experience is delegitimised because it contains too much emotional and sensitive data that belongs to the sphere of intimacy. For example, the suffering of residents exposed to violent transformations of their environment is often expressed in disjointed speeches, 'rants', some violence incompatible with a serene exchange of dialogue. To be considered in the debate and taken into account in public choices, this sensitive and emotional dimension requires prior treatment, cosmetic formatting that crystallises emotion, sensitive in a cooled form, detached from the subject. This is not however, intended to bypass all of the sensitive and emotional sphere in the public domain in the name of transparency. Indeed, the wealth of experience does not obey the non-contradiction principle that governs exchange of arguments as being part of the rational language with stable and well understood strategic interests. Two features of the experience resist: the necessary coexistence of contradictions within an individual or a community and the necessary reserve of latency to maintain such 'soft stuff', (such as atmosphere), which do not resist explanation. One must admit that it will be necessary to invent participation procedures that are not governed solely by a regime of transparency and give a legitimate or opaque place to what is implicit. Procedures, like the hybrid forums, do not assign a priori definitive identity or defined interests to the participants.

Note

1   Indebted to Romantic writers such as Novalis and Schiller, as well as the social ideas of anthroposophy and the work of Rudolf Steiner, in the 1960s Beuys invented the concept of social sculpture, in which society as a whole was to be regarded as one great work of art (the Wagnerian *Gesamtkunstwerk*) to which each person can contribute creatively (perhaps Beuys's most famous phrase, borrowed from Novalis, is 'Everyone is an artist'). In the video 'Willoughby SHARP, Joseph Beuys, Public Dialogues (1974/120 min)', a record of Beuys' first major public discussion in the US, Beuys elaborates three principles: freedom, democracy, and socialism, saying that each of them depends on the other two in order to be meaningful. The 7,000 oak trees project exemplified the idea that a social sculpture was defined as interdisciplinary and participatory. Shelley Sacks, UK based artist, founded the Social Sculpture Research Unit (SSRU) at Oxford Brookes University.

References

Bourriaud, N., 1998. *L'Esthétique relationnelle*. Dijon: Les Presses du Réel.

Doguet, J.-P., 2007. *L Art comme communication: Pour une redéfinition de l art*. Paris: Armand Colin.

Paquet, S., 2009. *Le paysage façonné: Les territoires postindustriels, l'art et l'usage*. Québec: Presses de l'Université Laval.

Van Westen, J., 2007. 'De Runde, une expérimentation paysagère avec l'habitant'. In Blanc, N. and Lolive, J., eds., *Cosmopolitiques 15: Dossier 'Esthétique et espace public'*. Rennes: éditions Apogée/Cosmopolitiques, pp. 73–84.

Wang, D. S., 2004. *Downtime at the Experimental Station: A Conversation with Dan Peterman*. Chicago: Temporary Services.

Part VI

Markets to micro-utopias
Contextualising values

The importance of the value of art, embedded in the cultural ways and locally invented, is the focus of this section. One could imagine that all art could sell the same, independently of its place of origin thanks to a globalised market. It is true that artists have long since learned to combine resources to create a product, to seek to control these resources and to want to guard against hazards and threats (copying, hacking, etc.), which involves being able to handle a variety of skills, enter into contracts, protect their rights, facilitate relationships and networks to achieve artistic and economic targets. Some have even endorsed the conditions of the global market, as a number of contemporary visual artists dramatically illustrate (Takashi Murakami, Jeff Koons, Damien Hirst). The artist is then placed at the intersection of two dynamics: the dynamic of artistic densification (of which he/she is the only master and judge) and the dynamic of economic development (determined by several factors, including the market).

Yet it is important to keep in mind that displacing a work of art, or a craftwork from its original context and selling it in another place is still to play with contextualised values. Brazilian artist Vik Muniz's *Waste Land* project is a perfect example of this recycling of both product and reverse systemic strategy. He has worked with men and women living in a garbage dump in Rio de Janeiro re-using waste and creating works of art, such as portraits of the workers who do the actual garbage recycling and live at/in the dump. Creating large-scale recreations of classical paintings out of garbage, then photographing the images from a high tower in order to view them, the scenes become collages of known 'masterpieces', with the local dump inhabitants as the models. Through his work, he transforms an abandoned class of society into works of art, which are then sold at auctions and the proceeds eventually given back (he donates the funds to his 'models') to the community that inspired the work. Projects like *Waste Land* use the value differential between the world of waste and the world of art in order to fund the local people's micro-utopias (Film *Waste Land*, 2010).

At the hour of disintermediation and dematerialisation enabled by the Internet, such creators as Muniz must rethink their activity directly and the distribution of their work, developing skills that enable them to understand and even manipulate the socioeconomic system in which they enrol their creation. The relationship between art and the economy is multifaceted, whether in the ways in which art, particularly contemporary art, has to contribute to the market, or in whose art is the object of trial evaluations through a system of public galleries, museums, critics, collectors. So we will explore how art and value are linked in different cultural systems (Chapter 15).

Second, we denounce the collusion of art and market through financial mechanisms. Art markets are places of disembededness, and the extreme financial value reached by works of art, as well as the collusion between the world of luxury (Kuspit's 'degenerate') and the life of the artists show how dysfunctional today's art market is. The authors question a speculative economic valorisation over local enhancement. At the other end of this broad spectrum, we also look at the contribution of art and artists to revitalising economically impaired areas. (Chapter 16).

Third, we propose the idea that certain artists may change their world (and its values) with their process of setting up micro-utopias (Chapter 17). Two key factors allow the artist to build his/her reputation: recognition and trust. The value is generally determined by recognising markers that constitute guarantees for the consumer, who in the cultural field, is not always able to determine the quality of what is offered (a book is purchased before it is read, a work of art requires a culture or expertise to be evaluated). Today, the choice can be anticipated by adopting upstream production values that allow marketing studies. One can also combine the consumer with the production of the work. The artist must therefore constantly find economic models for his/her work to make the best of it. Reaching out in order to create small 'holes' in the world fabric, micro-places where the hope for another society can happen, the artist plays with the environmental value and forces the recognition of his/her work.

15 The contextualisation of value

Recent geo-political movements, particularly in Central and South America, but spanning countries across the planet, are increasingly revolving around environmental justice, eco-aesthetics, and 'Rights of Nature'. They position the Earth as a living entity (mother, Gaia, Tlazolteotl, etc.), naming her as in ancient times and placing her with this new found identity at the core of a global art shift that is as economically driven as it is philosophically, ecologically and aesthetically.[1] Artists from the so-called developed countries (that is, former colonial powers) are increasingly creating works that are community based, process oriented, often anonymous, but tied to a desire to re-integrate daily life with that of nature and set up systems of stewardship and respect for the environment that supports human life. Equally, artists from cultures that are either indigenous and/or former colonies, or have other ancient ties to their environment, are also producing works that reflect native belief systems integrating respect of the natural world and its necessary guardianship.

The nineteenth century nature/culture divide seems missing in these current projects, blurring the lines between that artifice of westernised thought. Similarly, our increasingly globalised world has given indigenous artists access and voice to an audience at large, outside their own continents and reservations, where parallel activities and works that revere, reflect on and respect local ecologies as part of a greater whole also exist. What were once separate worlds are now united via the arts in a symbiotic push to protect the planet, or at very least call attention to her anthropocentric demise. It is a unique moment in time, not just the arts.

The definition of indigenous is multi-faceted and ever-changing in the twenty-first century. With global transmigrations, immigration, disappearing lands and entire ecosystems, forests and seas, the traditional identity with cultural landscape is often mitigated with displacement and disappearance. Yet, if we can use the term in its broadest sense – originating or occurring naturally in a particular place, native – then the similarities and comparisons with current ecological art movements become more obvious. A deep connection to *place*, the *genii loci*, is a primary indicator of a long tradition or even identification with the land. Recent environmental artists are creating an aesthetic to complement this system revolving around the concepts of complexity and resilience:

'Uncertainty/complexity means that there is always a uniqueness to specific places: a fruitful area for environmental art is investigations of how we discover, value and work with local places' (Phillips, 2015, p. 56).

In the northwestern corner of Cameroon in West Africa, in the Bui region, lies the ancient kingdom of the Nso peoples. Their traditions remain to this day, although now overlapped with Muslim, Christian, and other outside influences. In Nso, a dance performance and a ritual procession by the elders accompanied by a masquerade involves and absorbs people without their having any thought of the general usefulness of such an involvement and absorption (see Plate 25). To that extent, art is enjoyed intrinsically. That is, it could exist as an end in itself and not as a means to some other end (Wingo, 1998, p. 2).

What is being called in the West, 'socially responsible art', such as the eco-art experiments over the past thirty years, runs parallel to what Wingo emphasises in Nso culture where secret societies are the holders of 'art': 'which undergird and transmit the fundamental values of society, such as cohesion, the (spiritual) well-being of the members, entertainment, enforcement of laws and upholding of customs and values from one generation to another' (Wingo, 1998).

Art that embraces environmental justice issues, addresses climate change, rising sea levels, ocean acidification or loss of animal habitat, for example, embraces a similar responsibility of holding fundamental values of the society as in indigenous cultures throughout time. The creative works presented in this book that represent just a small intersection of contemporary projects and art happening globally, are intrinsically enmeshed in these 'traditional' issues of value and ethics, the Aristotelean *philia*, that many cultures never lost.

Copy from Cameroon

The word 'value', when associated with art has, at least since the Renaissance, been tied to economic systems. Western art objects have personal value, monetary value and perhaps cultural 'collateral' over time, but stewardship of the land, or valuing the environment has come late in the Westernised cultures that have (obviously) profited from its exploitation. Critiquing the capitalist structure of desire and demand is at the core of the 2010 work *I Want That You Want What I Want That You Want* by Belgian artist Maarten Vanden Eynde (born 1977) (see Plate 26). While working in a remote village in Cameroon, he set up an exchange with a local artisan, of an original Stihl chainsaw for a copy made in Eben wood by the Cameroonian artist. This humorous but poignant sculpture/intervention points out the profound connection of the capitalist market with poverty and economic imbalance, environmental devastation and economic growth. Not only are the two objects, placed side-by-side, a glaring reality of what a commodified international market has done to devalue local craft, destroy indigenous forests (with saws, by the way), and bring more destruction at the price of artistic loss, but they also bring full circle the obvious clash of traditional ways with those of the industrialised world.

Wood carving is a long tradition in West African art, obviously dating to times long into the past before deforestation began to encroach upon villages and regions. Carved masks, carriers of dance and ritual, are never realistically rendered in sub-Saharan art. This would be not only 'ugly', but taboo, useless and dismissed. An artisan who produced a realistic representation could even be shunned, if not punished. This is diametrically opposed to the rise of the idealisation of beauty in Western art over the last 2000 years, and the eventual glorification of the individual artist (reflecting the rise of the individual in general in the West) and his portrait since the Renaissance. Albrecht Dürer's self portrait in early 1500 opened the door, symbolically and literally, to the new found era of European exploration, exploitation, individualism, mechanical reproduction with printing and the rise of the industrialisation. Hitherto, the portrayal of the artist's self remained hidden in painting. It was still 'veiled', with only secret references or visual clues imbedded in the artworks to indicate an individual author. But Dürer's bold, frontal realistic representation of himself, placed the artist on a pedestal of capital and commerce, where he remained until the modern era.

Eynde's saw-exchange, therefore, is not only a clever critique of the market economy and colonialism, but also the modernist agenda, where so much sculptural influence was copied from African art (Picasso, Braque) eliminating all value from the aesthetic. The traded power saws create a simulacrum, where monetary exchange is eliminated. The 'trade' is equal as it was mutually agreed upon by both artists. The value of the Cameroonian artist's sculptural work, 'equals' the price of a saw in the West (approximately $350). The imbalance of the trade, made visual and 'real' in the objects, raises important issues of not only equity, but the very role of art. The indigenous artist is working in an age-old tradition of wood carving with techniques going back generations into his African heritage.

The 'commission' by conceptual European artist Eynde, illustrates the complete imbalance of the economies, the differentiated value of the artist in the societies, and the end of a millennium-old practice due to the cutting down of the ancient forests, which have provided the very material for the artistic expression of carving.

Traditional wood carving in sub-Saharan African art, was/is not only for everyday objects, but especially for objects used in sacred and religious practice. The famous masks and tribal images that are now often displayed in Western museums still have potent spiritual value for the members of the generation of those indigenous cultures that grew up with objects that were sacred to the community, and the religious elite. Endowed with 'mana', they are/were living with spirit. Because the masks, for example, are purposefully non-representational and do not portray individuals, they are able to communicate via what Wingo calls 'veiling'. The religious structure behind each mask, dance and ritual is complex and culturally specific. Secret societies, elders, chiefs and sorcerers all carry traditions of hidden knowledge that maintains balance within the tribal society. Rules and regulations are enforced and responsibilities are shared in dances and song that remind the members of the social group.

The excitement produced in attempting to decode the secrecy – and even the knowledge of the existence of the secrecy – is an aesthetic endeavour. Acknowledging, whether intellectually or not, the existence of the unseen – activated by something visceral which then activates the imagination and sensitivity – should also be considered aesthetic. The aesthetic is not restricted to beauty – beauty is just one aspect; it involves (shaped) feelings aroused by artworks of every genre (Wingo, 1998, p. 10).

The 'unknown' that contributes to the aesthetic of these traditional works, and therefore maintains social control within its native context, becomes devoid of power when removed to a museum or private collection. Or does it? What is the hidden element that allows works of art to create social change? And what are the repercussions for contemporary artists working in the field of environmental aesthetics?

> [B]y rejecting – along with Stengers, Latour, and Gordon – the clear separations between modern science and pre-modern animism, objective positivism and subjective belief, the real and the imaginary, then it corresponds, in my view, to an innovative approach to aesthetics that joins the factual and the fictional.
>
> (Demos, 2015, p. 17)

O2 Canal

The O2 Canal project, proposed by Indonesian artist Firman Djamil (born 1964) and other installations by him, create exactly such an aesthetic. After obtaining his master's degree from the Indonesian Institute of the Arts in Yogyakarta, he produced sculpture installation works with environmental themes for a number of international art forums. Working in traditional materials such as wood and bamboo, typical of architectural structures from indigenous people such as the Worok homes of the Rebos community in Flores Island, Indonesia, Djamil's objects are also conical in shape and architectural in size.[2] 'These methods of construction have been tested over hundreds of years, made specifically for that particular geographic area using materials found on-site' (artist's COAL proposal). The function of the artist's object is 'fictional' however, as it recreates a chimney-shaped structure, or even a nuclear reactor-like form, to call attention to the 'manifestation of a forest of trees and corals in a plankton-filled marine environment'. The artist compares this to a 'spirit producer' of oxygen (O_2), that could ostensibly reduce carbon dioxide (CO_2), in the fight against global warming. (COAL Prize, 2015).

The feeling of the structure is indeed animistic, recalling something ancient and unknown. Perhaps a totem or an altar, it does indeed resemble such altars and temples, *heiau*, used throughout Polynesia and Micronesia in pre-contact times. That the artist has chosen to name the work as a tribute to the biological and ecological process of nature confirms its connection to both the real and the imaginary, in Demos' definition. We are cognisant that climate change is real, the leap of faith with the artist to change or influence the viewer's belief of that status is embedded in the imagination.

Again referring back to Wingo's 'shaped feelings' that the work of art arouses, it is the critical ingredient of the experience to transform the audience. Modern archeological research of offerings left at ancient Hawaiian temples has found bundles of rather seemingly inconsequential materials. McAllister says:

> The bundles range in size from small packages containing perhaps a leaf wrapped in a piece of tapa, or a fish wrapped in ti [leaves], which measure on an average about 6 inches long, 3 inches wide, and 2 inches thick, to the large bundles of grass, ferns, and other plants, measuring about 1.5 feet long, 1 foot wide, and 0.5 foot thick.
>
> (McAllister quote in Hiroa, 1964, pp. 37–40)

Were the plant forms sacred to the ancient Hawaiians, and therefore a powerful offering, or was the content of the offering inconsequential, as McAllister notes: 'an examination of the contents shows that the objects were of no great value, even to the Hawaiian before the coming of Cook. Apparently it was the act and not the offering that was important' (ibid., p. 527).

One of the more famous modern Westerners to 'study' native culture was the anthropologist Margaret Mead. As a woman (pretending to be unmarried in order to further her research on adolescent girls and sexual mores in Samoa), Mead was particularly poised to record not only the 'social codes' she set out to document, but perhaps offhandedly for our purposes, the aesthetics of an indigenous art form: tapa cloth. The production and design of this highly important object across Polynesia cannot be more essential to the material culture. Tapa was used as clothing, as offerings, gift exchange, blankets, home protection and decoration. Tapa art, the practice of pounding the bark of the mulberry tree to create a cloth that is then decorated and designed in paint and beaten patterns, is still abundant throughout Polynesia, (although now more as commodity for tourists than for clothing). Bark cloth decoration is still carried out in many indigenous groups of the southern hemisphere. Dr. Mead was well versed in the importance of culture in the determination of human behaviour, and

> followed the metaphysical philosophers such as John Dewey, William James, and Charles Sanders Pierce, who from the late nineteenth century on argued for the importance of ideas and the imagination in shaping social life as well as individual behavior.
>
> (Lutkehaus, 2008, p. 112)

One of her research trips to Samoa in the 1920s produced a famous tale in the history of anthropology (Freeman, 1983), based on her documentation of the women making tapa cloth. The highly ornate graphic designs of worms, sea urchins, basketry weaves and dance moves are intricately transformed into patterns that barely changed over the generations of intact island culture, i.e., 'pre-contact' or 'pre-European' contact (Mead, 1929). The images were connected to stories and the surrounding ecosystems of sea life, hula moves, songs, food, relationships and nature. Indigenous Polynesian culture was imbedded in these designs, beaten into the bark cloth, then painted with a bud brush and perhaps sea urchin ink or other plant dyes, onto the dried cloth. They were then wrapped around the body in various ways for specific occasions, hung on the walls of the *halau* or folded into wedding blankets as prestigious gifts. The form was mandated by the cultural activity, place and time. All the materials were gathered from the land and sea, with specific meaning attached to their making, use and gifting.

For her research, Dr Mead created a series of questions that were translated to the women on each expedition to the island of Ta'u (Mead, 1929). She carefully documented the responses to the questions into an empirical system of research phenomena to add to her documentation of the Samoans. After Mead's death, Freeman famously denounced her findings after interviewing one of her main translators, a follow-up years later to the anthropologist's research. Was it that the women created stories about the tapa, new stories, about the designs and patterns, that they thought Dr Mead would enjoy? Did they respect and love her so much that these women began creating new chants and *her* stories that were as creative as the original meanings, yet not indigenous to their culture? Did they make up stories to make fun of her? We will perhaps never know if the stories behind the designs were 'fabricated' by the women of Samoa or not, but perhaps that is not the point.

Mead, who was a pioneer of gender issues in modern Western thought, and as a 24-year-old woman doing field work on women of approximately her own age group, promoted the interconnectedness of all aspects of human culture. Her holistic approach to culture perhaps allowed her to understand the production of tapa as an integrated part the entire society: fishing, religion, dance, rhythm and music. In pre-contact Polynesia, the beat of the tapa *tutua* anvil could send signals, like Morse code, across the island to announce a foreign visitor. The sense of sound, the cadence of a rhythm, therefore, was as important as the final tapa object. The entire production is tied to the social, political and religious life of indigenous Polynesia. To separate out one visual aspect of that process negates its efficacy and value completely into a reduction to solely visual terms. Aesthetic, in this way, is a cohesive flowering of the richness of human existence, of which beauty and visual pleasure are but one element.

This example raises not only the question of 'what' is 'indigenous', but at which point of contact with foreigners is said culture no longer 'indigenous', and becomes reflective of the questioner/interlocutor. Within this paradigm we may simultaneously begin in fact to designate the separation of 'art' from the culture into which it was indigenous itself. Just as the borders between an active life and art are blurred in much of the work explored in this book, so too are the designations of the so-called 'history of art' that reflects its local culture, yet transcends to 'high' art as the capitalist economy rose with industrialisation.

So, is a contemporary environmental aesthetics (Blanc, 2012) based on this pendulum of animism and modern science, where the *feeling* body is required to listen, see, and experience the work of art in a total, transdisciplinary way, also a force, as Wingo suggests, for social change? When we speak of a sustainable world (and that term too will be debated within this book), are we not calling for a complete social and economic transformation, that would demand life on our planet to exist in a different way? As Phillips presents, in her article:

> The aesthetics of contemporary environmental art has moved a long way from classical or neo-Kantian notions of beauty as unity, stability and balance ... through artworks this may be one way of *unsolidifying* the rational-economic basis of sustainability.
>
> (Phillips, 2015, p. 59)

Transdisciplinary and transcultural, sound, music, movement and dance are the non-objectified art forms that invite the audience's participation in a deep way. 'As a common denominator for human and non-human practices, dance comprises a particularly interesting example here, because it reflects part of the deep knowledge that is evolutionarily encoded in the brain' (Kalliwoda's COAL proposal, 2015, p. 4). Two artists, Hans Kalliwoda (Germany) and Akshay Raj Singh Rathore (India), each have worked with interventions of natural phenomena re/dis-placed from rural to an urban environment. Each artist presents a sensory experience (bird song and the dance of bees) as metaphor for biological health, both human and non-human.

If sense perception indeed lies at the 'etymological core of aesthetics (Gr. aisthesis, perception by the senses), and is central to aesthetic theory, aesthetic experience, and their applications' (Berleant, 2010), then we will find, in the aesthetic, like Berleant, 'a source, a sign, and a standard of human value'.

Rathore's proposal is to transform a part of urban Paris into a huge bird's nest made of hanging terracotta pots where various species of birds would be lured to nest, and eventually sing. This cacophony of song would then be broadcast to urban points normally void of nature, especially in the green-deficient Paris centre: train stations, metro lines, shopping areas, airports, etc. The experiential element of this work is key, for although it has aesthetic 'value' in the hanging pots beautifully sprawled across a t-bar and hanging in space, it is the sound of the birds that stirs the imagination and potentially creates an experience that is aesthetically connected to the environment that is ourselves.

The artist remembers his home in India, where:

> Sounds of nature are still omnipresent: calls of monkeys, cows, dogs, pigs, goats, elephants on the streets or hear [sic] peacocks, crows, parakeets, mynas, sparrows, lapwings, pigeons, owls, hawks, eagles and numerous other birds [that] fill [the] environment every dawn and dusk.
>
> (Artist's COAL proposal)

He wants to recall the 'deep affiliations' that humans have with nature, with his huge installation in the heart of Paris, where many species of birds are encouraged to nest and create new homes. Rathore quotes Edward O. Wilson and the concept of biophilia, which stems from Aristotle's proposition that *philia* – friendship with other beings – is an integral ethics, central to survival of the species. While Aristotle focuses on the interconnectedness of human beings, his concept leaves open room for expansion of the idea to a shared sentiment that creates obligation with other living things (Santas, 2014).

Since the mid 1980s, German artist Hans Kalliwoda has focused on the integration of the spectators into his art works, installations and interventions. His complex projects involve changing the systems of human interaction, both with the environment and one another, across cultures in an attempt at creating global understanding and empathy. Beginning with the dance of the bees, in the 'polliniferous project' he compares the catastrophic decline of our world's honey-bee population, (so-called 'Colony Collapse Disorder' or more appropriately 'Depopulation Syndrome'), with the increasing rate of suicide in indigenous peoples. If the bee population is self-destructing, in an 'epidemic of suicide', perhaps it can give us an indicator as to the human psychological and emotional angst now on the rise (not only in native populations). This is a multi-faceted project, which includes a completely off-the grid, high tech structure called World in a Shell (WiaS) for meetings, exchange of information, interventions, and what the artist calls 'swap-shop' situations. Kalliwoda also creates Bee-Sanctuaries in inner cities across Europe, himself acting as the pollinator of ideas, proposals and solutions between cultures, and public and private research.

The WiaS structure in Africa is based on the homeland of the San people, the Bushmen of the Kalahari Desert, where the artist has long been involved as both researcher and environmentalist. Said to be the Ur of human civilization, from

Figure 15.1 Hans Kalliwoda, *the Polliniferous Project, the World in a Shell*

whence we all sprang, this indigenous culture is still surviving today, despite loss of habitat and the forced re-settling of the people, shut off from hunting and gathering. Kalliwoda makes the connection of this disruption in the culture of both bees and indigenous peoples, as to the loss of dance:

> Reduction of complexity of the environment with both Bees and San leads to simple behavior that can be observed in the dances. In both contexts, a dance is a particular language that can be observed in the making, recorded and analyzed. Dances are mostly of significant meaning for telling a story, give directions and form an integrate part of well-being and development for the individual as well as for the colony or community. A quantitative decline on the occurrence of performing dances ultimately leads to a poorer quality of the performances. Over time, the availability of dancers may also be reduced. An analogy to what the decline of these processes can lead to be, a reextinct or dead languages, which by definition are languages that no longer have any speakers.
>
> (Artist's COAL proposal)

Just as the survival of the organic ecosystem is predicated on the spread of pollen, so too that of human civilization is dependent on cross-pollination between the conception and practices of indigenous cultures and those of industrialised, urban-centric culture. Both of these cultures are in a state of collapse, the former at the hands of the latter, and the latter from apparent unsustainability (artist's COAL proposal).

Human experience has a base in transcendence and transformation. Change is in our DNA. The decline in the experience of spiritualty (coincidentally parallel to the rise of mental illness) in the Western cultures could be equated with the phenomenal rise of prices on artworks for sale at market. Artists responded to this in postmodernism with a breakout from the gallery and museum system, and a 'return' to community, home, the earth, and local activity removed from a remote hierarchy, economic or political or both. If we can expand the definition of a twenty-first century 'indigenous' artist (with due respect to First Nation's Peoples) to a new generation of art-makers who are responding to their local environment and global ecosystems, then we are embracing the environmentally based work of today that is in fact tied to traditional criteria for exploring change and creating respect and harmony with a greater presence.

It can therefore be concluded that our senses are not for detached cognition but for participation, for sharing the metamorphic capacity of things that lure us or that recede into inert availability as our manner of participation shifts, never vanishes: we never step outside the 'flux of participation' (Isabelle Stengers quoted in Franke and Folie, 2011).

The creation of objects has historically been tied to the nature from which the culture sprang. The so-called nature–culture divide, when man began to create his own existence outside of the environmental parameters of place, could also be argued to be the point in time when art as artifice was born. An integrated culture, where many native peoples create traditional forms with *purpose*, or *spirit* will not necessarily label said objects, performances or music, 'art'. It is the outsider's structure imposed upon a foreign system that does so.

Contemporary environmental artists are seeking to re-integrate this nature–culture divide. As has been seen in the case studies of the previous chapters, there is a wide range of community activities, experiments, social engagements, research projects and scientific explorations embracing the environment. The enthusiasm of the works implores a love of the earth and her existence into the next generations. While the removal of a formalised religion from these artworks separates them from historical traditions, the very blurring of boundaries between social/political engagement and beauty might be said to transport the works to a new place of action, involvement and audience. The public is a present player in many of the projects. Nature and all her systems are celebrated and explored. As Gaia moves into the era of the 'Anthropocene', contemporary artists dismantle the name of their craft, throwing away the hierarchal structure of art's commodification and all it employed, in what could be seen as a parallel practice to indigenous cultures. Eco art is by definition engaged with the environment, which is at its most fragile moment in human history.

Notes

1   'My friend, I am going to tell you the story of my life, as you wish ... It is the story of all life that is holy and is good to tell, and of us two-legged sharing in it with the four-legged and the wings of the air and all green things; for these are children of one mother and their father is one Spirit' (Neihardt, 2008, p. 1).
2   http://webecoist.momtastic.com/2013/05/03/simple-and-beautiful-bamboo-frame-homes-in-indonesia/

References

Berleant, A., 2010. *Sensibility and Sense: The Aesthetic Transformation of the Human World.* Exeter: Imprint Academic.
Blanc, N., 2012. 'From Environmental Aesthetics to Narratives of Change'. *Contemporary Aesthetics*, Volume 12. Available at: www.contempaestetics.org/newvolume/pages/journal.php.
Demos, T. J., 2013, *Return to the Post Colony: Specters of Colonialism in Contemporary Art.* Berlin: Sternberg Press.
Demos, T., 2015. 'Rights of Nature: The Art and Politics of Earth Jurisprudence'. In: *Rights of Nature: Art and Ecology in the Americas.* Nottingham: Nottingham Contemporary.
Franke, A. and Folie, S., 2011. *Animism: Modernity through the Looking Glass.* Berlin: Verlag der Buchhandlung Walther Konig.
Freeman, D., 1983. *Margaret Mead and Samoa: The Making and Unmaking of an Anthropological Myth.* Cambridge, MA: Harvard University Press.
Hiroa, T. R., 1964. *Arts and Crafts of Hawai'i: Religion.* Honolulu: Bishop Museum Press.
Lutkehaus, N. C., 2008. *Margaret Mead: The Making of an American Icon.* Princeton: Princeton University Press.
Mead, M., 1929. 'Coming of Age in Samoa: A Psychological Study of Primitive Youth for

Western Civilisation'. *American Anthropologist*, 31(3), 532–534.

Neihardt, J. G., 2008. *Black Elk Speaks: Being the Life Story of a Holy Man of the Oglala Sioux*. New York: State University of New York Press.

Phillips, P., 2015. 'Artistic Practices and Eco Aesthetics in a Post-Sustainable Worlds'. In: C. Crouch, N. Kaye and J. Crouch, eds. *An Introduction to Sustainability and Aesthetics: The Arts and Design for the Environment*. Boca Raton, Florida: Brown Walker Press.

Santas, A., 2014. 'Aristotelian Ethics and Biophilia.' *Ethics & The Environment*, 19(1), 95–121.

Wingo, A. H., 1998. 'African Art: The Aesthetics of Hiding and Revealing'. *British Journal of Aesthetics*, 38(3), 251–264.

16 The great divide
Artist and art

Can we compare the commodification of art, and it's separation for the artist into a market economy based on a banal materiality, to the divide between humans and nature? Is there a relationship of the heart between creativity and how we live in the environment? Do emotions play a role in our decisions about how to live, work and make things? When art is only a product to be invested in, like a stock on the market, and the strings of the system are pulled by the same small one per cent that has stirred anger and protests across the United States. Since the Wall Street scandals plaguing the first quarter of this century, can the artist remain invested wholeheartedly in the work? If a collector sits on the board of a major museum, and his collection (it IS usually a man[1]) contains Artist X, then naturally his inclination will be to put Artist X in the museum, which will increase the value of his own painting at home by said artist. It is an old monopoly and a very old game. The lack of diversity on boards, leadership positions in the art world and even staff, all point to a power structure that is reflective of that small one per cent, and of not the artists.

In the belly of the beast

> Individual funders, who founded America's art museums and who remain their greatest hope as the tradeoffs of earned income become manifest, are more demanding of such proof as well. Self-described 'venture philanthropists' are just as determined to measure the value of their investment in non profits as they are in venture capital investments. This new generation of arts patrons, including influential collectors and trustees from the world of business, has an increasingly large share of attention in museum boardrooms.
>
> (Anderson, 2004, p.4)

Because of progressive tax laws in the US that carefully guard non-profit institutions and how they operate, museums must be very careful in their profit margins, where bookstores are selling more chachkas and postcards and silk scarves with a Renoir painting silkscreened on it, than is going into outreach and education programmes, conservation or collecting. While the museum has traditionally focused on collecting, and building a collection that is 'shared' with the public (and thus the non-profit status), for the betterment of the citizen, there was a shift in the last century when that focus became more on entertainment.

Not all boards, of course follow the profit-only pattern. Yet, as traveling exhibitions reached profit margins that were off the charts, starting with the blockbuster King Tut exhibition in 1974, (which was originally a diplomatic coup of the Egyptian President Anwar Sadat and Richard Nixon), checks and balances began to be challenged. As either 'soft diplomacy' or showing off 'cultural collateral', international exhibitions and individual lending have increasingly moved away from the culture and more toward the loan payoff. Boston's Museum of Fine Arts has admitted to the *Boston Globe* earnings of over $5 million in 2014 from lending out individual master paintings from its collection (Smee, 2014). Three board members resigned, citing a conflict of interest with the public trust. 'Our primary responsibility as Trustees is to safeguard the art. If these works are placed at risk too often and without sufficient justification, then we are not fulfilling that obligation' (ibid.).

The mandate in recent times, fortunately, is shifting towards more social 'outcomes' than 'outputs'. Like happiness and creativity, these outcomes are more slippery to measure, and therefore more difficult to report upon at a board meeting. Museums are beginning to compete with one another to 'make a difference' rather than merely having the highest attendance. Numbers are much easier for us to measure than a qualitative experience. Capitalism is built on production, not joy, equality, laughter, empathy or friendship, especially in the United States, where the production of gadgets fuelled the post-war economy. As Susan Sontag wrote in a New Yorker essay in 1967:

> American power is indecent in its scale. But also, the quality of American life is an insult to the possibilities of human growth; and the pollution of American space, with gadgetry and cars and TV and box architecture, brutalizes the senses, making grey neurotics of most of us, and perverse spiritual athletes and strident self-transcenders of the best of us.
>
> (Sontag, 1967)

Susan Sontag's critique of cultural and political inequalities is apropos today, as they have influenced the way that artists make art. Sold on a myth of fame and fortune, young artists in the US were tempted into the fantastic array of quality art schools across the country after the Second World War. From the New York Artist's League, to the Rhode Island School of Design, down to Black Mountain College and over the Chicago Art Institute, European émigré artists were flooding the US, ready to teach to earn a living. It was an incredibly rich time for the arts, and the market was only beginning to except 'avant garde' works such as those of Duchamp and Pollock. With Ed Kienholz and the Ferris Gallery out in Los Angeles, the Pasadena Art Museum opened and Chouinard Art Institute took off. By the 1970s there were five major art schools on the West Coast and LA was beginning to challenge the New York hegemony of the art market. Hollywood money fuelled the galleries and sales skyrocketed. The boom of the

1980s had a profound effect on the international market, with Japan, Europe and South America competing with the US in sales. This 'boom' is once again in process, especially for artists who were born about the time of the last one. The headlines are astounding; Picasso selling in 2015 for $179.4m, and Jeff Koons' *Balloon Dog* for $58.4m, the highest sum ever paid for a living artist's work.

But it is an art that is separate from the public. These are private collections for very private people, not unlike the entire history of western art, which was for the aristocratic elite. When Bill Gates bought Leonardo da Vinci's Codex Leicester on November 11, 1994 for $30,802,500 there was public outrage. Often cited as one of the most magnificent scientific journals of the Western world, it is comprised of eighteen sheets of paper, folded in half and then again, to create 72 pages, written and drawn on both sides in the artist's unique 'backwards' hand-writing and distinctive style. It is a treatise of observations on the moon, fossils, how water moves and what causes erosion. They are precious to the history of our civilization. Should they be locked away in a private collection to never be seen again by the public? Should money be allowed to buy anything? Or does art, especially something as precious as the Codex, belong to the commons?

This history is integral to what and how artists are creating today, as it is a form of protest against such corporate privatisation of culture. It offers a valuable example of who buys and sells art, property and people, and what our relationship is to those objects. Leonardo's notebooks were bought in 1980, from the estate of the Earl of Leicester, where they had been in quiet repose since purchased back in 1719, by another millionaire of the time, the oil magnate Armond Hammer (the museum in LA carries his name). The museum's trustees put them up for auction at Christie's (which caused another press scandal and some resignations from the museum board), in 1994. At first anonymous, and then publicly jubilant, Gates, the billionaire founder of Microsoft, promised to keep the Codex available to the public, to deflect the amount of bad press suddenly surrounding the sale and subsequent purchase. He does this once a year, and at different cities around the world, for a short amount of time. It reads, like so much of the Bill and Melinda Gates charitable activities, like a 'beneficient' action on the part of the world's richest man. He proceeded then to Xerox all the pages of one of the world's greatest artworks, and turned them into wallpaper and screensavers for his Windows95 program. Is this art for the masses or art for one man to make a huge profit on? Has the market economy (and Xerox machines) displaced Walter Benjamin's 'aura'?

Manifest destiny

Instead of theorising art's relationship to capitalism through the concepts of commodification, culture industry, spectacle and real subsumption, all of which have a superficial ring of truth, the key to understanding art's relationship to capitalism must be derived from questioning whether art has gone through the transition from feudalism to capitalism. This may not provide the whole account of how art has been penetrated by capitalist society, but it must be the foundation of any adequate account of the exceptional economics of art and for any politics of art within and against capitalism.

In *Art and Value*, Dave Beech interprets the history of the art economy via a Marxist spectrum (Beech, 2015). He uses culture and society as barometers, and asks us if indeed we are past basic feudalistic systems in how we buy and sell art. With secondary markets, many artists today never receive the huge sums from sales that their works from decades earlier are now fetching. While laws are in place in some states in the US (California leading the way in artist protections), copyright laws are still dismally antiquated or non-existent for visual artists.

If we are moving towards an art that is non-marketable in the future, by choice, then the paradigm of the 'poor' artist can no longer be accurate. Nor of the 'rich' artist either, for that matter. Because when the buy and sell quotient is removed from the formula there is only intrinsic value that remains. Before the genocide of First World Peoples in the Americas, there was the loss of land. Native Americans were first herded and hunted farther and farther from their homelands, as they were with disbelief and incomprehension, lost to the notion of land ownership. It did not exist in their culture or religion. One did not own 'god'. We might extend the metaphor to artists, who for the most part, until the late-twentieth century, did not make art because there was the possibility to become rich. The late twentieth-century mythos encircling art with fame and fortune, in part the responsibility of the art schools at the end of capitalism, runs a close parallel to colonialism's rise and fall.

Sontag talks of the poor immigrants from Europe, Mexico and South East Asia who fled to the United States, only to find more poverty, more segregation, and less culture.

> Even the poorest knew both a 'culture', largely invented by his social betters and administered from above, and a 'nature' that had been pacified for centuries. These people arrived in a country where the indigenous culture was simply the enemy and was in the process of being ruthlessly annihilated, and where nature, too, was the enemy, a pristine force, unmodified by civilization, that is, by human wants, which had to be defeated. After America was 'won', it was filled up by new generations of the poor, and built up accordingly to the tawdry fantasy of the good life that culturally deprived, uprooted people might have at the beginning of the industrial era.
>
> (Sontag, 1967, p. 52)

So while we imagine in the United States, that we have equality, freedom, and contact to great natural wildlife refuges and national parks, they are, in fact, owned by the Coke Brothers, Bill Gates or Monsanto. A recent battle to end the plastic bottles polluting the Grand Canyon is a case in point. When a small NGO in California, the 5 Gyres Institute, who has been working for years on plastic pollution in the oceans decided to tackle one-use plastic bottles, a hike at the Grand Canyon revealed an astounding number of plastic Coca-Cola bottles littering the cliffs and canyon floors; thirty per cent of the waste in the Park and the largest source of trash. After some research, it became obvious to campaign manager Stiv Wilson that the reason was due to the inordinate amount of Coca-Cola machines strategically placed at the top of every trail and tourist rest spot. After a highly successful campaign that garnered over 100,000 signatures on change.org, the Park decided to take the risk of offending its major supporter (Coca-Cola) and ban the bottles. That was not before there was a threatened lawsuit (filed by Public Employees for Environmental Protection) and major media documenting the battle. 'These documents confirm what appeared obvious – corporate donations influenced national park conservation policies,' said PEER's executive director, Jeff Ruch, referring to the email documents the group obtained after filing its lawsuit (Verespe, 2011). There is a direct historical line to the white man's relationship to nature throughout US history, in turn, directly imported from Europe.

If America is the culmination of Western white civilization, as everyone from the Left to the Right declares, then there must be something terribly wrong with Western white civilization. This is a painful truth; few of us want to go that far (Sontag, 1967).

Gorillas/guerillas

While much of the art in this book may not seem subversive, per se, it is. There are spectrums represented throughout, and colours, but the values are the same: that of respect for the surrounding environment that supports all life as we know it. Some of the art may be for sale, artists do have to eat, (fact). And the craft of drawing, painting, photography, building things around ideas, are the tools of the trade. Some of the work might look like commercial work from afar, until the intent is exposed. What separates these artists and their work from history, is that they (in Marxist terms) work with modes of production, and not modes of consumption (Beech, 2015).

They are aware of the intricacies of past empires and those inherent markets. They critique them, in small or large ways, blatantly or subtly, because ultimately those markets of profit are what have destroyed the planet. They imitate nature, while she survives, and invent new systems to co-create with her. Some artists reconnect to their art with the craft of it, some with the inherent category of change, at whose altar creativity must worship. Art's long relationship to political and social change is too long to record here, but it is much older than the bourgeois history of pretty paintings over the couch, or stilted portraits in the great halls.

To that end, some angry women artists in the 1980s decided to take matters into their own hands. With a press release listing their disgust at the lack of women artists in galleries and museum institutions, they were determined to take on the Che Guerera-like tactics of underground and anonymous revolt. The Guerillas Girls have called out inequalities in the art world ever since, from representation, to antiquated power structures, to the destruction of the natural environment and gender and race. In a recent 'interview' (in Gorilla masks), with the late-night talk-show host Stephen Colbert, they reported that thirty years after their start as an art group, only five women have had solo shows at the major US museums since 1985. As Gorilla 'Frida' said:

> Every aesthetic decision ... has a value behind it – and if all the decisions are being made by the same people then the art will never look like the whole of our culture. And right now, the art world is run by billionaire art collectors who buy art that appeals to their values ... we say art should look like all the rest of our culture. Unless all the voices of our cultures are in the history of art, it's not really a history of art, it's a history of power'.
>
> (The Guerrilla Girls, 2016)

First World artist Sonny Assu, based in Vancouver, Canada, uses the aesthetic images of the Northwest Coast tribes, (specifically his own Ligwilda'xw Kwakwaka'wakw), to critique the power structures that have tried for generations to destroy his people's nation and culture. Using all the techniques of Western art history (painting, drawing, trompe l'oeil, pop art) as well as iconography of the local indigenous peoples (birds, totems, salmon, bear), Assu has set up a double critique, that works within the aesthetic framework of the 'conqueror'. One insidious form of destroying the human body is through diet; malnutrition plagues both white and people of colour in the US who are at the poverty level (85 per cent of Americans do not get enough nutrients in their diet). Fast foods and sugary soft drinks have contributed to astounding numbers of diabetes and obesity in Native Americans especially. Assu has taken this to heart, creating a huge poster in the style of Coca-Cola, transcribing the local tribal name onto the poster instead of the soft drink (see Plate 27). The history of First World Peoples, who have been bought and sold, is summed up in this cynical pseudo-advert created in 2009 with some humour. Says the artist, 'By melding Kwakwaka'wakwak art, cultural and societal structures with various Western art movements, I am challenging and persisting that consumerism, branding, and technology are new modes of totemic representation'.[2]

Notes

1   In a report released in 2014 by the US based Association of Art Museums, only 25 per cent of major museums are run by women, who earn less than a third of what a male museum director makes. As the budgets get bigger for each museum, the gap grows: institutions with budgets over $15m are run by less than 25 per cent women. Gender ratios on the boards of museums (who hire the directors) remain very unbalanced. At the Metropolitan Museum of Art, for example, the ratio is 23 men to ten women.
2   See: www.sonnyassu.com

References

Anderson, M. L., 2004. *Metrics of Success in Art Museums*. Claremont, CA: Getty Leadership Institute at Claremont Graduate University.

Beech, D., 2015. *Art and Value: Art's Economic Exceptionalism in Classical, Neoclassical, and Marxist Economics*. Boston: Brill Press.

Smee, S., 2014. 'MFA Expands Loans of Well-known Works'. *Boston Globe*, 3 August. Available at: MFA expands loans of well-known works', https://www.bostonglobe.com/arts/2014/08/02/museum-fine-arts-controversial-lending-program-keeps-works-off-walls/9dsHEU1Faxh8AbKbGRN6LL/story.html

Sontag, S., 1967. 'On America'. *The New Yorker*, 34(1), 51.

The Guerrilla Girls, 2016. *Guerrilla Girls Talk The History Of Art vs. The History Of Power* [Interview] (14 January).

Verespe, M., 2011. 'Park Director feared Coke over Canyon Bottle-ban.' *Plastic News*, 12 December.

17 Micro-utopias

Value scales

Art can change values only partially. Extending the idea that art comes out of its status of exceptionality, and contributes to our ordinary lives, we will go to the encounter of how artists grasp specific issues, such as the ecological destruction of the Earth, denouncing the social and geographical injustices and irremediable losses. In this chapter, we will look again to the effects of political and social changes on art-making practices. American critic Clement Greenberg famously said in 1939: 'Today we no longer look toward socialism for a new culture – as inevitably as one will appear, once we do have socialism. Today we look to socialism simply for the preservation of whatever living culture we have right now' (Greenberg, 1939).

One cannot ignore the role of art during totalitarian regimes. In the former Czechoslovakia, for example, during the communist times, art was a micro-way to denounce injustices and to dream of another world with other values. Another way to act is global activism. Justice is thought at a global scale, and art contributes to denounce global degradation in favour of few. Do these multiple mobilisations transform art value? In what way can it change environmental values? The answer is very uncertain. We call 'micro-utopias' the artists' micro actions: how the artistic challenge is an ability to formulate an aesthetic environmental public space that attaches to places and modes of dwelling. Poetic production is so ordinary and seeks to redefine the requirements facing the living conditions. The two justices, trying to better the world and denouncing global failures facing justice claims, have one thing in common though, which is the relationship to the land, as one's own land, the right to live there under conditions set by the people who live there. The re-appropriation of land use is at the heart of these new arguments. In the following paragraphs, we would like to consider the different ways by which environmental art could be envisioned producing micro-utopias.

Parallel structures: art without a market

The first kind of mobilisation has been notably observed in totalitarian times in the former Soviet bloc. There is a stretch of land along the Czech–German border, some hundred kilometres long, that was alive with pristine forests and abundant healthy nature, the largest greenbelt left in Central Europe. The Šumava forest of former Czechoslovakia (today Czech Republic), or Boemenwald in German, is now sick, due to acid rain and air pollution from neighbouring Poland and the former GDR. The unique, comparatively healthy ecology of this greenbelt, ironically until recently,[1] is due to the tragic historical fact named the Iron Curtain. This was the no-man's land of the communist border zone separating Czechoslovakia from the West. For over forty years, few humans walked this space, nor had access to it due to the military presence.

> 'Today there is a No Man's Land ... At some places along the German and Czech border – my God, what a border it is, a piece of wire in the field, a barrier across a road, a rope from tree to tree, a pathetic border ... there is strip of land which belongs to nobody. When the Czech soldiers departed, German recruits brought Jews deported from the occupied area. Then some refugee Jews returned from the remnants of Czechoslovakia, and some because they heard rumors, some from fear for their property, together from fear for their loved ones who had stayed in the confiscated territory. They got through the barbed wire of Czechoslovakia, they did not get through the barbed wire of Germany. And then they could no longer get back across the Czechoslovakian wire. The barbed wire of 1938 is firm and impenetrable.
>
> (Hockaday, 1992, p. 182)

Since the opening of the borders in 1989, and then as the Czech Republic entered the EU in 2004, environmental projects and proposals working with the forest environment and region have been on the rise. Ecological groups and NGO's, such as Zelený Kruh, Pošumaví and the esky Les, for example, have established bike trails and are working towards eco-tourism to keep the forest region from suffering even more at the hands of human contact.[2]

Just as the border zone environment was 'protected' in some of the former Soviet-bloc countries in a historical irony, the cultural life and art-making practices also found a certain flourishing, despite the closed borders and enforced removal from life in the West. Because of the politically imposed sealing off of the culture from a top-heavy central communist government, the intellectuals and artists created was referred to as the 'parallel culture'. These structures worked economically, culturally and socially. The underground was able to bring in bootlegged popular music or machine Xeroxed books hot from the press, blue jeans, the ubiquitous cigarettes, or even people. Both 'protected' by their isolation and suffering under it, Czechs and Slovaks, like many of the rest of the countries behind the Iron Curtain, were able to find some semblance of cultural life in leading a double life: hidden from the secret cameras and microphones, out of the path of the secret police, and undeniably as creative as it was dangerous. Penalties for such disruptions could be as mundane as an interrogation (in itself psychologically torturous) to severe punishments like imprisonment, loss of income and job, or even, physical and bodily violence. The stakes were high, to keep culture alive.

Exposure to Western art trends was not insignificant. Visitors from the West could smuggle in art magazines and books, and while the glossy magazine images in the 1960s, 1970s and 1980s were small and often difficult to translate into two dimensions, the theories and ideas were large and well discussed in a culture that had nothing if not time. So, while Greenberg's pre-Second World War statement seems as dated as much of his formalism, turning to post-communist societies for comparison to the West's post-industrialised culture of the future may not be. The alternative structures created under totalitarianism may offer new paradigms for culture making in the 'post-post-modernist' paradigm of environmental art that is similarly working outside of a traditional art-market economy.

Although Czechoslovakia's history from 1938 to 1989, like much of Eastern Europe, was often inhuman and anti-productive, most of these countries had a long and accumulated 'cultural capital', which allowed them the foundation to continue making art under surveillance. Up until the Second World War, Prague in particular, with its long ties to Italian and particularly Parisian artistic trends, was a leader in modern art. As modernism opened up the parameters of art in the West, we were forced to 'examine ... the relationship between aesthetic experience as met by the specific – not the generalized-individual, and the social and historical contexts in which that experience takes place' (Dewey, 1980). This led to the previously discussed expansion of art into the environment, out of the gallery and off the pedestal. The experience of the audience's involvement with the work of art surpassed the object's historical 'value', and the process of creating a work eventually displaced or at least equalled the final design.

Czech and Slovak so-called 'Land Art' had a very specific history that was related to movements in the West, yet embedded in the fabric of dissident life that was constantly seeking to escape socialist Big Brother surveillance. Art was forced out of the urban environment since it was illegal (which included most work that was not supporting the Party line and was therefore considered 'against the state'.) Impromptu installations in the hops fields or in barnyards across the countryside were by nature subversive, temporal and reflective of the surrounding environment.

Theoretically, the conceptual base for such ephemeral works were indeed already in place, since the 1920s when Structuralism began in Prague (Mukarovksy, Jacobson). Aesthetics had a long and distinguished presence in Prague, where since the mid-nineteenth century the discipline had been taught and developed by followers of J. F. Herbart (1776–1841). He gave a stark objectivist account of knowledge and experience. In aesthetics, he was himself a kind of proto-structuralist, stressing that beauty was not an intrinsic quality of anything in particular but of relations between images (Merquior, 1987, p. 25).

Denunciations from North to South: justice at a global scale

Another way to observe art in the making of another world is to look at environmental artistic practices trying to denounce global injustices. Art is linked with political ecology and that ecology, especially in its most recent developments, is integrally associated with a vision of North–South and South–North. Any political decolonisation goes along with severe critical examination and awareness of the relations of domination and geopolitical, socio-political exploitation, as well as those related to gender, racism, or class struggles. The 'artivism' or artistic activism denouncing these defects in the making of justice, is not new. Hans Haacke's artwork, previously cited for its pioneering place in the domain of ecological art, also are the fruits of an active denunciation of conditions of exploitation of natural resources, which, besides causing environmental disasters, supports the development of social misery.

The artworks testing activism are numerous. Some try reviewing exploitative conditions, highlighting the relationships between large industrial groups and situated environmental and social misery. Environmental policies and sustainable development involve serious distribution conflicts, like those that have been instituted at the first Earth Summit in Rio in 1992 through the Framework Convention on Climate Change and the Convention on Biological Diversity (Martinez-Alier, 1993). The first was driven by the idea of tradable permits CO_2 emission; the second by bio-prospecting contracts that deal with property-rights exchange on genetic resources and knowledge associated with them. However, as Martinez-Alier points out, 'The poor do sell cheap'.

Following the work of R. Guha, with whom he worked, Martinez-Alier has put forward the concept of 'environmentalism of the poor' (Martinez-Alier, 2002), which is a form of environmentalism among 'others', often an 'environmentalism of mere survival' that is designed to defend against oikonomia chrematistics, through access to natural resources, water, land, forests, and pastures. Martinez-Alier demolishes the idea that environmentalism is a movement borne exclusively by the middle classes – that the environment would be a 'luxury good' – an idea that is to be found in the Brundtland report (World Commission on Environment and Development, 1987).

Believe and It Will Happen: this is the ironic formula which opens the site of the Mexican artist Minerva Cuevas (born 1975). Each word appears successively in white on black, the sentence being followed along the same rapid advertising blinking process, through a series of symbols and abbreviations seemingly unrelated (five-pointed star, euro, Star of David, encircled A of anarchism, Latin cross, crescent and star of Islam, Jerusalem Cross, NATO symbol, dollar, communist hammer and sickle, taijitu Taoist). The images embedded in the collective unconscious are indeed often the source of the work of the artist who intends to denounce and raise awareness of an often insidious propaganda. Minerva Cuevas was particularly illustrated in France in 2007 by the installation *Equality* at the Grand Café in Saint-Nazaire, offering the reactivation of a work consisting of 2004 bottles stamped with the logo of the usurped famous Swiss mineral water brand Evian (see Plate 28). The work invites reflection on the sharing of this vital natural resource and the threat of privatisation: simply installed bottles on pallets are distributed free to visitors.

In 2002, the logos of multinational oil companies were affixed on the small cars of the theme park in Mexico City, in order to draw attention to the war they engaged in the global market. For Minerva Cuevas, environmental issues cannot be separated from a reflection on globalised capitalism and worldwide social inequality. One of her first diversions concerns the brand of canned tomatoes Del Monte, for which the reproduction as a mural includes the terms 'criminal' and 'pure murder' to denounce the murder in 1954, sponsored by the CIA, of a leader democratically elected who had the project to nationalise the company acquired by the brand. The institutions are not spared, as the billboard *Nuclear Winter* (2004) reminds us, by the use of the NATO logo, a stylised silhouette of bird skeleton and a hook, that the organisation reserves the right to use nuclear weapons in its statutes and registering the assumption of 'environmental holocaust'. However, the artist, who considers herself an activist, did not stick to a rebellious posture. With Mejor Vida Corporation (Corporation for a Better Life), Cuevas created by the group of artists Irrational.org, proposes to concretely improve the lives of users by distributing free coupons, metro tickets, lottery tickets and fake student cards. The variety of media used (web, video, installation, painting), or by the artistic command or by the gift, but also by simultaneous action in and out of the art world, the work of Minerva Cuevas use of a strategy that by mimicry and movement, allows her to infiltrate her context.

Photographic or videographic documentation are consistent. The documentary essay connects remote places and causalities, for example the efforts of people of the South to withstand the consequences of climate damage mainly caused by the North. Spectacularisation of environmental damage causes some discomfort; these beautiful images depict dramatic events. Yet to be afraid of voyeurism is also to refuse to see. In fact, the show has never been so great, so beautiful, so extreme in its disproportion in its meaning. The sublime is reached. Edward Burtynsky, born in 1955 in Canada and who lives and works in Toronto produces photographs, often taken from above revealing the imprint of human activity on the planet. Gideon Mendel, born in 1959 in Johannesburg, studied psychology and African history, in Cape Town. He began photographing in the 1980s during the final years of apartheid. On the border of action, reportage and art, he implements a committed practice, reporting to international major global scourges such as historical apartheid, the AIDS virus and more recently climate change, filmed at eye level as a modern flood. Since 2007, the artist has travelled the world; for his *World Drowning* project we see men and women facing floods more frequent and violent. For Climate Paris 2015, Gideon Mendel completed his first seven films (*Haiti, Pakistan, India, Thailand, Nigeria, United Kingdom, Germany*). The set was projected in multi-screen, so that the public views a phenomenon that is growing, sparing no region of the globe. A poster campaign could accompany the project to reach the widest audience. Frauke Huber and Uwe H. Martin are documentary photographers and visual storytellers working on long-term, in-depth, documentary photographic projects that combine photography with documentary film, text and sound. Currently they are partnering on a set of multimedia documentaries about the global commons: water, seed, and land. In 2010, they founded Aggreys Dream, a project supporting a school in a slum in Mombasa, Kenya which became the blueprint for the establishing of the Freelens Foundation (Demos, 2013). These testimonies have in common the cross-regards between spectacular images and narrative essays mixing socio-historical intellectual constructs and emotions, through interviews and portraits.

Utopias: for what to hope now?

What do I hope for now? I, and in the name of which utopia? Indeed, one of art's strengths is to reconnect with the utopia as a present laden with alternatives. These can be micro-utopias centred on the transformation of local realities. Although, there is not a single way of understanding utopia.

The first utopias (More, Campanella) do not have the role of building an artificial world, but to offer a critical reflection of society, thanks to the imaginary development of a counter-society through the establishment of an urban space. Utopia can be considered a place of happiness or a space that has no place. Yet the urban utopias have become part of urban planning theories which they precede and are then labelled with an indelible seal. Indeed, as the French theorist of urbanism Francoise Choay says, they have 'two features common to all urban writings: the critical approach of this reality and the spatial modeling of a future reality.' They offer 'on an imaginary level, a priori design tool of the built space, the model' while the treatise on architecture or urban project offers principles and rules (Choay, 1965).

Gilbert Hottois, the Belgium philosopher of technology, has an optimistic view. According to this author, utopia refers to the functioning of modern societies (Hottois, 1986). Technology pushed to excess invades all areas of daily life in our societies. In other words, utopia is the present dream that societies are doing for themselves. But this contemporary utopia is very much linked to the idea of a technological self-sufficiency. Gilbert Hottois' 1980s views seem prescient today. The technique aims to organise independent handling of an amorphous 'energy and material'. In this way, nature is integrated into the making of the habitat systems, urban as well as rural, to the point of its erasure. The reality of our life is near a 'technocosm': Hottois continues that the apartment or house is our basic technocosm. It is increasingly closed and self-sufficient with respect to nature (thanks to the insulation and the thermostatic packaging) at the same time it is more and more intensely connected to other elements of technocosms or integrated into larger networks. This vision of contemporary utopia compromises the comprehension of the living conditions since the habitat is a:

> Hyper-systemic and technical object. Thus, the natural environment, as well as the artificial environment, are real puzzles. The urban environment, among others, is a fact that only experts know how to produce and maintain. One difference between these two environments, however, plays a crucial role on the political level: the natural environment was not produced by man and speaks for itself. But the use of technology over nature made

thereof a technical product which also needs to survive to be maintained and managed by human beings.

(Hottois, 1989; authors' translation)

The relationship with nature requires a high degree of technicality and expertise, therefore denying the symbolic issues. This logic is now pushed to its extreme. Ecology and environment are issues primarily for a technique focused on solving environmental problems. Highlighting issues and setting nature to work (calculation of services provided by nature, for example, phyto-purification) show an under-representation of how the problems are ordinarily formulated at the expense of technical solutions. This leads to forgetting the human relationship that passes through stories, narratives, always at work. The opposition between the ways engineers problematise and artists dramatise is easy but effective. The engineer and political actors seek solutions to problems while the artist seeks a way to deploy an emotional story. You would think that for the former, any solution is a solution to a problem, that is to say the resolution of a coherent set of proposals in one or more proposition. This pattern of scientific problematisation is perhaps not applicable to the extreme complexity and singularity of malfunctions and ecological issues. How to represent these environmental changes? While it is true that in the case of a techno-nature, a symbolic relationship does not have an operative character, the operational nature of the technical relationship is partial because each individual being expert holds only a part. Thus, utopia is also a counter-utopia, a black dream within reach of a technological civilization.

This criticism of the modern world and its technique is also to be found in the International Situationist. However, these authors did not mind using the word to describe their utopian productions. In the 'planning' chapter of his book *The Society of the Spectacle* (Debord, 1970), Debord describes how the procedure of planning becomes the production of spectacular places which oppose the idea of daily life in favour of control and an ever-greater mastery of the environment: 'Thesis 169: urbanism is this taking possession of the natural and human environment by capitalism which, while developing logically into absolute domination, can and should now redo the entire space as its own decor' (Debord, 1970). In contrast, Unitary Urbanism brings together all members of the International Situationist around the city utopias that would change lives. The prototype of this new utopian city that struggles against functionalism is called the New Babylon, designed by the artist Constant. The 'Situationists' think of the urban masterwork as a lifestyle in spaces that are irreducible to spectacle. This group explores a lived utopia, as an experiment, as opposed to the alienated and alienating structures considered typical of modernity.

Micro-utopias

Ecological artists not only imagine utopias on the model of a successful whole in another place, even imaginary, like Thomas More's Utopia. Utopias are experienced as life situations, new ways to experience and live the city. The assumption is that the passage of an aesthetic mode of intervention, based on the artistic style to a pragmatic mode of intervention, which is based on a presumed need for action, plays a major role in the fabric of daily life. This change involves the role of actors of aesthetics in collective mobilisations (artists, architects, landscape architects) that redefine their practices and know-how based on an understanding of urban ecology and the need to give it a place in public life.

Thus, urban planning becomes an evolutionary/revolutionary challenge. Local spaces' ownership then passes through the takeover of territories. If AVL, first of our following examples, criticise ecology as setting up a totalitarian model of urban space, Natalie Jeremijenko and Valentina Karga propose, even within urban areas of life, new ways of living in cities. This brief review provides an understanding of the importance of artists in both developing utopian models and critic counter-models. Utopia is dealing with the social, geographical, and political to explore its potential. Utopia is secured towards a critical approach that reaffirms the possible from the real-life situations. It is a 'real and active' utopia, which allows hope from the reality (Bloch, 1995). The experimental utopia, according to H. Lefebvre, returns to the exploration of a possible human, using the imagination, in the context of a critical stance firmly rooted in reality (Lefebvre, 1992). The experimental utopia differs from prospective thoughts, extending present trends often unimaginative of a change in society, and which preside in the post-Second World War in the development of urban plans. It is also from the 'abstract' experimental utopia in a fictional space time which imagines a possible world detached from real conditions.

AVL, created in 1995 by Joep van Lieshout (Netherlands), is working on a business model. Its team includes artists, architects, designers and workers, but also a librarian, a chief financial officer and trainees, making it especially suitable for realising the more fanciful proposals. Since its founding, AVL proposes drawings and sculptures but also furniture, housing equipment, mobile homes and cities which can operate. However, the solutions appear quickly ironic or even disturbing. The reception building (*Welcoming Center*, 2007) sorts out the prospective visitors: the old, the sick, the crippled and the 'bad taste people' are immediately 'recycled' for biogas, the healthy people, (but unintelligent) being transferred to the meat factory. The healthiest young people can participate in the programme of organ transplantation, the most intelligent being oriented to the 'call center'. Could ecology be considered as a totalitarian tale of science fiction? This seems to be the question raised by the design and the architecture projects of the Atelier van Lieshout where the theme is fleshed out. This is the case of the urban structures proposals in closed circuit such as *Slave City* (2005-) or *The Technocrat* (2003). Taking at face value the issue of overcrowding, the first is described as 'a sinister dystopia project, very rational, efficient and profitable.' Designed for 200,000 inhabitants, it intends to manage the vital factors but also social, food, energy and the economy, all the way to ethics, morality and aesthetics. The goal is to achieve a model of Green City 'at zero energy' where everything is recycled and does not waste the world's resources. The other *Slave*

City buildings are dominated by two universities for male slaves and female slaves, strictly regulated in increments of seven hours between studies, work and rest, plus three hours to eat, wash and relax. To this end, *Slave City* provides brothels for women and men, in which are offered several types of pleasures. Their satisfaction, thus, involves alienation as counterparty: this could be the motto of the ecological city of *Slave City*.

The Technocrat (2003) project also insists on the issue of recycling, rendered absurd by its reduction to body waste. 'In this system, the human citizen is the biological cog that produces enough raw material to produce biogas not only used to cook food, but to get alcohol capable of ensuring the proper functioning of people.' The Total Faecal Solution provides video surveillance controlling the use of separate toilets for faeces or urine for recycling. In doing so, AVL says 'the ecology friendly borders on voyeurism.' The Alcoholator in return allows the production of 1800 liters of alcohol at 40 degrees distributed three times a day to residents for their welfare.

These ecological city projects could simply be humorous denunciation if they were not from a group that was also shown successfully in the field of public and private commissions, including the production of objects on the boundaries of art and utility for hotels, offices and industries. In 2001, the establishment of AVL in the port city of Rotterdam points to its success. A proclaimed 'free state' with its own constitution, flag and currency, AVL-Ville is already the laboratory of an ecological self-sufficient life.

Besides the creative workshop, the community produces its food there, its medication, its alcohol, its purified water and electricity. Closed after eight months as a result of conflict with the authorities, including the confiscation of defence weapons. AVL-Ville is now franchised and a unit has been erected in Belgium.

Cities and AVL objects evoke a search of a refuge that is not without resonance with the climate of fear created in Western societies. The furniture and housing structures often resemble cells enveloping shapes and materials like sheepskin, leather and velvet, but they also avoid the decorative drawing on industrial forms. Between libertarian humour and reactivation of the ideal of reconciliation of art and life, recurring themes from romanticism to the avant-garde, AVL projects and achievements are as much fun as they do disturb, partly because they question the move between ecological ideology and technical solutions.

Another way to approach these issues is highlighted by Natalie Jeremijenko (born 1966), pioneer artist at the art-technology–environment intersection (COAL Prize, 2015). She is the Director of the Environmental Health Clinic at New York University, a laboratory that wants to show that external ecosystemic factors are more important than genetic biology in environmental design. Students/residents take an appointment at the clinic, not to discuss their own health but that of their environment. It is not to be prescribed medication, but actions to accomplish. Natalie Jeremijenko somehow renews the model of design and points toward a craft as a locally embedded engagement. Utopia is more modest, and perhaps lighter. Criticism is less noticeable while the idea of game is very present. The artist says:

It's a particularly urban design challenge to transform our relationship with the ecosystem to become a form of cultivation rather than damage with gold mining … Through thesis lifestyle experiments – which must be playful, enjoyable, interesting, compelling, wondrous, otherwise people are not going to do them – people are getting a real empirical sense of how we might improve things.[3]

For the artist, it is no longer possible to rely on existing political systems. The ecological fabric of the everyday life requires engaging collectively and individually. So creativity, invention and imagination are essential. Like a traditional zoo, OOZ is a series of sites where animals and humans interact, except that these sites do not have cages and the animals remain there by choice. The human–animal interactions on a website for OOZ differ substantially from that of a zoo: they are based on the principle of reciprocity, that is to say, any action may direct them to an animal, the animal can direct it to you, and information based on observations and collective interpretations can be exchanged. Jeremijenko has implemented OOZ in the Netherlands and in the United States (Chicago). Among the many attractions of OOZ, there are three flagship products: Moth Cinema, a night celebrating the nocturnal pollinators facility; the Butterfly Bridges, gateways connecting to facilitate gene flow in populations of butterflies; and the Resilience Tower, a seven-storey resource for birds, insects and other flying urban bodies, which aids in the creation of plant associations and nesting sites. The participatory project Butterfly Bridge illustrates this model of micro-utopia. This intervention of three months in Washington, DC, has helped butterflies to navigate in the city including planting vegetation on specific routes; the idea was to build an infrastructure for this 'small staff'. This work is part of an 'activist' movement of design, which aims to reconfigure the design of objects or common spaces to intervene in the production of ecology. The artist's position is pragmatic. Whether mussels, butterflies, flowers or other living things, the objective is to improve reasonably the conditions of local life, and overall using the intelligence of nature, mutualism being present everywhere. The artist intervenes without claiming political position: the ecological-minded technology is at the heart of these changes. This intervention model is now spreading to other cities.

Valentina Karga (COAL Prize, 2015), born in Greece, is an artist and architect based in Berlin. Through collaborative actions, her work addresses issues such as autonomy, education, sustainability, communication, the DIY, rural practices in urban space, the commons and the role of engagement and participation in the contemporary society and the arts. She is the founder of the Summer School for Applied Autonomy in Berlin, a research initiative interested in capturing the technical know-how but also the social, political and affective aspects involved in autonomous living. The summer school was the aftermath of Valentina's interdisciplinary seminar at the Universität der Künste Berlin (UdK) and was built in collaboration with the students. Its functioning is largely self-sufficient, tending towards environmental sustainability, and it is based on

Figure 17.1 Valentina Karga, *The Institute of Placemaking, Summer School of Applied Autonomy*

feedback loop circuits where its different outputs (from garbage to words) become inputs that re-feed the social and material body of the garden. Exploration of thematic fields such as self-sufficiency, open source knowledge, collaboration, self-reflection, urban development and exchange and gift economy is at the very base of the curriculum. The school welcomes everyone, but its capacity is small; it can support only two residents per rotation. Residents must engage for a stay of one or two weeks. After the end of each rotation and the beginning of the other, the two groups overlap for one day, so that the first group transfers their knowledge to the next one. The days are structured via tasks and lessons, while each person is free to propose his own topic of research. The project was born in an artistic–academic context and completed the circle by becoming a learning site in its own right and aesthetics; a school promoting alternative pedagogies, learning-through-experience and self-reflection, very much linked to the topics of the commons, environment and collaboration.

Responses to the ecological crisis

What do we learn from these artistic experiments? Environmental aesthetics produced a new way of stating the ecological drama. We must assume an overflow of the human drama on the technical approach to a situation. Where it is believed that the issue of a dam is technical and concerns a confined natural area, it turns out that we are faced with a complex ecological and human entanglement. Or art, called to magnify complex situations, to offer new frameworks of reading emerging representations, highlights the sensitive values involved in the environmental issues regarding nature. The language itself, as Joseph Beuys said, is involved in the construction of ecological facts (Beuys, 1988, pp. 19–43). Thus, work on language, poetic work, not just to denounce tucking the ecological literature in the era of suspicion, is at the heart of the ecopoetics. For Jonathan Bate (Bate, 2000) who evokes the literary process of creating an ecological language that would complement (or even challenge) the scientific or policy approaches, as for many other ecocritics, it comes to lending a human language to natural processes and therefore to strive to represent them. Utopia rooted in the present, concrete and experimental, retrieves the *oikos* ways. Indeed, art as an activity specialised in the production of new systems of representation, playing of fabric modes and formal vocabularies, helps to anchor anew a reconnection to inhabit. This requires some new narratives produced by the encounter with works of art.

According to the philosopher Henri Lefebvre, the appropriated space-time is an œuvre, and art is a form of appropriation of nature, of social relations, of the relationship to one's own body. Therefore, producing space is not to build monuments, or houses and technical infrastructure. It is to produce space-time, combined with sensible phenomena, projects and projections, symbols and utopias. A critical theory must highlight the process of space production, which is unintentional, and should be the project of a collective action. In short, the imagination is the creative ability of human beings to the extent that the living space is the imagined space. The aesthetic experience involves the senses and emotions, projections in utopias, narratives, images. The concept of 'dwelling' captures this relationship of humans to the appropriated space. This is the insertion of the human being into a world that challenges the production of an appropriated space. This implies to consider space and time together. This inseparability of space and time is difficult to consider in modern philosophy that seeks to distinguish them, since Kant. The space would be the order of the reversible and distinction, so that time would be the order of the irreversible and continuity. The idea of production of space challenges this idea, since the space has also a dimension of permanence and irreversibility, which the environmental issues remind us of today. The ambition of an environmental aesthetics would be not to describe the aesthetics of the environment, but to know the rules of its production and reproduction.

Notes

1   In the mid 1990s, the nation had the world's highest industrial carbon dioxide emissions, totaling 135.6 million metric tons per year, a per capita level of 13.04 metric tons. Like the Slovak Republic, the Czech Republic has had its air contaminated by sulfur dioxide emissions resulting largely from the use of lignite as an energy source in the former Czechoslovakia, which had the highest level of sulfur dioxide emissions in Europe, and instituted a programme to reduce pollution in the late 1980s. Western nations have offered $1 billion to spur environmental reforms, but the pressure to

continue economic growth has postponed the push for environmental action. See: www.nationsencyclopedia.com/Europe/Czech-Republic-ENVIRONMENT.html# ixzz3hqoih8yT

2 In the mid 1990s, an international group of artists were invited by the Goethe Institute in cooperation with Siemens Company, to install outdoor artworks in the northern part of the Czech lands. The Zeleny Kruh group renovated decades-old bike trails from the Austrian border up through Moravia, and eventually into SW Bohemia.

3 Interview with Patrick Degeorges on the portal of environmental humanities: http://humanitesenvironnementales.fr/

References

Bate, J., 2000. *The Song of the Earth*. Cambridge, MA: Harvard University Press.

Beuys, J., 1988. *Par la Présente, Je n'Appartiens plus à l'Art*. Paris: L'Arche.

Bloch, E., 1995. *The Principle of Hope*. Cambridge, MA: MIT Press.

Choay, F., 1965. *L'Urbanisme, Utopies et Réalités, une Anthologie*. Paris: Seuil.

Debord, G., 1970. *The Society of the Spectacle*. Detroit: Black and Red.

Demos, T. J., 2013. 'Contemporary Art and the Politics of Ecology.' *Third Text*, 27(1), 1–9.

Dewey, J., 1980. *Art as Experience*. New York: Perigee Books.

Greenberg, C., 1989. *Art and Culture, Critical Essays*. Boston: Beacon Press.

Hockaday, M., 1992. *Kafka, Love, and Courage, the Life of Milena Jesenská*. New York: Oxford University Press.

Hottois, G., 1989. 'Le Technocosme urbain. La ville comme theme de philosophie de la technique, texte roneotype, conference donnee dans le cadre de la 17ieme Ecole urbaine de l'ARAU'. In P. Ansay and R. Schoonbrodt, eds. *Penser la ville, Choix de Textes Philosophiques*. Bruxelles: AAM.

Lefebvre, H., 1992. *The Production of Space*. London: Wiley-Blackwell.

Martinez-Alier, J., 1993. *Ecological Economics: Energy, Environment and Society*. London: Blackwell Publishers.

Martinez-Alier, J., 2002. *The Environmentalism of the Poor: a Study of Ecological Conflicts and Valuation*. Cheltenham: Edward Elgar.

Merquior, J., 1987. *From Prague to Paris*. London: Verso Books.

World Commission on Environment and Development. 1987. *Our Common Future*. Oxford: Oxford University Press.

Conclusion

Art's sustaining blossom

Environmental art is at a turning point in its history and evolution, which reflects the cataclysmic climatic and cultural changes of our times. This art is no longer an isolated practice, yet it is still an unorthodox field with respect to all art practices. It is no longer the pioneering practices as in 1960s and 1970s. These practices however, which we have designated as environmental art practices, participate more fundamentally in a deeper transformation of our relationships to nature and the environment.

We are fully aware, nonetheless, of the risk of greenwashing practices; it is not the time, in these concluding remarks, to give examples of such practices: that environmentally focused works are not necessarily by definition, either art or creating social change. Sometimes, environmentally focused artworks are done in response to calls for proposals by political institutions or the corporate world.

There is a second point that is important to establish. Social representations and practices are evolving (albeit slowly), taking into account environmental issues. The concerns generated by the many environmental problems such as climate change, air pollution, biodiversity loss, etc., force us to reinvent our relationship to the environment by taking into account the many injunctions and transformations affecting housing, transportation or energy consumption.

These social changes, working deep in our cultural referents, lack guidance and assurance in the choices made. The Western standards and lifestyles must be completely disowned if a new relationship to the environment is to be invented. Therefore, this invention that requires trust in one's aesthetic and sensitive judgment, to experience anew what it means to build a world, specifically requires reliance on a conceptual framework that defies the norms and customs, to try to invent modes of intervention, sculptural forms involving experimentation. The vanguards in terms of passive housing, or permaculture or environmental community at different scales and in a variety of cultures draw their resources in experimentation, which is one of the guides that includes the development of an aesthetic mode of life.

Many of the artists discussed in this book claim an expressive autonomy, maintaining independence from traditional art structures, and re-inventing how they engage, become involved and change the social systems around them. It can be a spontaneous involvement or a highly developed plan calling on government bodies and civil society members for expertise and cooperation. Their works can be a call to an artist proposal or a response to a totalitarian regime. But more broadly, aesthetic intervention can be described as a way to react to norms, customs, habits, and even extremely restrictive policy frameworks. In this context, the artists involved in the environmental field are developing proposals, which are often thought of as being alternatives to problematic environmental situations.

Rather than simply responding to a series of environmental problems, artists are trying to invent a collaborative and interdisciplinary approach in terms, not only of works of art but also of life forms that call for unprecedented aesthetic modalities and new representations.

Response to the future

Further remarks should be noted. We tried to grasp how environmental art should be contextualised. At the same time, we are fully aware of a progressive homogenisation of the formal and contextual repertoires of artworks. Even though, to intervene in Africa has nothing to do with an eco-intervention in the Arctic, it seems to a certain extent, that a globalised repertoire is indeed formulating in our time.

Can we then respond to what we therefore wanted to express in the title chosen for this book: *Form, Art and Environment: Engaging in Sustainability?* The form is a concept that provides an operative way to go beyond the work of art, while remaining attentive to the issue of sensitivities and emotions. In addition, any reflection on form, more specifically, environmental structures, harkens back to a collective understanding of the forms created and the judgements made on them. The highlighting of these forms shows their collective and common character. The 'common' form emerges from the fact that we have in common environmental forms to which art contributes, and the repertoires and settings necessary for their creation. Similarly, the capacity of judging proceeds from a culture. Aesthetic competence refers to the idea that there can be no question of referring the judgement of taste beyond the democratic sphere, on behalf of the extreme singularity of issued judgements. Form is in fact created by context, surroundings, light and shadow.

To enrich the reflection, we should also reconsider the possible parallels between the history of forms in art history and a history of ecosystems. In the story of progress, the succession of aesthetic styles has been little taken into account, even by the art historians.

Ecological models analyse the evolution of socio-natural systems trying to determine the factors that led to changing phases (development, stabilisation, degradation, renewal) and modelling possible development scenarios. However, the difficulty of defining the phase plan is rooted in the practical impossibility of knowing all the variables that are part of the analysed system.

Like the description of these ecological cycles, a formal approach linking environmental and art history could be imagined. The forms are organised spatially and temporally. It is indeed the structuring of discrete times playing on the configuration of the beings that are part of the arrangements.

The description of the formal qualities of ecological cycles, but also the depiction of ecological relationships produced by the implementation of these forms in history, gives full value to the relationship between aesthetics and ecology. The organisation of sensitive environments (not just the description of their features) would allow theorizing about environmental forms. The movement uses an internal 'r/evolutivity', an incessant 'differing', which combines gradually. The form is the interface, which is the movement; their dynamic meaning mixes attraction, extraction and contraction.

In this very particular context, the two authors of the book who make environmental aesthetics tools and theoretical terms for their investigation, not only want to be able to mobilise in favour of the environment, but want also to reflect on the meaning of their action, claiming both the pragmatic and the theoretical framework. This commitment also means to test the knowledge of their respective ability to renew the forms of the environment in collective action. This book is therefore an active mode of intervention by showing alternatives. It is to renew the forms of repertoires, action contexts, enunciation modes thereof. How can one think otherwise, to enrich the way we represent the environment in which we operate and on its terms of production? These analyses must be consistent with larger investigations, and make more general tools and procedures for testing the waters.

At this point in the conclusion, it remains open to debate what form a political community would take that would involve environmental forms in its heart, that would involve as well ethical changes, and therefore rules of behaviour towards the community. Environmental forms, those that allow us to see how we will live, or the context in which we want our lives to incarnate, can be the subject of collective discussion. It is not so much to return to the expression of a political community without intermediaries and which satisfy the expression of passions and feelings and sensations, but a rise of the environment perceived as both a social and natural resource anchored in a territorialised relationship between global and local as well as a relationship between material and virtual. The entry into environmental policy consists not only in the implementation of public policies on issues defined by a set of actors or experts, but also of the expression of a way of living in the environment both practical and symbolic that do not meet contemporary living conditions. This is important in facing the challenges ahead, but also in a crisis of political regimes and withdrawal of territorialised communities. Aesthetics is part of political choice. This work is not the subject of the book, but indicates the direction of future work.

A second theme is a reflection on ethics, which is not an abstract environmental aesthetics devoid of a relationship to proximity, but rather an environmental ethic that grows *in relation* to proximity. In the continuity of the relationship of art and ethics, in some way, the aesthetic regime analysed by Jacques Rancière would follow a pragmatic regime or to be solidaristic, which would be guided by an ethics agreement involving all the concrete aesthetic attachments.

What then is the revival in the arts? Is it the extension of the principles of a democratic engagement with all of the social actors participating equally? Have the artist and audience today reached an historical moment of balanced dialogue, where each action and reaction are fundamentally dependent upon one another? Many of the works and projects described in this book have indeed emphasised this, in both rural and urban environments. Community and consensus building have become the new norm in artworks that seek to engage a more ambitious and broader public than traditional museums and galleries could support. And in fact, this trend is re-invigorating the arts economically, as structures for creating are superimposed and extended way beyond studio work and the making of things into the fabric of the society at large. Works that are processes of action, often extending over several years or lifetimes, are not only recorded documents of civil involvement and change, but form relationships amongst people across wider panoramas of the community than ever before. Artists working in these environments, be they local or global, are often seeking to create changes in the traditional discourses of class, privilege, power, or possession, as the earth's future is now being debated across all continents and countries. The old colonial paradigm of ownership is confronted with a newer revival of an ancient one: that of stewardship.

An aesthetic that is grounded in craft, the craft of making, is not at odds with the process orientation of many environmental artists. Creativity, the fountainhead of all works of art, is as much endangered as the planet. What the new aesthetic of environmentally based art is bringing, including what we might describe as 'sustainable creativity', is an aesthetic that endures.

The ecological transformation (or metamorphosis)

In the Introduction, we talked of metamorphosis. Each culture deals with metamorphosis specifically, as a transformation between the ages, the passage from life to death, the recycling of objects and events. Finally, we would like to show that the artist contributes to environmental transformations through the fabric of environmental forms, between nature and culture. By 'environmental forms', we mean forms relating to the production of ordinary environments or to environmental issues. Although the term 'form' is commonly used and scientifically discussed, when seen in a contemporary perspective taking into account the environment, it could widen the interdisciplinary debate and outweigh the *aporia* created by underestimating the potentialities of the humanities and social sciences concerning environmental questions. Earth and life sciences could benefit from the manifold considerations of biological and physico-chemical forms. Using environmental forms (such as the Earth, nature writing, the landscape, the urban garden, etc.), our aim is also to propose knowledge modes and modes of assessment and action that are different from those usually mobilised by public environmental action. It involves bringing together cultural and environmental approaches, while respecting the diversities contained within each of them.

In the field of forms, art is often mentioned: however, we consider the aesthetic experience in order to enrol in the study of life, not to hide it in books or art museums. The exploration undertaken in this book concerns the production of everyday-life environments through their artistic forms. Thus we go against a reductionist approach, as morphological theories view the forms at the organisation level where they occur. To adopt a morphological approach amounts to embracing a qualitative theory, which opposes the techno-scientific approaches more focused on solving problems than on understanding phenomena. To develop a morphological approach is to hope for a renewed environmental geography that illuminates the sensitive dimensions; the essence of geography is defined by the interaction between naturalness and spatiality that comes in different processes and modalities of humanisation. In terms of spatiality, the Anthropocene involves considering both the horizontality, the verticality, and to question this process of humanisation by examining the created environments. This creative geography gives power to the idea of formatting, as a result of art, but also of the invention of the ordinary. Human activities can only be exercised in materialising operations, that is to say, movements to culminate in works; but it is only by being so that the work becomes in its unique reality, now detached from its author and living its own life, contained in the indivisible unity of consistency, open to the recognition of its value and able to demand and obtain.

Therefore, the environmental process is placed at the centre of attention, erasing the separation between human beings and other living beings, and the nature/culture divide. The formatting activity is systemic, connects the parts to the whole. Thus, the environmental process involves different kinds of aesthetic investment, and a focus on production activities that involve both aesthetics and ethics.

The environmental transformation involves changes in individuals, institutions and cultures through fundamental alterations to existing feedbacks and power relations and in thinking, values, consciousness and the questioning of key assumptions that underpin contemporary societies and economic systems. Here a distinction between 'ecological transition', a terminology that is often used to qualify public policies, and social/environmental transformations is important. The former tends towards technological advances that are easily dominated by existing discourses and which often favour existing concentrations of privilege and power. The latter implies greater emphasis on experimental innovations, new ways of thinking, challenging the existing socio-political structures. The question therefore is not just reducing the impacts of the symptoms of particular patterns in the way things are done in that society, but a political imagination of what could be done to address the contemporary challenges. It is important to stress this distinction and to clarify the structural aspects of the time perspective specific to a transformative approach as well as its political consequences.

Deliberate practices of transformation are really political actions when they aim to take a political stance, to bring back into the realm of a possible decision the dimensions of our existence that 'transitional' policies have systematically pre-empted. We should insist on this democratic quality of transformation. Because, if our critical moment occurs only once, if there will be no repetition that would allow a change in government to reverse the mistakes of the past, if political defeat is not a temporary and remediable setback, then the political stakes of the 'now' are so high that implications for a democratic system become disturbing; extremist authoritarian politics are usually called upon in such situations of 'emergency'. We need to make an explicit link between transformation and democratic (pacific) emancipation.

The challenge to face is to recognise what is common. Our human condition is associated with the creation of environmental forms. Some forms, related to the way we recognise ourselves and make a world that we share, are also common forms: landscapes, stories and atmospheres. Today however, these forms, linked with the discriminated or rejected sensitivity in the direction of aesthetics and consumerism, are ignored in favour of a logic of a geo-engineer. So is a design in terms of operating systems, with the aim of a better regulation, as well as a managerial definition of a relationship with the environment, and inhabited worlds. In the area of environmental aesthetics, the tragedy of the commons involves a specific resource: the 'capability' – the capacity – born of a link to environmental opportunities in a very broad sense, to shape environments. This tragedy would result in environmentally impoverished communities, according to Garrett Hardin (1968). Without appearing naive with respect to a generalised creativity, it is quite remarkable that the modern age has contributed to the specialisation of knowledge, and privatisation appraisals. Art forms have become specialised forms of aesthetic experience, prey to art historians and curators in the context of state or private institutions. Folk arts found themselves disqualified in this regard. The specialisation of knowledge, particularly of aesthetic experience, produced dimensional agents (Marcuse, 2002), skilled workers or producers and consumers. This is to reflect on the links between autonomy and consciousness of particular ecological interdependencies.

Far from recognising the knowledge produced in specialised force (and thus the Fordist scheme of predominant specialisation of tasks, looking for economies of scale and equipment investment), a common aesthetic connects with repertoires and contexts. From there expressive patterns, bio-semiotics are generated. The repertoires involve a number of expressive possibilities in a given situation. We draw in repertoires that provide a basis for feeling and creating. The contextual determinations and the skills needed to maintain these repertoires as they were alive, as languages of generative model, are of utmost importance. Perhaps the most traditional and established communities will focus on the integrity of the repertoire level, while the most fragile collective will promote the role of the contextual level in the optics of renewing the formal commons. All aesthetic processes operate through specific forms and skills, which work with existing language patterns. These language patterns, these narrative forms and narrative modes of construction are common. In Western societies, these commons were privatised, socialised, marking the membership of social groups that differ politically. The twentieth-century avant-garde movements exceeded the boundaries of aesthetic experience, but also created new forms of authentication. From there, we must not forget that forms combine ecological and aesthetical expressivities in three main areas:

1   The relationship of individuals in-and-with their environment. It still needs to be explored how the different elements of intra-agentivity give life to forms for individuals. For example, we grow up knowing the grass is dirty or clean and act accordingly.
2   The relationship of different collectives in-and-with the environment.
3   The way landscapes, narrative processes combine natural and cultural diversity, playing a role in the community, begetting process, must be examined from many perspectives.

Reflection on intra-agentivity can be used to describe an environmental mode of production. It is well to stage and reflect intra-agentive relations, without losing sight of what we produce and also what we are and want to be. Therefore, to highlight a new kind of common means, at all levels, aesthetic, ethical, economic, to think about human history in its formal dimensions, coupling and support. For example, a human being needs air, but also bacteria that are in the body. A human being needs a soil or some space to live in. This formal need refers to the kind of fair forms that would be needed, from a socio-ecological point of view. Thus contemporary aesthetics refers to both environmental and individual normative ethical issues.

Art and community

Art can be part of this ecological transformation. We cannot just teach art, it is not enough anymore. There are tools, forms, histories to be learned, but without the overall ability of the individual to create within a community, the creations are not sustainable. For it is in the local that we discover the universal, and the intricacies and subtle patterns of each location, every site, each tree. Like the bees and the ants, change is then multiplied through the chain reaction of united organisms making something as a whole. It is not that artists are returning to a romanticised craft of native cultures, but that they are engaging traditional practices that still remember how to make, build and exist beside nature. The weaving of bamboo poles to create a sturdy roof, or the introduction of charcoal on tilled soil to reinvigorate its mineral content, or the distribution of objects underwater that will create new reefs, are all ancient practices reformulated into a frame that inspire them into an aesthetic life for today's world. Environmental art is therefore directly related to local, indigenous production histories, embedded in a sustainable culture.

We are at a point in human civilization where the individual self-portrait (today's selfies, the Renaissance's Dürer portrait), and the decadence it represents, could be a dead trope. Artists' collaboratives, neighbourhood actions, anonymous graffiti (Banksy, et al.), social works that reach broad-based audiences that cross all economic groups, are the harbingers of a sustainable creativity that can propel our species to think and live creatively in an environment that we protect and steward for the future. In this way, the current artistic modes examined in this book are not ascribing to the 'resilience' theory of survival. They are not climbing the highest mountain to eat the last fruit from the tallest tree as the waters rise around us. Indeed, the art of our times that imbues meaning and value to the earth, continues to challenge and struggle with uncertainty, re-inventing definitions of existence in collaboration with nature, grounded in suspended sustainability.

References

Hardin, G., 1968. 'Tragedy of the Commons'. *Science*, 162(3859), 1243–1248.

Marcuse, H., 2002. *One-Dimensional Man: Studies in the Ideology of Advanced Industrial Society*, 2nd edn. New York: Routledge Classics.

Bibliography

Abbing, H., 2002. *Why are Artists Poor? The Exceptional Economy of the Arts*. Amsterdam: Amsterdam University Press.

Adorno, T., 2013. *Aesthetic Theory*. London: Berg.

Agamben, G., Badiou, A., Bensaïd, D., Brown, W., Nancy, J.-L., Rancière, J., Ross, K., Zizek S., 2012. *Democracy in What State?* New York: Columbia University Press.

Alloway, L., 1968. 'Interfaces and Options: Participatory Art in Milwaukee and Chicago'. *Arts Magazine*, 43(1), 25–29.

Anderson, M. L., 2004. *Metrics of Success in Art Museums*. Claremont, CA: Getty Leadership Institute at Claremont Graduate University.

Andrews, M., ed., 2006. *LAND, ART: A Cultural Ecology Handbook*. London: The Royal Society for the Encouragement of Arts, Manufactures and Commerce.

Anon., 2012. 'Chennai Professor R Vasudevan Invents Plastic Monoblock Technology'. *The Economic Times*, 3 January.

Anon., 2014. '"Robert Smithson's New Jersey" at the Montclair Museum'. *The New Yorker*, 7 March.

Arendt, H., 1978. *The Life of the Mind*. New York: Harcourt.

Arendt, H., 1991. *Juger: Sur la philosophie politique de Kant, suivi de Deux essais interprétatifs par Ronald Beiner et Myriam Renault d'Allonnes*. Paris: Seuil, Points Essais.

Arendt, H., 1998. *The Human Condition*, 2nd edn. Chicago: The University of Chicago Press.

Austen, B., 2013. 'Chicago's Opportunity Artist'. *The New York Times*, 20 December.

Baker, K., 2005. 'Talking with Robert Smithson'. In K. Kelly and L. Cooke, eds. *Robert Smithson: Spiral Jetty*. Berkeley: University of California Pres.

Barad, K. M., 2007. *Meeting the Universe Halfway: Quantum Physics and the Entanglement of Matter and Meaning*. Durham, NC: Duke University Press.

Barreras del Rio, P. and Perreault, J., 1988. *Ana Mendieta: A Retrospective*. New York: The New Museum of Contemporary Art.

Bate, J., 2000. *The Song of the Earth*. Cambridge, MA: Harvard University Press.

Baumgarten, A. G., 1750. *Aesthetica*. Frankfurt (Oder): I. C. Kleyb.

Becker, H., 1982. *Art Worlds: 25th Anniversary Edition*. Berkeley: University of California Press.

Beech, D., 2015. *Art and Value: Art's Economic Exceptionalism in Classical, Neoclassical, and Marxist Economics*. Boston: Brill Press.

Berger, J., 1972. *Ways of Seeing*. London: Penguin.

Berleant, A., 1991. *Art and Engagement*. Philadelphia: Temple University Press.

Berleant, A., 1992. *The Aesthetics of Environment*. Philadelphia: Temple University Press.

Berleant, A., 2010. *Sensibility and Sense: The Aesthetic Transformation of the Human World*. Exeter: Imprint Academic.

Berleant, A., 2012. 'Beauty and the Way of Modern Life'. In *Aesthetics Beyond the Arts: New and Recent Essays*. Aldershot: Ashgate Publishing.

Beuys, J., 1988. *Par la Présente, je n'appartiens plus à l'art*. Paris: L'Arche.

Blanc, N., 2012. 'From Environmental Aesthetics to Narratives of Change'. *Contemporary Aesthetics*, 12. Available at: www.contempaestetics.org/newvolume/pages/journal.php

Blanc, N., 2016. *Les formes de l'environnement. Manifeste pour une esthétique politique*. Lausanne: Métis Presses.

Blanc, N. and Emelianoff, C., 2008. *L'investissement habitant des lieux et milieux de vie: une condition du renouvellement urbain? Etude européenne et prospective (France, Pays-Bas, Allemagne, Russie)*. Paris: PUCA, Université du Maine.

Blanc, N. and Lolive, J., 2007. *Cosmopolitiques 15: Esthétique et espace public*. Rennes: éditions Apogée/Cosmopolitiques.

Blanc, N. and Ramos, J., 2010. *Ecoplasties: Art et Environnement*. Paris: Manuella.

Bloch, E., 1995. *The Principle of Hope*. Cambridge, MA: MIT Press.

Boetzkes, A., 2010. *The Ethics of Earth Art*. Minneapolis: University of Minnesota Press.

Bohumil, H., 1990. *Too Loud a Solitude*. San Diego: Harcourt Brace.

Boltanski, L. and Chiapello, E., 2006. *The New Spirit of Capitalism*. London: Verso.

Bonacossa, I. and Latitudes, eds., 2008. *Greenwashing Environment: Perils, Promises and Perplexities*. Turin: The Bookmakers.

Bourdieu, P., 1984. *Distinction: A Social Critique of the Judgement of Taste*. London: Routledge and Kegan Paul.

Bourdieu, P., 1992. *Les Règles de l'art: Genèse et structure du champ littéraire*. Paris: Seuil.

Bourdieu, P., 1993. *The Field of Cultural Production*. New York: Columbia University Press.

Bourriaud, N., 1998. *L'Esthétique relationnelle*. Dijon: Les Presses du Réel.

Bourriaud, N., 1999. *Formes de vie: L art moderne et l invention de soi*. Paris: Denoël.

Bourriaud, N., 2003. *Postproduction*. Dijon: Les presses du réel.

Brautigan, R., 1967. *All Watched Over by Machines of Loving Grace*. San Francisco: The Communication Company.

Breidbach, O., 2006. *Visons of Nature: The Art and Science of Ernst Haeckel*. Munich: Prestel Verlag.

Brown, A., 2014. *Art and Ecology Now*. London: Thames & Hudson.

Brown, L., 2006. *Art en ecologie - Un laboratoire d'idees sur l'art et le developpement durable, rapport sommaire* (report summary). Vancouver: UNESCO.

Buck, L., 2009. 'The group show that takes to the stage'. *The Art Newspaper*, Art Basel Daily edition, 10 June 2009, p.4.

Burnham, J., 1967. *Hans Haacke, Wind and Water Sculpture*. Evanston, IL: Northwestern University Press.

Burnham, J., 1974. *Great Western Salt Works: Essays on the Meaning of Post-Formalist Art*. New York: G. Braziller.

Capra, F., 2002. *The Hidden Connections: Integrating the Biological, Cognitive, and Social Dimensions of Life into a Science of Sustainability*. New York: Doubleday.

Carlson, R., 1962. *Silent Spring*. Boston: Houghton Mifflin.

Choay, F., 1965. *L'Urbanisme, utopies et réalités, une anthologie*. Paris: Seuil.

Cometti, J.-P., 2002. 'La monnaie de la pièce: remarques sur l'art, l'échange et la valeur'. *Parachute*, 106, 70–85.

Darwin, C., 1881. *The Formation of Vegetable Mould, through the Action of Worms, with Observations on their Habits*. London: John Murray.

Daston, L. J. and Galison, P., 2007. *Objectivity*. Cambridge: MIT Press.

Davies, D., 2008. *Art as Performance*. New York: Wiley-Blackwell.

Debord, G., 1970. *The Society of the Spectacle*. Detroit: Black and Red.

Debord, G., 1955. Introduction a une critique de la geographie urbaine. *Les levres nues*, 6, 11–15.

Deléage, J.-P., 1991. *Une histoire de l'écologie*. Paris: Editions du Seuil.

Demos, T., 2007. *The Exiles of Marcel Duchamp*. Cambridge, MA: MIT Press.

Demos, T., 2013. 'Contemporary Art and the Politics of Ecology'. *Third Text*, 27(1), 1–9.

Demos, T., 2015. 'Rights of Nature: The Art and Politics of Earth Jurisprudence'. In: *Rights of Nature: Art and Ecology in the Americas*. Nottingham: Nottingham Contemporary.

Derrida, J., 1967. *Of Grammatology*. Paris: Les Éditions de Minuit.

Dewey, J., 1980. *Art as Experience*. New York: Perigee Books.

Di Maggio, P., Ostrower, F. 1992. *Race, Ethnicity, and Participation in the Arts: Patterns of Participation by Hispanics, Whites, and African-Americans in selected activities from the 1982 and 1985 surveys of Public Participation in the Arts*, Research Division Report 25, National Endowment of the Arts, Washington DC: Seven Locks Press.

Dissenayake, E., 1992. *Homo Aestheticus: Where Art Comes from and Why*. Seattle: University of Washington Press.

Doguet, J.-P., 2007. *L art comme communication: Pour une redéfinition de l art*. Paris: Armand Colin.

Dolphijn, R. and Tuin, I., eds., 2012. *New Materialism: Interviews and Cartographies*. Ann Arbor: Open Humanities Press.

Durozoi, G., ed., 2002-2006. *Dictionnaire de l'art moderne et contemporain*. Tours: Hazan.

Eddy, M., 2009. 'A Brief History of Somatic Practices and Dance Historical Development of the Field of Somatic Education and its Relationship to Dance'. *Journal of Dance and Somatic Practices*, 1(1), 5–27.

Ellul, J., 1977. *Le système technicien*. Paris: Calman-Levy.

Foster, H., ed., 1983. *The Anti-Aesthetics: Essays on Post-Modern Culture*. Port Townsend, WA: Bay Press.

Foucault, M., 1988. *History of Sexuality*. New-York: Vintage.

Fowkes, M. and Fowkes, R., 2006. 'The Principles of Sustainability in Contemporary Art'. *Praesens: Contemporary Central European Art Review*, Issue 1, 5–11.

Franke, A. and Folie, S., 2011. *Animism: Modernity through the Looking Glass*. Berlin: Verlag der Buchhandlung Walther Konig.

Freeman, D., 1983. *Margaret Mead and Samoa. The Making and Unmaking of an Anthropological Myth*. Cambridge, MA: Harvard University Press.

Friedman, G., 1953. *Villes et campagnes:. Civilisation urbaine et civilisation rurale en France*. Paris: Armand Colin.

Gablik, S., 1984. *Has Modernism Failed?* London: Thames & Hudson.

Gablik, S., 1991. *The Reenchantment of Art*. London: Thames & Hudson.

Gadamer, H.-G., 2013. *Truth and Method*. London: Bloomsbury Academic.

Grande, J. K., 2003. *Balance: Art and Nature*, Revised edn. Montreal/New York: Black Rose Books.

Grande, J. K., 2004. *Art Nature Dialogues: Interviews with Environmental Artists*. New York: State University of New York Press.

Greenberg, C., 1989. *Art and Culture, Critical Essays*. Boston, MA: Beacon Press.

Guattari, F., 2005. *The Three Ecologies*. London: Continuum International Publishing Group Ltd.

Halloway, D., 2016. 'Staying with the Trouble: Anthropocene, Capitalocene,

Chthulucene.' In J. Moore, ed., *Anthropocene or Capitalocene? Nature, History and the Crisis of Capitalism.* Oakland: PM Press, pp. 34–76.

Hanson, J. and Steinman, S., 2004. *Women Environmental Artists Directory.* Oakland: Steinman.

Hardin, G., 1968. 'Tragedy of the Commons'. *Science*, 162(3859), pp. 1243–124.

Havel, V., 1985. 'The Power of the Powerless'. In J. Keane, ed. *The Power of the Powerless: Citizens against the State in Central-Eastern Europe.* New York: M. E. Sharpe.

Hess, D. J., 2009. *Localist Movements in a Global Economy: Sustainability, Justice and Urban Development in the United States.* London: MIT Press.

Hiroa, T. R., 1964. *Arts and Crafts of Hawai'i: Religion.* Honolulu: Bishop Museum Press.

Hockaday, M., 1992. *Kafka, Love, and Courage: The Life of Milena Jesenská.* New York: Oxford University Press.

Home, S., 1991. *Assault on Culture: Utopian Currents from Lettrisme to Class War.* Edinburgh: A. K. Press.

Honneth, A. and Rancière, J., 2016. *Recognition or Disagreement: A Critical Encounter on the Politics of Freedom, Equality, and Identity.* New York: Columbia University Press.

Hottois, G., 1986. 'Le Technocosme urbain. La ville comme theme de philosophie de la technique, texte roneotype, conference donnee dans le cadre de la 17ieme Ecole urbaine de l'ARAU'. In P. Ansay and R. Schoonbrodt, eds. *Penser la ville, Choix de textes philosophiques.* Bruxelles: AAM.

Humboldt, A. v., 2014. *Cosmos: A Sketch of the Physical Description of the Universe.* s.l.: Create Space Independent Publishing Platform.

International Organisation for Migration, 2008. *IOM journal: Migration Research Series,* Geneva: International Organisation for Migration.

Jarry, A., 1997. *The Ubu Plays.* London: Nick Hern Books Ltd.

Jauss, H. R. and Shaw, M., 1982. 'Poiesis'. *Critical Inquiry*, 8(3), 591–608.

Johns, J., 1996. *Nature and the American Identity.* Available at: http://xroads.virginia.edu/~cap/NATURE/cap2.html

Jones, A., 1994. *The En-gendering of Marcel Duchamp.* Cambridge: Cambridge University Press.

Kagan, S., 2011. *Art and Sustainability: Connecting Patterns for a Culture of Complexity.* Revised edn. Bielefeld: Transcript Verlag.

Kant, I., 1951. *Critique of Judgement.* New York: Hafner Publishing.

Kaprow, A., 1991. *7 Environments: Introduction to a Theory.* Milan/Naples: Fondazione Mudima and Studio Morra.

Kepes, G., 1972. *Arts of the Environment.* New York: George Braziller.

Kurt, H. and Wagner, B., 2002. *Kultur - Kunst - Nachhaltigkeit.* Essen: Klartext Verlag.

Kwon, M., 2004. *One Place after Another: Site-Specific Art and Locational Identity.* Cambridge, MA: MIT Press.

Lebowitz, C., 2009. 'Review at Ronald Feldman Gallery'. *Art in America*, 4 May.

Lefebvre, H., 1962. *Introduction a la modernite: Preludes.* Paris: Editions de Minuit.

Lefebvre, H., 1992. *The Production of Space.* London: Wiley-Blackwell.

Levin, K., 2010. 'Where are all the Great Women Pop Artists?' *ArtNews.* Available at: www.artnews.com/2010/11/01/where-are-the-great-women-pop-artists/.

Levine, L., 1988. *Highbrow/Lowbrow: The Emergence of Cultural Hierarchy in America.* Cambridge, MA: Harvard University Press.

Lewitt, S., 1969. 'Sentences on Conceptual Art.' *Art-Language*, 1, 11–12.

Liebgott, N., 2000. 'The Representation of Nature in Art'. *Naturopa*, 93, 14–16.

Lippard, L., 1973. *Six Years: The Dematerialization of the Art Object from 1966–1972*. New York: Praeger.

Lippard, L., 1998. *The Lure of the Local: Senses and Place in a Multicentered Society*. New York: The New Press.

Lippard, L., 2007. *Weather Report: Art and Climate Change*. Boulder: Boulder Museum of Contemporary Art.

Lippard, L., 2014. *Undermining: A Wild Ride through Land Use, Politics, and Art in the Changing West*. New York: The New Press.

Lippard, L. and Chandler, J., 1968. 'The Demateralisation of Art'. *Art International*, 12(2), 31–36.

Lodé, T., 2011. *La Biodiversité amoureuse: Sexe et évolution*. Paris: Odile Jacob.

Lutkehaus, N. C., 2008. *Margaret Mead: the Making of an American Icon*. Princeton: Princeton University Press.

Macel, C. and Guillaume, V., 2007. *Airs de Paris, exhibition catalog*. Paris: Centre Pompidou.

Marcuse, H., 2002. *One-Dimensional Man: Studies in the Ideology of Advanced Industrial Society*. New-York: Routledge Classics.

Margantin, L., 1999. *Système minéralogique et cosmologie chez Novalis, ou les plis de la terre*. Paris: L'Harmattan, Ouverture Philosophique.

Margolin, V. and Smith, S., 2006. *Beyond Green: Toward a Sustainable Art*. Chicago/New York: Smart Museum of Art at University of Chicago and Independent Curators International.

Martinez-Alier, J., 1993. *Ecological Economics: Energy, Environment and Society*. London: Blackwell Publishers.

Martinez-Alier, J., 2002. *The Environmentalism of the Poor: A Study of Ecological Conflicts and Valuation*. Cheltenham: Edward Elgar.

Matilsky, B. C., 1992. *Fragile Ecologies: Contemporary Arists' Interpretations and Solutions*. New York: Rizzoli.

Mead, M., 1929. 'Coming of Age in Samoa. A Psychological Study of Primitive Youth for Western Civilisation'. *American Anthropologist*, 31(3), 532–534.

Meillassoux, Q., 2006. *Après la finitude: Essai sur la nécessité de la contingence*. Paris: Seuil.

Merleau-Ponty, M., 2000. *Nature: Course Notes from the Collège de France*. Evanston, IL: Northwestern University Press.

Merquior, J., 1987. *From Prague to Paris*. London: Verso Books.

Miles, M., 2014. *Eco-aesthetics: Art, Literature and Architecture in a Period of Climate Change*. London: Bloomsbury.

Morganova, P., 2014. *Czech Action Art, Happenings, Actions, Events, Land Art, Body Art and Performance Art Behind the Iron Curtain*. Prague: Karolinum Press, Charles University.

Neihardt, J. G., 2008. *Black Elk Speaks: Being the Life Story of a Holy Man of the Oglala Sioux*. New York: State University of New York Press.

Novalis, 1997. *Philosophical Writings*. Albany: State University of New York Press.

O'Doherty, B., 1976. *Inside the White Cube: The Ideology of the Gallery Space*. Santa Monica, CA: Lapis Press.

O'Hagan, S., 2013. 'Ana Mendieta: Death of an Artist Foretold in Blood'. *The Guardian*, 21 September.

Panofsky, E., 1938. *Meaning in the Visual Arts*. Chicago: University of Chicago Press.

Paquet, S., 2009. *Le paysage façonné. Les territoires postindustriels, l'art et l'usage*. Québec: Presses de l'Université Laval.

Pareyson, L., 2007. *Esthétique: Théorie de la formativité*. Paris: Éditions Rue d'Ulm.

Pehe, J., 2014. 'The Czech Republic and the EU: Democracy Without Democrats'. *The Huffington Post*, 10 August.

Phillips, P., 2015. 'Artistic Practices and Eco Aesthetics in a Post-Sustainable Worlds'. In C. Crouch, N. Kaye and J. Crouch, eds. *An Introduction to Sustainability and Aesthetics: The Arts and Design for the Environment*. Boca Raton, FL: Brown Walker Press, pp. 55–68.

Pincus-Witten, R., 1971. 'Eva Hesse: Post-Minimalism into Sublime'. *Artforum*, 10(3), 35–40.

Prigann, H., Strelow, H. and David, V., 2004. *Ecological Aesthetics: Art in Environmental Design: Theory and Practice*. Basel: Birkhäuser.

Ramade, B., 2011. 'Mierle Laderman Ukeles: après la révolution, qui ramassera les poubelles?' *02*, Autumn, 36-49.

Ramos, J., 2000. 'Romantic Landscape in Europe'. *Naturopa*, 93, 10–11.

Rancière, J., 2000. *The Politics of Aesthetics, the Distribution of the Sensible*. London: Bloomsbury Press.

Rancière, J., 2009. *The Emancipated Spectator*. London, New York: Verso.

Ranciere, J., 2010 *Dissensus: On Politics and Aesthetics*. New York: Bloomsbury.

Reuters, 2015. 'Hopi Sacred Masks Auctioned in Paris Despite Protests'. Reuters, 11 June. Available at: www.reuters.com/article/us-france-auction-masks-idUSKBN0OR1DG 20150611

Rifkin, J., 2009. *The Empathic Civilization: The Race to Global Consciousness in a World in Crisis*. London: Tarcher.

Santas, A., 2014. 'Aristotelian Ethics and Biophilia'. *Ethics & The Environment*, 19(1), 95–121.

Sante, L., 1998. 'Robert Smithson: The Monuments of Passaic, 1967. (Art Photographer; Passaic River in New Jersey)'. *Artforum International*, 36(10).

Schaeffer, J.-M., 2007. *La fin de l'exception humaine*. Paris: Gallimard.

Schumacher, F. E., 1989. *Small Is Beautiful: Economics as if People Mattered*, 2nd edn. New York: Harper Perennial.

Schwendender, M., 2014. 'New Jersey Images, Unbound by Galleries'. *New York Times*, 7 March.

Sloterdijk, P., 2014. *Globes: Spheres Volume II: Macrospherology–Bubbles: Spheres Volume I: Microspherology*. Los Angeles: Semiotext(e), Tra Edition.

Smee, S., 2014. 'MFA Expands Loans of Well-known Works'. *Boston Globe*, 3 August.

Smithson, R., 1996. 'Conversation in Salt Lake City'. In J. Flam, ed. *Robert Smithson: Collected Writings*. Berkeley: University of California Press, p. 298.

Sontag, S., 1967. 'On America'. *The New Yorker*, 34(1), p. 51.

Sooke, A., 2009. 'Eva Hesse: Her Dark Materials'. *The Telegraph*, 4 August.

Spaid, S., 2002. *Ecovention: Current Art to Transform Ecologies*. Cincinnati: Contemporary Arts Center.

Thomas, H., 2004. *Somatics: Reawakening the Mind's Control of Movement, Flexibility, and Health*. Cambridge, MA: Da Capo Press Inc.

Vartanian, H., 2013. 'Exclusive Video: James Turrell Talks About Working with Light'. *Art21*, 8 May.

Verespe, M., 2011. 'Park Director feared Coke over Canyon bottle-ban'. *Plastic News*, 12 December.

Villiers de l'Isle, A., 2000. *Tomorrow's Eve*. Champaign: University of Illinois Press.

Wang, D. S., 2004. *Downtime at the Experimental Station: A Conversation with Dan Peterman*. Chicago: Temporary Services.

Weintraub, L., 2006a. *Cycle-Logical Art: Recycling Matters for Eco-Art*. Rhinebeck, NY: Artnow Publications.

Weintraub, L., 2006b. *ECOcentric Topics: Pioneering Themes for Eco-Art*. Rhinebeck, NY: Artnow Publications.

Weintraub, L., 2007. *EnvironMentalities: Twenty-Two Approaches to Eco-Art*. Rhinebeck, NY: Artnow Publications.

Weintraub, L., 2012. *To Life!: Eco Art in Pursuit of a Sustainable Planet*. Berkeley, CA: University of California Press.

Wingo, A., 2010. 'The Odyssey of Human Rights: Reply to Diagne'. *Transition*, 202, 120–138.

Wingo, A. H., 1998. 'African Art: The Aesthetics of Hiding and Revealing'. *British Journal of Aesthetics*, 38(3), 251–264.

Wyatt, M., 2004. *A Handbook of NGO Governance*. Budapest: European Center for Not-for-Profit Law.

Index

Page numbers in *italics* denote an
illustration

1200 Bags of Coal (Duchamp) 17, *18*
21st United Nations Conference on
 Climate Change, Paris 60, 121–2, 160
350.org 106
5 Gyres Institute 140, 187–8
7000 Oaks (Beuys) 20, 170n

Abeles, Kim 132
aesthetics: aesthetic activity 53, 56n;
 beginnings of 12, 38; contemporary
 importance 43–4, 209–10;
 environment, renewed relationship
 57–8, 88–90, 179–80; environmental
 aesthetics 58–9, 175–6, 178–9;
 Herbart's influence 193; participatory
 169–70; relational 163–4; sensitivity
 64n; skills development 83–4;
 sustainability factor 54, 178–9
Ahumada, Carolina Pino 98–9
Alves, Maria Thereza 86–7
American Renaissance 15–16
animals: deformity visualised *74*, 74–6;
 farming culture 78–9; scientific
 inspirations 137–8; sculptured nesting
 boxes 137; sounds of nature 179–80
Anthropocene, hypothesis of 22, 39, 208
Arendt, Hannah 54, 61, 62, 64
art, definition of 49
art and science: changing perceptions
 128–9; design and engineering 136–7;
 ecosystem activism 75–6; landscape
 painting 12–13, 16; lithographs,
 influence of 38; living systems and
 resources 132–6, *133*, *135*, 137–8;
 modern perspective 57, 102; nature,
 opposing interpretations 39–40; nature

expeditions 11–12, 38–9, 74; research
 value 131–2, *132*, 158–60; Romantic
 scientists 13–14; theoretical
 contributions 74; urban space 196–7
ArtCOP21 30
art experience: cultural value 41–2, 44;
 multiple senses 17; natural element
 re-framed 26; olfactory 79; receptive/
 active process 162–4; soundscape
 13–14, 76–7, 179–80; static vision
 16–17
artist's self 19, *41*, 41–2
art market: artist's financial status 117;
 museum patrons 184–5; private
 collectors 42, 185–6; US art schools
 185; women underrepresented 188–9
art under oppression 112–15, 191
Assu, Sonny 189
Atelier Gras 88
Atelier van Lieshout 198–9
Audubon, John James 74

Baj, Enrico 19
Ballengée, Brandon *74*, 74–6
Bate, Jonathan 202
Baumgarten, Alexander 57, 64n
Beech, Dave 187
Beehive Design Collective 109–10
Beuys, Joseph 20, 27n, 163, 170n, 202
Bierstadt, Albert 16
BioArt *74*, 74–6, 96
Blanc, Nathalie 30
Boccioni, Umberto 19
Boetzkes, Amanda 31
Bonacossa, Ilaria 29, 33, 36n
Bonneval, Karine 98, *98*
Bourriaud, Nicolas 58, 65n
Boutonnier, Thierry 89
Bové, Charles 97

Brautigan, Richard 67
Bret, Michel 97
Brewster, Michael 13–14
Brown, Andrew 31
Brundtland, Gro Harlem 32
buildings: above water 123; community
    regeneration 110–11, 118; waste into
    architecture 109
Burtynsky, Edward 195

Caillois, Roger 39
Capitalism and art: anti-corporate critique
    189, 194–5; museum and arts patrons
    184–5; ownership and value 186–7;
    private collectors 185–6; women
    underrepresented 188–9
Caretto, Andrea 94–5
Carson, Rachel 121
Carus, Carl Gustav 12
Chevalier, Miguel 97
Chin, Mel 131–2, *132*
Chivialle, Daniel 88
Choay, Francoise 196
Church, Frederic 16
cities *see* urban space
citizen science: ecosystem activism 75;
    land reclamation 159–60; olfactory
    experience 79; organic recycling and
    cultivation 94–5; waste into
    architecture 109
civil society: artist collaborations 101–2,
    105, 115; political oppression 111–14
climate change: art-activism 106, 160–1;
    climate migrants 152, 153n; coasts and
    sea-level rises 77–8, *78*, 151; UN
    agreements 60, 121–2, 194
Cole, Thomas 15
conceptual art 26
Cooper, Lilian 77–8, *78*
corporeality 88–9
Couchet, Edmond 97
Cragg, Tony 139
Cuevas, Minerva 194–5
curiosity cabinets 76
Czechoslovakia: art and literature under
    oppression 111–15, 192–3; ecological
    legacy 192–3

Dada 145
Dangelo, Sergio 19
Dare-Dare 166
Darné, Olivier 89
Darwin, Charles 138

Daudelin, Charles 166
Davis, Lucy *124–5*, 125–6
D'Caires Taylor, Jason 126
Debord, Guy 82–3, 197
deconstruction 26
Defoe, Daniel 122
Denes, Agnes 21, 29
Dewey, John 62
Digital Farm Collective 91
Dion, Mark 158–9
Djamil, Firman 176
documentaries see photography and film
Domingues, Diana 97
Duchamp, Marcel 17, *18*, 27n, 145, 147
Dürer, Albrecht 19, *41*, 41–2, 175

earth art: associated artists 20, 31, 147,
    155–6; definition 4, 32; mystical
    connections 156–7
ecoinvention 28
ecological art: biodiversity and ecological
    flow *84*, 84–6, 86; community
    collaborations 159–60; definition 32;
    ecological documentary *124*, 125–6;
    invasive species, floral/cultural debate
    86–7; land art, assimilation issues 22,
    30; living processes 23–4, 132–4, *133*,
    137–8, 154; maintenance art 22–3,
    126–7; nature as medium 22; original
    artists 21, 130–1; pollution issues
    131–2, *132*; psychogeography and drift
    method 83; resource management
    121–2; sculpture as wildlife habitat
    24–5, 126–7, 134–6, *135*, 137; site-
    specific 34, *132*
ecology, definition 3, 32
eco-poetics 202
Eliasson, Olafur 14
Ellul, Jacques 40
Emerson, Ralph Waldo 15
environment, definition 3, 32
environmental aesthetics: aesthetic
    experience 209–10; artistic practice
    58–9, 175–6; concept and scope 59–61,
    201–2; political change 82, 178–9
environmental art: anti-corporate critique
    189, 194–5; artistic activism 193–6;
    artist principles 110, 117, 188, 204–5;
    changing perceptions 19–20, 43–4,
    118–19, 147–8; community based
    collaborations 101–2, 105, 159–60,
    164–5, 171, 207; community
    regeneration 110–11, 166–9; definition

4, 32; design and engineering 136–7; disruptive decline *180*, 180–1; early depictions 15; ecosystem's connectivity 123–4; environmental responsibility 33, 34, 69–70, 107–8, *108*; female pioneers 20–1; indigenous inspiration 123; interactive cultivation 98–9; Joseph Beuys's contribution 20; keys to interpreting practices 33–5, 42; landscapes revisualised 120–1; localism 117–18; local space, global issues 150–2, 173, 176–7, 181–2, 191, 207; mystical and religious influence 13, 79–80, 148, 150–1, 156–7; natural activity, mediation and interventions 51–2, 73, 93–4, 204–5; nature, cultural changes towards 34–5; Other Earth art 20–1; pioneering exhibitions and books 28–9, 35n, 130; plastic pollution artists 139–41; political risks 111, 193; politics unchanged by 40–1; process art 158–60; public involvement and experiences 163–4; recognition issues 55–6n, 108–9; recycling projects 94–5, 109, 111–12, 167–9, *168*; resource management 121–2, *141*, 141–2, 150–1; sculptural origins 19; Smithson's land art 147–50, *149*; social change commitment 150–1, 159–60; terminology confusion 40; virtual environments 97; working with scientists 102; written accounts and criticisms 30–1
environmental creativity 62–4, 70–1
environmental forms: aesthetic relationship 57–8, 205–6; art/crafts, value to material world 52–3; manifestations 50; system of interactions 50–1, 205, 207–8
environmental justice and 'artivism' 109–10, 119–20, 150–1, 173, 193–6
environmental transformation 208–9
Erikson, Markus, Dr. 140

Fabriques Architectures Paysages 90–1
farming culture: art-farmers 90–1; documented practices 78–9, 91–2; global monocultures 119–20; urban agriculture 87–90
female pioneers: environmental art 20–1, 154–6; The Women's Building 157
Floc'h, Nicolas 134, *135*
Florians, Martina 79

Flottemesch, Robert 150–1
Fontana, Lucio 19
form, definition 50
Foster, Hal 55–6n
Fowkes, Maja and Rueben 28
'Fragile Ecologies' exhibition 28
Friedman, Georges 81–2
Friedrich, Caspar David 14–15

Gablik, Suzi 30, 41
Galtier, Eva 78–9
Gates, Bill 186
Gates, Theaster 110–11
Gibson, John 22
Godde, Robin 151
Goethe, Johann Wolfgang von 14, 39–40, 51
Goya, Francisco 128, *129*
Greenburg, Clement 191
Gregory, Celia 134–6
'Groundworks' exhibition 28
Guerilla Girls 188–9
Guo-Qiang, Cai 29
Gutherie, Karen 111, *112*

Haacke, Hans 85, 86, 131, 194
Haeckel, Ernst 32, 38
Hanna, Thomas 88
Harrison, Helen and Newton 130–1, 142n, 151–2
Havel, Vaclav 105, 112–13
Herbart, Johann 193
Hesse, Eva 157–8
Holt, Nancy 22
Hottois, Gilbert 196
Houle, Karen 98, *98*
Hrabal, Bohumil 111–12
Huber, Frauke 195–6
Hull, Lynne 24–5
Humboldt, Alexander von 12–13
Husky, Suzanne 77
Hutton, Eileen 137, *138*

indigenous cultures: anti-corporate critique 189; connectivity to environment 80, 122, 173–4, 177–8; installations inspired by 123, 147, 176–7; value of art 41, 174–5
International COAL Prize 29–30
International Situationist 82–3, 197
Irwin, Robert 26, 157

Jarry, Alfred 145, *146*

Jeremijenko, Natalie 199–200
Johanson, Patricia 21, 23–4
Jordan, Chris 107–8, *108*

Kac, Eduardo 96
Kafka, Ivan 111, 114, 147
Kagan, Sacha 31
Kalliwoda, Hans *180*, 180–1
Kant, Immanuel 38, 61, 62, 64, 67
Kaprow, Allan 19–20, *21*
Karga, Valentina 200–1, *201*
Kepes, György 130
Kim, Walter 77
Klein, Yves 19
Kühn, Björn 121
Kultivator 92
Kurt, Hildegard 28

Laimanee, Suwan 123
land art: artist practices 40; art under
    oppression 193; associated artists 21,
    147, 148–50; definition 4, 32;
    ecological art, assimilation issues 22, 30
Land Art: A Cultural Ecology Handbook 28
landscape painting 12, 14–16
Latitudes collective 29, 33, 36n
Lefebvre, Henri 56n, 82, 83, 198, 202
Leonardo, da Vinci *49*, 53, 186
Lieshout, Joep van 198–9
Lindmark, Maria 92
Lindmark, Marlene 92
Lippard, Lucy 30
lithographs, influence of 38
living beings: artistic attention on
    environment 69–71; ecological theories
    68; process of life defined 67–8
localism 117–18

Maathai, Wangari, Dr. *106*, 106–7
Margolin, Victor 33–4
marine environments: coral reef
    protection 126–7, 134, *135*; plastic
    pollution 107–8, *108*, 139–41
Martin, Uwe H. 195–6
Martinez-Alier, Juan 194
Marx, Karl 53
matter: definition 158; material
    exploration 159; organic recycling
    94–5, 138; process of life 67–8, 158–9
McKibben, Bill 60
Mead, Margaret 177–8
Mendel, Gideon 195
Mendieta, Ana 20–1, 150, 154–6, *155*

micro-utopias 101, 105, 197–201, *201*
Milde, Krystina and Marek 123–4
Miles, Malcolm 31
Montag, Dara, Dr. 122
Moore, Charles, Captain 139–40
Moore, Matthew 91, *91*
Moran, Thomas 15, 16
Motta, Liliana 86–7
movimento d'arte nucleare 18–19
multi-cultural hybrids 25–6
Muniz, Vik 171
museum management 54, 184–5, 188–9

Nancy, Jean-Luc 62
nature (*physis*): artistic documentation of
    expeditions 11–12, 15, 38–9, 74;
    collection of elements 39; cultural
    change towards 34; definition 3; forms
    and movement 39–40; Romanticism's
    interpretation 14–15, 16; symbolic
    representation 11, 15
Nietzsche, Friedrich 39
non-government organisations (NGOs):
    corporate battle 187–8; educational
    programmes 109–10; mobilising
    communities 105; operational strategies
    110, 193; UN recognition 107
Novalis 13

O'Doherty, Brian 157
Orta, Lucy and Jorge 160–1
Other Earth art 20–1

Palma, Miguel 123
Palmer, A.Laurie 159
Panhuysen, Paul 14
Paquet, Suzanne 166
Peterman, Dan 167–9, *168*
photography and film: aerial pictures 195;
    documentary photographs 133–4;
    documentary projects 78–9, 91–2,
    195–6; live video plays 120–1;
    photographic diary 159; scanner prints
    75; time-lapse film 91
physis (nature) 3, 53
Pincus-Witten, Robert 154
plant life: audible communication 98, 98;
    bamboo's sustainability *141*, 141–2;
    community gardens 111, *112*, 118;
    cultivation via social networks 98–9;
    ecological documentary *124*, 125–6;
    ecology through education 106–7,
    158–9, 160; ecosystem frailty 158–9;

ecosystem's connectivity 123–4; historic and political significance 77, 119–20; organic recycling and cultivation 94–5; virtual gardens 97
poiesis 53
pollution: air 132, 192, 202–3n; awareness through art 69, 73; plastics 107–8, *108*, 139–41, 187–8; reclaimed land 131–2, *132*, 159–60; water 131
Pope, Nina 111, *112*
Post-minimalism 154
process art 158–9
psychogeography 82–3
public involvement: aesthetic experience 163–4; artistic action 163; land restructuring, locally valued 164–5; participatory aesthetics 169–70; recycling projects 167–9
public space: aestheticisation of 64; revitalisation through art 166

Ramos, Julie 30
Rancière, Jacques 43, 61, 118, 206
Rathore, Akshay Raj Singh 179–80
relational aesthetics 163
'relational art' movement 26
Ring, Heather 118
Riopelle, Jean-Paul 166
Roden Crater (Turrell) 20, 30, 156
Romanenko, Anna 121
Romanticism 13–14, 16
Ruller, Tomaš 120–1
Runge, Philipp Otto 14–15
rural space interventions 79, 90–1

Sacks, Shelly 28
Saint Simon, Claude de 128
Samakh, Eric 76–7
Schafer, R Murray 30
Schiffers, Antje 79
Schumacher, E.F. 117, 121
sensitive sharing experience 60–1, 63
Shankland, Stephen 109
sharing: democracy 62, 65n; environmental creativity 62–3; political judgement 61; sensitive sharing experience 60–1, 63
Smith, Stephanie 28
Smithson, Robert 20, 22, 31, 147–50, *149*, 151
'social art' 128
'Social Sculpture' 20, 163, 170n
Sonfist, Alan 21, 22, 84, 84–5

Sonjasdotter, Asa 119–20
Sontag, Susan 185, 187
soundscape 13–14, 76–7, 98, 179–80
Spagna, Raffaella 94–5
Spaid, Sue 28, 64, 84
Spiral Jetty (Smithson) 20, 22, 147, 148, 150
Sprenger, Thomas 79
Stephan, Elodie 136–7
Stigeborn, Henric 92
Stimmung (atmosphere) 13
Survival International 42
sustainability: aesthetic value 54, 59; culture's role, UN recognition 108–9; definition 3–4, 32
sustainable development: associated issues 32; undermined measures 59–60

Thoreau, Henry David 15
Time Landscape (Sonfist) 22, 84, *84*
Tiravanija, Rikrit 25–6
Titlova-Ylovsky, Margita *114*
tribal artefacts, ownership debate 42
Turrell, James 14, 20, 156

Ukeles, Mierle Laderman 21, 22–3, *24*
United Nations: culture, recognized contribution 108–9; environmental terminology 32; NGO's, working with 107
urban agriculture 87–90
urban space: biodiversity record 84, 84–5; city, a technical environment 81–2; community centre and garden 118; ecological city models 198–9; ecological productions 199–201; invasive species, floral/cultural debate 86–7; psychogeographical studies 82–3; restorative installations 89; urban agriculture 87–9; utopian productions 196
utopias: micro-utopias 101, 105, 197–201, *201*; modern perspective 196–7

value of art: aesthetic qualities 54–5, 59; cultural interpretation 41–2, 44, 174–5; intellectual property 171–2, 187; museum and private collections 184–6
Vanden Eynde, Maarten 140, 174, *175*
Vasudevan, R. Prof. 140–1
virtual gardens 97
Voyt chovský, Miloš 13–14

Vrijman, Mathieu and Malin 92

Warburg, Aby 74
Warhol, Andy 19
Was Getekend to Runde project 164–5
Webber, John 38–9
Weintraub, Linda 30
Westen, Jeroen van 164–5
Western art: Dada 145; early
   'installations' 17; landscape painting
   and Romanticism 14–15; modernism
   118, 120, 157; movimento d'arte
   nucleare 18–19; nature in context
   79–80; objectification 42;
postmodernism 147; rise of the
   individual 19, 41, 175; value of objects
   174; WWII atrocities, effect on 17
Whitehead, Frances 159–60
Wightman, Jennifer 132–3
Williams, William Carlos 148
Wingo, Ajume H. 175–6
Women's Building, The 157
world events and art: emigration post
   world wars 145–7, 185; global
   realignments 20; nuclear war threat
   (1950's) 18–19; WWII atrocities 17
Wyatt, Jon *141*, 141–2
Wyatt, Marilyn, Dr. 110

For Product Safety Concerns and Information please contact our EU
representative GPSR@taylorandfrancis.com Taylor & Francis Verlag GmbH,
Kaufingerstraße 24, 80331 München, Germany

Printed and bound by CPI Group (UK) Ltd, Croydon, CR0 4YY
08/05/2025
01864352-0001